LIVE WELL, RETIRE WELL

LIVE WELL
RETIRE WELL

Strategies for a Rich Life and a Richer Retirement

PATRICIA LOVETT-REID

with JONATHAN VERNEY

KEY PORTER BOOKS

Library and Archives Canada Cataloguing in Publication

Lovett-Reid, Patricia
    Live well, retire well : strategies for a rich life and a richer retirement / Patricia Lovett-Reid ; with Jonathan Verney.

Includes index.
ISBN 1-55263-749-2

1. Retirement — Planning. 2. Saving and investment. 3. Finance, Personal.
I. Verney, Jonathan II. Title.

HG179.L683 2006   332.024'014   C2005-906487-0

The author, Patricia Lovett-Reid, is a Senior Vice President with TD Waterhouse Canada Inc. While every effort was made to ensure the accuracy of the material in this book, investors' situations are different and rules change. TD Waterhouse Canada Inc., a sub-sidiary of The Toronto-Dominion Bank, assumes no responsibility or liability arising from the use of the material in this book. The material is for information purposes only, and you should consult your own professional advisors.

Key Porter Books Limited
Six Adelaide Street East, Tenth Floor
Toronto, Ontario
Canada M5C 1H6

www.keyporter.com

Text design: Marijke Friesen
Electronic formatting: Jean Lightfoot Peters

Printed and bound in Canada

06 07 08 09 10 5 4 3 2

TABLE OF CONTENTS

Acknowledgements / 9

Introduction / 11

CHAPTER ONE / 13
   Retirement: Bring it on!

CHAPTER TWO / 19
   Attitude? What attitude?

CHAPTER THREE / 35
   PICTURE Go ahead: Picture yourself in retirement

CHAPTER FOUR / 47
   ARM (Part 1) Arm yourself with the *investment knowledge*
   you need

CHAPTER FIVE / 91
   ARM (Part 2) Arm yourself with the *investment tools* you need

CHAPTER SIX / 119
   ARM (Part 3) Arm yourself with the *insurance tools* you need

CHAPTER SEVEN / 143
   ARM (Part 4) Arm yourself with the *tax strategies* you need

CHAPTER EIGHT / 193
   TRANSITION Move seamlessly into retirement

CHAPTER NINE / 221
   HARMONY Leaving a legacy: estate planning

CHAPTER TEN / 261
   LIVE WELL, RETIRE WELL Make it happen

Bibliography / 273

Appendices / 277

Index / 291

"It sounded an excellent plan, no doubt, and very neatly and simply arranged: the only difficulty was that she had not the smallest idea how to set about it."
—LEWIS CARROLL, *ALICE IN WONDERLAND*

ACKNOWLEDGEMENTS

Many busy professionals contributed to making this book possible, and I'm grateful to all of you for your time and commitment.

I'd like to acknowledge and thank TD Bank Financial Group for its unwavering support and encouragement in my quest to inform and empower Canadians about their finances and retirement. More specifically I'd like to thank John See for his inspiring leadership. As President of TD Waterhouse Discount Brokerage, Financial Planning and Institutional Services, John is a pioneer in educating clients and investors and his commitment to education is unparalleled in the industry. John truly believes, as do I, that retirement is not about the money, it's about quality of life.

My special thanks to Ryan Lewenza, whose boundless energy, attention to detail and common-sense approach were integral to the completion of the book. His technical expertise, supported by the CFA Level III candidacy, helped greatly in guiding the technical sections of the book, as was his ability to garner support and input from so many key investment, tax and insurance specialists. I could not have done this without him.

Thank you also to those who were kind enough to assist me "behind the scenes": Craig Alexander, Jean Estabrook, Tanya Gilroy, Sandeep Goel, Robert Gorman, Bryan Lee, Robert Murray, Steve Pitts, Daniel Prosser, Scott Sullivan, Juanita Soutar, David Van Der Brug and Allan Vlah. And a special thank you to those Canadians who shared their retirement stories with us. My heartfelt thanks to all.

To Jonathan, with whom I wrote this book: I thank you for your creative energy, but especially for helping me understand the "inner game within the game."

Finally, I'd like to thank my husband, Jim, and our children, Carolyn, David, Jane and Kevin. I'm away a great deal and work long hours, and their love, patience and support allow me to follow my passion.

INTRODUCTION

"'Then there is the future,' said the Very Young Man. 'Just think! One might invest all one's money, leave it to accumulate at interest, and hurry on ahead!'"
—H.G. WELLS, *THE TIME MACHINE*

I'll let you in on a little secret. Studies show that a large percentage of non-fiction book buyers only read the first one or two chapters. Sound familiar? I'm guilty of doing it myself. I don't want that to happen with this book, which is why I've tried to do two things:

1) Create a different kind of reading experience: a guide that not only informs but entertains.
2) Make a promise to you: if you follow and stick with the four-step PATH outlined in this book, you'll be on the path to achieving all your retirement desires.

Everyone likes to eat, but I've never met anyone who likes to be force-fed — whether they're five or fifty-five. As a Certified Financial Planner and broadcast interviewer, I've had the privilege of meeting and talking with thousands of Canadians and their families. My experience is that when it comes to financial advice, most people like a little sugar with their coffee.

As a financial planner my goal is to inform you about your retirement options. But I want you to know more than just the facts. I want you to meet other Canadians whose life stories and financial successes will provide inspiration as you begin to shift focus, plan for the future, execute your plan and finally (and most importantly) stay the course.

While the book is written primarily for "Boomer" men and women between the ages of 40 to 60 years, I believe the insights, stories, perspectives and statistics found within will appeal to Canadians of all ages.

There's a lot of talk these days about what "path" people are on, or what path they are going to take in retirement (if they ever get around to it). I don't just want to talk about the path, I want to *show* you the path! In fact, this entire book is structured around finding and choosing the right PATH to a successful retirement.

PATH stands for Picture, Arm, Transition and Harmony: the four essential steps you need to retire in style. Just as no two people are alike, there is no single, universal path for all of us. But relax. This book is not about how to understand actuarial tables and present-value risk factors. It's about giving real people with real needs the ability to make the right choices.

To inspire you to make those choices, Chapter 1 explains the natural human need to live for today and downplay tomorrow. It explores the role our attitude plays in financial decision-making, and then relates stories of Canadians who have successfully chosen their own path to financial independence.

Chapter 2 introduces the PATH, a simple, effective and easy-to-remember strategy to help you retire in style.

Chapters 3 to 9 explore the retirement PATH step-by-step, so you can achieve the life you want when you retire.

The final chapter explores how our current perceptions about life and living affect the way we plan and make decisions. We're living in an unprecedented era. It's not only acceptable to reinvent yourself, it's okay to do it more than once. You'll learn how other successful Canadians — Boomers and retirees both — adjusted course and set sail for brighter horizons.

I've called the book *Live Well, Retire Well* because I don't believe you should sacrifice your life today just so you can live like a king or queen when you're retired. What kind of a life would that be? But neither do I want you to live for today and say to heck with tomorrow. That's a recipe for disaster and we both know it. There *is* a middle ground. You can live well *and* retire well, but only if you decide to get focused now, and keep focused tomorrow and next week and next year.

Those are the ultimate goals of this guide: to inspire and motivate you now, and then inspire you again and again so you'll stay on track and make it happen. Because retirement is a process, not a result. It's a journey, not a destination. No longer the "final frontier," retirement is an opportunity to enjoy our second adulthood.

Let's make the most of it!

CHAPTER
ONE

"The good news is: we're all going to live a long, long time.
The bad news is: we're all going to live a long, long time."
—WAYNE RUSSO, FINANCIAL CONSULTANT

RETIREMENT: BRING IT ON!

"Although he was in retirement and had now no influence in political affairs, every high official appointed to the province in which the prince's estate lay considered it his duty to visit him."

—LEO TOLSTOY, *WAR AND PEACE*

Retired. The R-word. A close cousin of "retread" and "reject." Yikes! It even contains the word "tired." Small wonder no one ever wanted to admit they were retired. Who would want to admit they were (according to *Funk & Wagnall's Dictionary*) "withdrawn from circulation; existing in seclusion"? Not so long ago, many people thought retirement was the kiss of death, the end of the road, the ultimate conversation stopper — to be avoided at all costs.

Remember the reaction when someone was asked what they did, and they said they were retired? It went something like this: "Oh.... Nice talking to you." Or maybe: "How do you keep yourself busy?" Or perhaps the unkindest cut of all: "So...what's it like to be put out to pasture?"

But all that negativity is changing — and fast. We're living longer, healthier lives, and our world (at least in the West) has transformed into a service-oriented society. Retirement has begun to evolve as well. It is now associated with a new group of R-words like "reenergized," "revitalized" and "rejuvenated."

RETIREMENT IS SUCH A "TIRED" WORD
Instead of deciding to re*tire*, maybe we should decide to re*live*. After all, retirement gives us a unique opportunity to truly live our lives again by experiencing things in a completely different — and hopefully better — way. But — and there's always a "but"— to make sure we take advantage of this opportunity, we need to do a little advance planning. First we

need to learn to relax. Retirement isn't the end of the world. It can be the beginning of something potentially very special. Few people do something well when they *have* to do it. If they *want* to do it, however, there's usually no stopping them.

Okay, before you say "Whoa, Pattie — take off those rose-coloured glasses," let me say this: When it comes to financial planning, I've always been a realist. Unlike some writers, I don't believe money magically appears in your life as soon as you decide to "attract" it. You have to do something first. What, you may ask? You have to do a little work. As the great South African golfer Gary Player once said, "The harder I work, the luckier I get."

Sounds simple, and it is — as long as you have the right attitude. Being a realist does not make me a defeatist or a pessimist. On the contrary, I'm a positive person who is grounded by facts and reality. You'll discover exactly what that means when you hit the core of the book, especially Chapters 4, 5, 6 and 7. Because once you're armed with the facts, you'll suddenly find yourself in a new position — halfway down the road to financial success.

There are only four basic ways to gain wealth: you can win it, inherit it, create it or save it. I can tell you that less than 1 percent of the population is lucky enough to win the lottery and less than 5 percent ever inherit a life-changing sum of money. Not good odds in my opinion, not to mention that I've never experienced either one. But creating enough money and saving enough money so you can retire in style — those are areas I know something about.

And while we're on the subject of reality, here are some facts that may either whet your appetite or give you an anxiety attack, depending on your attitude and state of mind. According to a recent study by David Bach, author of *The Automatic Millionaire*, a remarkable 46 percent of single Canadians aged 45 to 64 have *not* saved enough for retirement. In addition, 41 percent of Canadians with pre-retirement income of $75,000 or more may not be able to replace two-thirds of their income (a figure many pundits suggest is adequate to maintain your retirement needs).

Every year since 2001, consumption has risen faster than income. Many experts are beginning to question Canadians' ability to keep meeting future financial obligations if interest rates rise. It's well known that many people are over-extended on low-interest lines of credit as well as credit cards. Questions also surround potential pension fund shortfalls. Some say ballooning payments to Boomer retirees who will be living longer, combined with fewer employees to foot the bill is going to bankrupt the system. I am not one of those doomsayers, but there *is* a lot to be concerned about — especially Canadians' lack of awareness and attitude toward their finances.

But if you're proactive, follow the PATH outlined in this book and thus choose to do something about your situation, these negative stats simply won't apply to you. That's why you picked up this book, isn't it? To help you take action? Hopefully you will be inspired to follow the lead of the many successful Canadians you will meet in the book. Believe me, I know from personal experience there are lots of success stories out there. So before we explore current attitudes to retirement, I'd like to tell you the story of a retired Canadian widower who managed to fall in love again and eventually retire to his dream location a happy man.

RICHARD AND COLLEEN

Richard and his wife Colleen are both professors of economics. They met while he was living and teaching in Montreal, and she was in Boston. Richard, then 50, met Colleen (who was ten years younger) when they both were invited across the world to a Distinguished Scholar's Retreat in Bellagio along the beautiful shores of Lake Como in northern Italy.

They fell in love, but there was yet to be a happy ending. Because of ongoing teaching commitments, they began a commuting marriage between Montreal and Boston that was to last for over fourteen years! US Airways was most pleased to add these frequent flyers to its passenger list until Richard retired (actually he semi-retired), sold his house and moved to Boston.

Aside from the Montreal house proceeds, and her house in Boston, they had little assets or additional savings. They were by no means a financially sophisticated couple. Fortunately, Colleen continued to teach and Richard could draw on his Canadian pension, although the continually shrinking loonie (this was the 1990s) didn't help their cause, as practically all their expenses were in U.S. dollars. Now that they were finally living together, they yearned to fulfill a dream — to have their own retreat; although this one would prove to be much closer to home than Bellagio.

Through careful planning, saving and shrewd investing, they managed to save enough to buy an acre of prime land on lovely Martha's Vineyard, an island paradise situated just off the Massachusetts coast. But they could not afford to build a house on the land they had purchased, so it sat, tantalizingly dormant, for months, then years. What would they do now?

In a later chapter we will learn how sticking to a plan allowed these two hardworking academics to retire in style. But right now, I'd like to introduce you to a critical topic when it comes to retirement: attitudes. I said earlier that I was deeply concerned about Canadians' lack of awareness and attitude towards their finances. The following chapter will explain why.

CHAPTER
TWO

"The only way people (particularly baby boomers) are
preparing for [retirement] is by wearing upscale designer clothes,
buying sports cars and getting plastic surgery."
—WAYNE RUSSO

ATTITUDE?
WHAT ATTITUDE?

What happens in the United States deeply affects us here in Canada, whether we like it or not. There is a very disquieting trend going on south of the border. Americans are spending more than they earn. Michael Hodges says America is becoming a debt "junkie." On his Web site (Grandfather Economic Report: America's Total Debt Report, June 2005) he says total consumer, government and corporate debt is a staggering $136,479 per man, woman and child.

More than two-thirds of this debt has been created since 1990, and by the way, this figure excludes the huge unfunded contingent liabilities of social security, government pensions and Medicare.

Business Week quotes studies by Yale University political scientist Jacob S. Hacker, showing that finances of two-earner households are being stretched to the limit. In the past fifteen years, mortgage and home-equity borrowing has risen from 35.1 percent of home values to 43.9 percent.

I doubt this trend is significantly different in Canada, which leads to the question: Is another real estate bubble forming? Excessive borrowing by Canadian homebuyers coupled with the exceptional liquidity provided by financial services firms is pushing prices higher and higher. Only time (and interest rates) will tell us if a bubble has indeed formed.

I give you all these numbers not to scare you but to try and ground you in reality. Why? Because, according to a recent poll, a reality check may be in order for Canadian investors.

POLLS SUGGEST CANADIANS ARE SURPRISINGLY STRESS-FREE ABOUT THEIR RETIREMENT

According to the findings of a recent survey carried out by TD Waterhouse Canada, two-thirds of Canadians aged 18 to 69 found investing for retirement "not very or not at all stressful." Are you surprised? I am. The reasons for their complacency about retirement may be reflected in their answers to the subsequent poll questions, including the following:

1) The investors polled indicated they will be relying on *other* sources to supplement their retirement income, specifically:

- CPP: 41 percent
- Company pension plan: 39 percent
- Home equity: 27 percent

Interestingly, none of the above sources are under the investor's control.

2) Nearly half do *not* know their "retirement number"— that is, the amount they'll need to retire comfortably. This of course begs the question, how can you worry about saving "X" amount of dollars if you don't know what "X" is?
3) Canadians feel that they are investing as much as they can afford today. Up to 40 percent will only think about investing more once they make more money.

To me, the above trends are troublesome. It seems Canadians aren't stressed, but for all the wrong reasons. Either they figure they'll put adequate money into their retirement fund later, or as needed. Or more likely, they don't have a clue how much they'll really need.

Yes, the house will help them big time, provided of course that it's not financed to the hilt. But remember, not everyone owns a house. And if they sell it, they still have to pay to live somewhere. The Canada Pension Plan? Can anyone really expect to live on $456.92 per month (on average) up to the maximum possible amount of $828.75, which happens to be the 2005 Government of Canada CPP payment rate.

What about the Old Age Security pension? OAS is a monthly benefit available (if applied for) to most Canadians 65 years of age or over. OAS residence requirements must be met to collect on average $449.55 a month.

What about employee pensions? According to *Fortune* magazine, in 2005 only 21 percent of American investors had a defined benefits plan! In Canada, a recent survey from William M. Mercer Limited revealed that 39 percent of defined contribution plan sponsors offer no invest-ment education at all. On a more positive note, defined contribution (DC) plans, which include group registered retirement savings (RRSP) plans, have become a popular alternative to traditional defined benefit plans because DC plans promise greater autonomy and portability.

Underlying the polled investors' optimism may be some profound assumptions that they will never be laid off, get sick or, as they get older or head into retirement, be rejected for a job for which they are emi-nently qualified because of potential ageism or myopia on the part of corporate North America.

The stress levels of these polled may also be low because Canadians just don't want to think about retirement right now, or because they have no intention of *not* working when they retire. But how easy will it be to find work if ageism becomes a growing trend or unemployment figures rise? Have we figured out how to assimilate millions of working retirees back into the workforce?

We've all heard the expression that ignorance is bliss. Well, procrasti-nation is also a habit that is near and dear to many of us. Because retirement is such a "distant" place for many Boomers, perhaps it barely registers as a speck on their financial horizon. But a million-ton asteroid is just a speck, too — that is, before it enters the atmosphere and plummets to the earth at 65,000 miles per hour! Some experts are highlighting the potential for a massive shortfall in Canadians'— especially Boomers'— nest eggs.

Now, having said all the above, I want you to understand I haven't joined the doomsayers just yet. I don't agree we'll have a shortfall. I think the majority of us are gradually becoming more aware of our current and future financial condition through books like this. And it's impor-tant to note that (as we'll see shortly), we're in better financial shape than we think we are.

Believe me, I'm not here to use scare tactics. Just the opposite. If I'm right about why you picked up this book, you're already anxious and willing to learn something — and do something. It's important that you experience the process as positive, exciting and proactive. Why? Because our *attitude* to money plays a huge role in the quality and quantity of our decision-making.

You can have either a positive or a negative attitude to money. Few are neutral about it, no matter what they may say in public. It's your choice to be negative or positive, of course. But I can tell you from my own experience that negative attitudes to money — or life — will be mirrored back to you in spades through negative results. A positive attitude is not only attractive to others; it has a way of eliminating so many of the self-imposed obstacles that derail us at the most inopportune times. But to retire in style, you need more than a positive attitude. You need to *act*.

We don't need psychologists to explain to us the human instinct to live for today and downplay tomorrow. If you're like many Canadians I come across in my travels, planning for your retirement is one of your "back-burner" to-dos. It may nag at you from time to time, and depending on your age, it may have even reached the point where it's beginning to cloud your sunny outlook on life, but you haven't got around to any serious thinking just yet. Or perhaps you know you need to do something, but you just don't exactly know what.

My suggestion?

RELAX.... IT'S JUST THE REST OF YOUR LIFE!

That's right. Relax. It helps to have a sense of humour about the whole thing. Retirement is a serious issue, make no mistake, but let's not forget an important fact. Retirement is a journey, not a destination. When you retire, you don't suddenly disappear from the face of the earth — unlike our ancestors, for whom retirement and death were often a simultaneous event.

The Population Reference Bureau forecasts that the population of the United States will rise by 19 percent by 2025, compared to 13 percent in Canada, 7 percent in the United Kingdom, 6 percent in France and fractionally negative growth in Japan, Germany and Italy. For North America, these growth rates are a good thing. The higher the population, the more of a future tax base to support an ever growing retiree population. In other countries, particularly Germany, Italy and Japan, negative population rates are decidedly not going to ease the burden on their pension and infrastructure systems.

Retirement today, especially in North America, can be a decades-long period of productivity and freedom because life expectancies have risen, and continue to rise, changing the landscape forever. Middle adulthood is now being defined as 50 to 64. Late adulthood is 65 to 79. Old is thought of as being over 80. According to a government of Canada policy paper, "Life Expectancy, Health Expectancy and the Life Cycle," Canadians retiring in 2046 can expect to live seventeen years longer than the cohort that retired in 1989. Seventeen years in little more than two generations! That's a lot of extra time. What are we going to do with it? Are we really going to spend all those years doing nothing but playing golf and going fishing?

Of course, what you do depends on the size of your nest egg and your personal preferences. But it also depends on your financial acumen and risk tolerance. If you are an active investor, retirement is certainly not the end of your investing cycle.

If you want to begin the planning process on the right foot, you must find out where you stand in these critical areas. So let's get down to business and discover your financial acumen — whether you are a beginner investor, a moderately sophisticated investor or an experienced investor.

HOW FINANCIALLY SAVVY ARE YOU?

How knowledgeable an investor are you? The following simple quiz, courtesy of the Financial Planners Standards Council, will help determine where you fit on the "Financial Expertise Scale."

Test your financial I.Q.

	Always	Usually	Sometimes	Never
I balance my cheque book every month.		✓		
I understand the financial jargon in the newspapers and on television.		✓		
I know what types of insurance I need.		✓		
I pay off my credit card balance monthly.		✓		
I know the value of what I own (property, savings, investments).			✓	
I have money saved for the unexpected and I save regularly for my vacation.			✓	
I am able to cope financially with life's changes.			✓	

	Always	Usually	Sometimes	Never
I feel I will be able to retire when I want.			✓	
I take the time to consider what my financial needs will be in the future.			✓	
I feel that my financial affairs will be in order when I pass on.			✓	

Source: Financial Planners Standards Council (FPSC)

The left-hand column ("Always") counts for 4 points. The next column ("Usually") counts for 3 points. The next column ("Sometimes") counts for 2 points. The right-hand column ("Never") counts for 1 point. Total your answer scores to each question. Out of a possible total of 30 points:

If you scored 26 or more....
Congratulations! You are definitely on the right financial track.

If you scored between 20 and 25....
Not bad, but not great. You may need to rethink your finances as well as your investment strategy.

If you scored less than 19....
You need to be *very* careful about your finances. To get up to speed on some of the basics of investing, I suggest you read the many excellent articles to be found in the Investor Education Fund Web site (www. investored.ca).

YOUR RETIREMENT NUMBER

Okay, now that we've determined your financial I.Q., let's see if we can determine your "retirement number"— that is, the dollar amount you will need to save, or accumulate monthly, to live comfortably in retirement. As I always say in my seminars, retirement planning is not about doing one big thing right but about doing a lot of little things right. In other words, baby steps. But these baby steps must be in the right direction or they are of no help at all. In order to plan your retirement journey properly, *you must begin with the big "picture" in mind.* In other words, you should know your retirement number. As I mentioned earlier, nearly half of Canadians polled did not have any idea what their retirement number was.

First, let me tell you something: the number isn't hiding in a thousand-page actuarial table or a private banker's preferred customer file. In fact, the question isn't *where* do I find my number, but *how* do I go about estimating it?

Your retirement number doesn't just come out of thin air; but, as any experienced financial planner will tell you, it's not all that easily quantifiable. However, when you try to calculate it, then set a number in front of you as a target, a wonderful thing begins to happen. Making your number visible begins to take a big chunk of uncertainty away.

Imagine your retirement needs

- Are you debt-free?
- Do you know what your future cash flow (incomes less expenses) will be?
- Are you prepared to realign your current expenses with projected future expenses?
- Do you know where your income will come from (i.e., CPP, OAS, RRIFs)?
- How will you integrate your various income sources?
- What is the most tax-efficient way to do this?
- How many years remain until you expect to retire?
- Do you know your current net worth? (See Appendix 1)
- What will you need to live on at retirement?
- Will you travel?
- Will you help pay for your grandchildren's tuition?

These are just some of the questions that you should be asking yourself before you sit down and actually work out your retirement number. Once you feel comfortable answering most of these questions, you can calculate your retirement contribution number by going to www.tdcanadatrust.com/planning and working through the questionnaire.

Interest rates may ultimately prove to be the single biggest factor in determining the size of your nest egg, especially if you started saving and investing at an early age. This is due to the magical power of compounding, a concept which I will explain in detail later. Let's assume interest rates remain as low as they are now. That's not really a bad assumption if you consider that the G7 central banks have adopted a global policy to keep inflation in check at all times.

The Bank of Canada (Canada's central bank) aims to keep inflation at a 2 percent target, the midpoint of the 1 percent to 3 percent inflation-control target range. The central bankers as a group believes — and most economists agree with them — that spiralling inflation can do more damage to a country's people and their standard of living than virtually any other single factor. As an example, just look at how Brazil's decades-long inflationary spiral has eroded that country's living standard. Low inflation is the G7's policy, and they've done a pretty good job of it for the past ten years by also carefully monitoring inflation levels on a monthly basis, and not hesitating to raise interest rates immediately if they see inflation rearing its ugly head.

In Chapter 4 you will find much of the information you need to know about portfolio construction, asset allocation, diversification, risk/reward scenarios and rates of return.

Many pundits believe you will need about two-thirds of your current income to live comfortably in retirement, because travel, car, dry cleaning and other costs are reduced. However, this doesn't factor in the effect of inflation over a lengthy number of years to retirement — and during retirement — so keep that in the back of your mind for now. Also, some retirees want to completely scale down and simplify their lives, while others may want to spend more on long trips and other luxuries now that they have real freedom for the first time in their lives. This means some may need 50 percent of their pre-retired income, and others may need 100 percent. We will revisit this two-thirds estimation in a later chapter.

Yes, if you were to work out the present value of the cash needed to fund two-thirds of your current income, your retirement number might appear a little intimidating — or a lot! But before you panic, I want to mention a couple of important points. First, you don't have to find that kind of money today, or tomorrow. You just have to *start* building it from this point forward. Later in this book (in Chapters 4, 5 and 6) I'm going to give you the tools you need to make it happen. Lastly and most importantly, you have to decide whether you want to use all your capital or preserve most of your capital to give to your heirs, or charity, or both.

LISA AND BILL

Here are a couple of real-world examples. Meet Lisa and Bill, two Boomers who don't know each other, even though Lisa is a dog trainer and Bill is the superintendent of her apartment building. Hey, what can I tell you, they live in the big city!

Lisa is 50, and earns a "conservative" rate of return of 6 percent on her life savings of $50,000. Compounded over fifteen years to retirement, what do you think her nest egg would be? Now if Lisa *also* contributed $5,000 per year in her RRSP every year for fifteen years to retirement, how big would her nest egg be then? (There's a reason I've illustrated Lisa's scenario, and the answer is in Chapter 4.)

What about Bill? He's 40, and earns 6.73 percent with a more aggressive "balanced" portfolio, on his life savings of $50,000. Compounded over twenty-five years to his retirement, what do you think his nest egg would be? And if Bill also contributed $5,000 per year in his RRSP every year for twenty-five years to his retirement, how big would his nest egg be then? (There's also a reason I've illustrated Bill's scenario, and again the answer is in Chapter 4.)

Your retirement number is your financial goal, but you also need a strategy to ensure you achieve it

For many of you, your savings rate and/or income level will be sufficient to achieve your retirement number. But for some of you, it may not. Your current assets, savings rate and income level may prove to be inadequate. Either on your own or with a financial advisor, you can work out any potential discrepancy by determining your net worth and comparing that to your retirement number.

Factors that affect your retirement number

If your strategy is overly ambitious — meaning it doesn't match your savings rate, income or investment returns, you may have to save more aggressively or increase the equity portion your portfolio. A financial advisor can work with you to develop a realistic plan based on your age, occupation, risk profile and investment horizon.

Are you really prepared?

Maybe Canadians feel they are prepared. Many surveys indicate that is the case. Not so fast, says the Principal Financial Group. Their third annual Global Financial Well-Being Study found that only a minority of workers worldwide (22 percent) feel very confident they will have enough money to pay for basic expenses like food, shelter and clothing during retirement.

This leads me to ask you another important question relating to your investment style and investment objectives. How much investment *risk* can you tolerate? This is one of the most important questions you can ask yourself. Many people overestimate their risk tolerance, often because they've been lucky enough not to have lost much in the stock market, or they've never been in the market in the first place. Whatever the reason, if you want to grow the kind of nest egg that lets you sleep at night, you need to address this thing called risk.

If you want to check your risk tolerance, go to the Investor Education Web site (www.investored.ca) and fill in the three quizzes you'll find there.

IT'S ALL ABOUT ADJUSTING YOUR EXPECTATIONS

Risk is one thing. But expectations are quite another. The Canadian Labour Congress says that today, three out of every four Canadians worry that a secure retirement will be out of their reach. Is it really so bad?

Yes and no.

According to a CBC News online report entitled "Golden Years: Baby Boomers and Retirement," by the year 2030 there will be only *two* workers per retired person, compared to four today, to pay rapidly rising CPP costs.

A national poll conducted for Investors Group by Decima Research indicates that over 18 percent of Boomers said they had household savings and investments worth over $250,000. Another 21 percent said they had saved between $100,000 and $250,000. But Debbie Ammeter, Vice President of Advanced Financial Planning for Investors Group, cautions that while many Boomers have done a good job of saving, without a plan their expected retirement income may not support their desired lifestyle.

"Will Canadians outlive their assets?" That was the question posed by a recent survey commissioned by Desjardins Financial Security. According to Monique Tremblay, Senior Vice-President at Desjardins Financial Security, respondents said they were generally optimistic about their retirement, but less than 20 percent reported being "very confident" in their ability to save enough.

Okay, have I managed to thoroughly "ground" you with these facts? More likely, I've thoroughly depressed you. So let's switch gears and return to some more positive retirement trends.

In the past ten to fifteen years, as the Boomer generation has reached what used to be called middle age, the negativity that used to surround the R-word has begun to disappear. A new group of R-words has entered our vocabulary: words like revitalize, reenergize and rejuvenate. This is no coincidence. Thanks to significant improvements in diet, exercise and health care, life expectancies have risen substantially. Smoking is on the decline — a recent Statistics Canada report indicated that the percentage of smokers over the age of fifteen had dropped to a new low of 20 percent.

Boomers in particular are revisiting the whole concept of retirement, turning it on its ear the way they have with child rearing, later marriage and double-income families. As University of Toronto Economics Professor David Foot states in his book, *Boom, Bust and Echo*:

> …the aging of the massive 10-million-strong Boomer generation (born from 1947 to 1966) has left indelible marks. After the Boom came the Bust. Maternity wards and schools emptied, house prices crashed and auto sales sagged as the Boom genera-tion was replaced by the smaller Bust generation (born from 1967 to 1979) moving through these stages of their lives. It is not until your 50s when the kids leave home, that you start to build up your financial assets for retirement, build up your nest egg for retirement that you are going to live off.

Fair enough. But what about those who choose *early* retirement? Are an increasing number of people retiring *before* the traditional retirement age of 60? Statistics Canada answered the question in a 2001 study by Patrick Kieran.

- Between 1987 and 1990, only 29 percent of people who recently retired did so before the age of 60.
- Between 1997 and 2000, however, that rate grew to 43 percent.
- The early retirement rate was much higher in the public sector than in the private sector. The most popular retirement age for public-sector employees was 55. Most private-sector workers still retired at age 65, while the majority of self-employed retired even later.

- The Atlantic provinces had the highest early retirement rates, while the western provinces had the lowest. The many early retirements in the Atlantic provinces may be related to their higher unemployment rates.
- More women than men retire early. Two factors may be involved — the greater number of women in public-sector jobs and the two-year age difference between spouses.
- Early retirement was popular among people with higher levels of education and those with higher incomes. The early retirement rate was also high in industries with workers in utilities, public administration and educational services.
- People in the agriculture sector are the least likely to retire early. Workers in this industry are primarily self-employed. Also, many farmers do not earn high incomes and postpone retirement until they can collect Canada or Quebec Pension Plan benefits.

What effect will these trends have on Boomers' retirement plans? I said earlier that I was deeply concerned about Canadians' awareness and attitudes toward their finances. Apparently I'm not alone. Mike Hendricks, editor of *The Business Review*, reminds us that Boomers were raised on the notion that early retirement was a virtue, and as a result "they're going to need a big attitude adjustment."

All is not doom and gloom, however. A recent HSBC study revealed that Canadians lead the world in planning for retirement. What that says about the rest of the world is for you to decide. But from my point of view, I think we as Canadians have a lot of things going for us. In later chapters, you're going to meet some of these Canadians, both retirees and non-retirees. They're going to share with you some of their inspirational, intriguing and thought-provoking stories about retirement, their expectations and attitudes to planning.

There are ways to simplify your life, especially from a financial viewpoint. And while there's no cookie-cutter, one-size-fits-all approach to retirement, there are some very important, tried-and-true solutions that can help guide you toward a richer retirement. I've incorporated them into an easy to follow, four-step plan called the PATH.

THE PATH AND HOW TO FIND IT

The PATH is your essential four-step guide to a successful and financially predictable retirement. In the following chapters we'll discuss each step in detail, beginning with the big "Picture." But for now it is important to understand that they go together *in sequence*, just like four notes in the right sequence can make a beautiful melody (four little notes make up the memorable opening to one of Beethoven's most famous compositions — his *Fifth Symphony*).

1. Picture yourself in retirement
2. Arm yourself with the right financial and planning tools
3. Transition into retirement with style
4. Harmony: Put it all together and leave a legacy

Let's begin with the big "Picture." In other words, where are you going? When you go on vacation, you can't get to your destination if you don't know where it is, can you? Likewise, if you can't picture yourself having and doing and being in a successful retirement, I guarantee you won't get there, either. Let's see how "picturing" the future, and using a proven concept called guided imagery, can help you focus and succeed beyond your wildest dreams.

CHAPTER
THREE

"Imagination is everything. It is the preview of life's coming attractions."
—ALBERT EINSTEIN

PICTURE

GO AHEAD: PICTURE
YOURSELF IN RETIREMENT

Over a decade ago, a *Fortune* magazine article inelegantly entitled, "Americans don't have nearly enough savings for their longer lives," began with these alarming words:

> It's tough to contemplate retirement. At 25, the idea's remote. At 35, paying off a mortgage consumes all your thoughts — and much of your cash. At 45, kids' tuition bills loom. At 55, it's time to indulge — that is, if you haven't been restructured or down-scaled. At 65, hindsight hits with a vengeance.... Survey after survey reveals that working Americans know their retirement plans are inadequate. Yet fully 39 percent of U.S. households have no retirement savings at all, according to a study by Raddon Financial Group. Out of the 61 percent that do, most underestimate how much they'll need.

What have we learned about retirement planning over the past decade? Not too much, apparently. Earlier, I said that an attitude shift may be in the cards for some Canadians, depending on their expectations and savings rate. Unfortunately, as the above excerpt highlights only too well, changing one's attitude, behaviour and habits is one of the hardest things on earth to do.

But there is a way to change, and it's relatively painless if you have an open mind. It's all about concentrated visualization. It's amazing how many people say they have an open mind, when in fact they've developed rigid opinions on any number of subjects. With that thought in mind, if you are interested in learning how the concept of visualization through guided imagery can help you achieve your financial goals, read on. If you are not, by all means skip right to the next chapter. But if you've read this far, my guess is you're open to change, or at least curious about it. If you are, this chapter is definitely for you. It's about how visualization has the potential to significantly enhance the financial and emotional quality of your retirement.

Visualization is a concept that's proven itself over and over again in the sports world. Many of the most successful professional and amateur athletes create a positive picture of the expected result in their minds before they even hit the shot or call the play in the huddle. In 1988, Canadian sport psychologists Terry Orlick, Ph.D., and John Partington, Ph.D., found that 99 percent of the 235 athletes they surveyed relied on mental rehearsal to prepare for a high-stakes race.

In a *Psychology Today* interview dated June 2000, Dr. James Bauman, a sports psychologist attached to the U.S. Olympic Training Center, said, "I have seen how 'mental management' contributes to an athlete's performance. Some Olympians even say it accounts for 90 percent of their success."

Visualization is all about focus. Have you noticed if you ask a friend who is notoriously unfocused to concentrate on something, he can't do it for more than an instant? This chapter is highly relevant to you if you're trying to visualize your retirement picture, or it has not yet come into focus. A simple quiz may help you move ahead. It's divided into three parts, based on your retirement plans.

Complete Part A if you expect to retire the traditional way; complete Part B if you expect to have a phased-in retirement; and complete Part C if you never plan to retire. Be as honest as possible with your responses. There is no pass or failure.

A) For those who plan to retire the traditional way:

1) How old will you be when you retire?
2) What kind of leisure activities do you see yourself doing?
3) What kind of, and how much travel do you see yourself doing?
4) How big a role will family activities play in your week-to-week activities?
5) How big a role will friends and social activities play in your week-to-week activities?

6) Do you see yourself mostly alone?
7) Do you see yourself and your spouse mostly alone?
8) Do you see a full slate of social activities?
9) What kind of work — volunteer or paid — do you see yourself doing?
10) Where do you see yourself doing all the above? Where you are now or in some other geographic location?
11) If you see yourself in some other place, where do you think it will be?
12) Will you live there full-time, part of the time, or will you try to evenly split your time between two or more places?

If you answered all or most of the above the questions very quickly, there's no need for you to do any further visualization at this time. You may skip to the next chapter. However, if you answered "I don't know" a lot, or had to think hard about many of the questions, then you need to work on your retirement "picture."

B) For those who plan to phase in their retirement:

1) How old will you be when you retire?
2) What mix of work and leisure activities do you see yourself doing? Half and half? Mostly work? Mostly leisure?
3) What kind of, and how much travel do you see yourself doing?
4) How many years do you see yourself in semi-retired mode?
5) Will family activities play a larger role in your week-to-week activities?
6) Will friends and social activities play a larger role in your week-to-week activities?
7) What kind of volunteer work, if any, do you see yourself doing?
8) When you finally retire (fully), will you stay where you are or move away to another geographic location?
9) Will you live there full-time, part of the time, or will you try to evenly split your time between two or more places?
10) Do you see yourself mostly alone?
11) Do you see yourself and your spouse mostly alone?
12) Do you see a full slate of social activities?

If you answered all or most of the above the questions very quickly, there's no need for you to do any further visualization at this time. You may skip to the next chapter. However, if you answered "I don't know" a lot, or had to think hard about many of the questions, then you need to work on your retirement "picture."

C) For those who never plan to retire:

1) If you never plan to retire, what will you be doing after the age of 65 or 70 — in other words, during your non-retired "retirement" years?
2) How many hours a day/week/month will you be working during your "non-retired" years?
3) What mix of work and leisure activities do you see yourself doing? Half and half? Mostly work? Mostly leisure?
4) What kind of volunteer work, if any, do you see yourself doing?
5) What kind of, and how much travel do you see yourself doing?
6) When you are "non-retired," will family activities play a larger role in your week-to-week activities?
7) When you are "non-retired," will friends and social activities play a larger role in your week-to-week activities?
8) When you are "non-retired," will you stay where you are or move away to another geographic location?
9) Will you live there full-time, part of the time, or will you try to evenly split your time between two or more places?
10) Do you see yourself mostly alone?
11) Do you see yourself and your spouse mostly alone?
12) Do you see a full slate of social activities?

If you answered all or most of the above the questions without much hesitation, there's no need for you to do any further visualization at this time. You may skip to the next chapter. But if you're like many, and you answered "I don't know" to a lot of the questions, or had to think hard about most of them, then I think we need to work together to clarify your retirement picture.

THE POWER OF VISUALIZATION

Do you ever unconsciously sabotage your best efforts by either over-thinking or trying too hard, whether it be in sports, relationships, career decisions, business deals — in fact, just about any aspect of life? I know I have, and more often than I want to admit. Here's an example from my own life.

One of my hobbies is golf. In fact I have a passion for the game. It's a frustrating game but also an exhilarating one. A friend of mine named Bill, who plays both golf and tennis, says they're much more similar to each other than people think. He says in both sports, the mental aspects of the game limit us far more than our physical abilities.

For example, he's always telling me I should visualize the golf shot I'm about to play before I play it. He says it makes all the difference in whether I make the shot or not. Well, guess what? I didn't take his advice, partly because I wasn't sure I understood him, and partly because I thought I was doing okay at the game without any "gimmicks." But as the weeks went on, my game stopped improving. If anything it was getting worse. So one day, I went out and decided to play golf the way he said.

Before I got up to the first tee, I visualized my shot rising up into the air like a graceful bird and then landing softly in the centre of the fairway. So I got set, calmed my nerves, took a practice swing, pictured the shot and then hit the ball. I topped it! I dribbled the ball down the slope and it ended just a few yards off the tee. If you don't play golf, let me tell you, that is an embarrassing shot. But I didn't give up. That's not my nature. I tried again on the next shot from the fairway, visualizing my shot rolling through the fairway and right up to the green.

Wham! I sliced the ball to the right; it disappeared through the trees and out of bounds.

I stopped visualizing after that.

When I told Bill what had happened he laughed and then apologized for not "teaching" me properly. He told me there's more to visualization than people think, and promptly sent me a couple of books by someone named W. Timothy Gallwey. Perhaps you've heard of him. His first book was called *The Inner Game of Tennis*. He wrote other books afterward, and then came out with one called *The Inner Game of Golf*. A professional tennis instructor in the 1970s, Gallwey was the first to combine the principles of Zen and sport psychology into the sport of tennis.

I read both books, and as a result I began to observe my behaviour closely for the first time. I heard a little voice inside me whenever I was swinging badly — or about to swing badly! Gallwey says there's a little critic inside virtually every one of us who appears whenever we try to do something that requires skill and/or dexterity, or is new, or is outside our comfort zone. As a writer, I can tell you the biggest cause of writer's block is the voice in the writer's head that says, "The writing isn't good enough," or "I've got to stop writing garbage and wait for the muse to hit." Gallwey says there is no muse. That's just the ego getting in the way of the natural self, which not only prevents the smooth flow of writing, in some cases it can prevent any writing at all.

It's no different with sports. My (little voice) ego says things like, "Pattie, you can't play this shot because you've never played it before." But my natural self says, "Go ahead and play it. What have you got to lose?" But as I step up and hit the ball, the more powerful little voice in my head jumps in and says, "Look out! There's no way you're gonna make this." And, *voilà*, I flub the shot. Gallwey tries to keep things simple. He calls the ego "Self 1" and the natural self "Self 2."

I realized that in order for me to picture my shots successfully, I had to block out the little voice. Easier said than done, but Bill (and Gallwey) showed me how. Onto the practice range we went, where Bill reintroduced me to the concepts of rhythm and relaxation.

Instead of concentrating on the ball — which most people do — he had me think about where my club head was during my swing. To help me out, he showed me a drill — what Gallwey calls the "Back-Hit-Stop"— in which I would actually say the word, "Back" the instant I felt my club head reach its maximum extension at the top of my swing. Then I would say, "Hit" the moment the club face met the ball. Then I would say, "Stop" the moment I felt the club head stop at completion of my swing.

What did this do? It made me think about my swing, not about hitting the ball. It let me swing beautifully and make crisp contact with the ball. It blocked out my controlling little voice which wanted to say (in the middle of my swing!) things like, "Left arm stiff! Right leg quiet! Head still! Stay behind the ball!" No one can swing a club well with all that going on in their head!

Our judgmental little voice can never be silenced, however. It can only be blocked out. Why does this perfectionist or negative thinking arise, you ask? What does it matter? says Gallwey. It isn't necessary to know why; it's enough to recognize that this thinking exists. Analyzing the source of those thoughts is a fruitless exercise.

"PICTURE YOURSELF IN A BOAT ON A RIVER WITH TANGERINE TREES AND MARMALADE SKIES."

Okay, so what does all this have to do with retirement planning? Simple. In golf if you know how to picture the shot, and block everything else out of your mind, the shot will happen. If you know how to effectively picture yourself in retirement, doing the things you really want to do and blocking out negative or distracting thoughts, then it will happen.

When John Lennon and Paul McCartney wrote "Lucy in the Sky with Diamonds," they knew how to evoke beautiful images. It was part of the creative process for them. But tangerine trees and marmalade skies won't do us much good when we're picturing our retirement, because this isn't fantasy time, it's reality time. Try to imagine what you actually see yourself doing during your retirement. Is it a dream house in the Caribbean? Fine. Then make it a reality by introducing specifics: Decide where it is in the Caribbean, how big it's going to be and how much it's going to cost.

Or maybe it's simply a move away from the suburbs to the sophisticated conveniences of a luxury condo in the heart of downtown. Then make it happen. Is it living in the same house and working at the same job, and continuing to socialize with the people at work who became your friends? Good for you. But you may need to prepare yourself for a consulting role with that company, depending on their retirement rules.

Whatever the case may be, you need to decide financially, emotionally and psychically what it is you need to make this happen. In other words, establish a comprehensive, step-by-step process. To help you, I've repackaged the key sports principles espoused by Dr. Bauman and his colleagues and incorporated them into the following financial scenario:

Your pre-retirement planning strategy

- Attitude. Make sure you begin with a positive attitude; at the very least have an open mind. The more open you are to the process, the faster it will take hold and become easily achievable in your mind.
- Set realistic goals. Be specific about what you want to accomplish, whether it's keeping the exact same lifestyle you have now, downsizing or even upsizing.

- Picture your retirement. Find a quiet place and begin to dream about what would make you and your spouse happy. Visualize the result over and over so it starts to feel like a comfortable reality. If you haven't talked to your spouse about your picture, or learned what his or her retirement picture is, now is most definitely the time.
- Calculate your retirement number. Focus on the contribution number that makes this picture achievable.
- Establish a strategy. Develop (on your own or with an expert) a financial and lifestyle plan to achieve this number.
- Adjust your budget. If your strategy does not match your savings rate, your income level or your investment rate of return, you may have to adjust your savings, income potential or enhance your rate of return (depending on your age, occupation and risk profile). A financial advisor can work with you to develop an optimal scenario.
- Commit to a start date. By far the most effective way to do that is to begin right now — not Friday, Saturday or someday, but today!
- Relax. It's not the end of the world. It's the beginning of something new. There are a lot of ways to invest and save. Before you begin, think about things that put you at ease. Interestingly, what Bauman says about sports applies equally well to the process of establishing a retirement strategy: "Breathe easily and fully. Picture the muscles in your body as being loose and limber. Conjure up soothing images — scenes that make you feel genuinely good."
- Decide on your comfort level. What is your investment comfort level? Would you prefer to manage your own investments, have them managed for you or something in between? It's your choice, but if you have any doubts, begin with a planner and as time goes by and your investment sophistication increases, you can always opt out and go solo.
- Arm yourself. Learn about your investment options and then choose the investment, savings and protection tools you need. I will explain your options in detail in the next few chapters.
- Imagine your performance. Rehearse in your mind what your rate of return will be, and how you will feel as each year goes by and your nest egg swells. See yourself doing it, then do it.
- Control distractions. Make a checklist of everything that might derail you from accomplishing your goal. To paraphrase Bauman:

Eliminate the things you can't control, focus on those you can, concentrate on enjoying the here and now, but stick to your plan.

Your at-retirement strategy

- Pre-planning. Cover all contingencies. Make the transition a smooth one.
- Tax strategies. Convert RRSP and investment income to annuities and RRIFs.
- Portfolio composition. Remember to apply the concepts of asset allocation and diversification.
- Creative options. Reverse mortgages, part-time work, expectation adjustment, tax planning.
- Structure. Structure your days and weeks and make your attitude adjustment a reality.
- Close to home? Do you want to live close to friends and family or move to your dream location? The choice is yours, but income demands can vary considerably.
- Gifts. Gift planning and the tax implications.

Your in-retirement strategy

- Budgets. Simplify your life: Map out a monthly budget that works for you.
- Integration of income. CPP, OAS, RRIFs, and so on.
- Taxes. Not just income taxes but gifts and investments.
- Estate Planning. Leave a legacy without leaving half to the taxman.
- Philanthropy. The gift that keeps on giving.
- Work. To work or not to work, that is the question.

The above will be explored in detail in the following chapters. But if you're beginning to think this retirement planning gig is an enormously complex process, don't worry. All you need to remember is the PATH: Picture, Arm, Transition and Harmony. Remember these four simple steps and you won't lose your way.

And now it's time to move on from "P" to "A." Let's get you "Armed" for the journey ahead.

CHAPTER
FOUR

"Before you invest, investigate."
—WILLIAM ARTHUR WARD

ARM (Part 1)

ARM YOURSELF WITH THE *INVESTMENT KNOWLEDGE* YOU NEED

Now that your retirement picture is beginning to come into focus, I want to talk about the investments you'll need to help make that picture a reality. Specifically, I want to arm you with the fundamental concepts that successful investors use every day of their investing lives — concepts like risk and return and the magical power of compounding. If you want to be a savvy investor, you need to be well versed in the subtleties of investing. But before we discuss these subtleties, I need to ask you a very important question.

Are you debt-free?

By that I mean, aside from a possible house mortgage, have you paid off all your outstanding loans? If you have a secured or unsecured line of credit, are you paying it down? Do you promptly pay off your credit card loans? (Because that's what they are. Don't ever call them credit card balances.) If you answered no to any of these questions, you should rethink your financial situation before thinking about a long-term investment strategy. Why? Because not only are each of these loans likely to be non-tax-deductible, they'll most certainly eat up your capital faster than you can grow it through your investments.

PAY YOURSELF FIRST

"Canadians don't rely on luck to build wealth. They know that by following basic rules of saving they can get to where they want to go. It's about setting realistic goals and making tough choices." So says Jacqueline C.

Orange, President and Chief Executive Officer, Canada Investment and Savings. In a speech kicking off the 2004 Canada Savings Bond campaign, Orange went on to say that in her experience, two clear strategies work best: Pay yourself first, and start early. "An automatic deduction plan — where money comes off our paycheque before we can see it, or spend it — is the best way to go. It's a painless way to get there, and a great way to stay disciplined." She also feels we need to do a better job of teaching the basics of financial management, especially to young people, so they're encouraged to start investing as early as possible.

If truth be told, forced savings may be the only way many people *can* save. According to a new survey of 38 countries by ACNielsen, the United States ranked *first in the world* with the highest percentage of consumers living paycheque to paycheque. More than a quarter of Americans said they "have no spare cash" after paying for essential living expenses. What about Canada? We also ranked near the top in the survey. It's clear that North America (with the exception of Mexico) is a consumption-driven society where the more we make the more we spend.

SAVING IS NOT THE SAME AS INVESTING

Allow me to review a couple of basic but often misunderstood concepts. The big one is this: saving is *not* the same as investing. When you put your savings away, whether it be into a savings account or in a jar or under the mattress, you'll get back what you put in — and very little else. Saving is preserving from *loss*.

Investing, on the other hand, means to purchase something in the hope that it will either generate income or appreciate in value in the foreseeable future. There's always a certain amount of *risk* attached with any investment. That is, investments may grow a little or a lot, but they can also fall in value a little or lose their value altogether. The greater the risk, the higher the potential *return* must be in order to attract you as an investor. This is the classic risk/return trade-off that we all know and love.

We can invest in a stock, invest in a fund, invest through an advisor, invest in ourselves through education and training and even invest in others (children, colleagues, and so on). And in every case, the risk is counterbalanced by the hope or expectation of some kind of a payoff.

In recent years, there has been a lot of talk about the concept of risk — especially market risk. In fact, whole books have been written about the subject. After the recent shellacking many of us took during the 2000–2001 stock market meltdown, a new attitude of caution has begun to prevail. Some experts have even become bold enough to insist we stay out of the stock market altogether.

AVOID THE LOW-INTEREST TRAP

Where to put all your hard earned money, then? In low-interest money market funds and GICs?

In today's low-interest environment, I believe anyone with a long-term investment horizon should avoid the low-interest trap. Let's use a simple example of why you should avoid the low-interest trap. Let's say you're 40 years old and have $50,000 saved. You decide to put all of it in a 3 percent interest-bearing money market fund. If you don't contribute another dime until you retire, how much do you think you'll have saved by the time you retire at 65?

You would have $104,688.90 (before tax) at age 65, which is double your initial savings. Pretty good. But wait — hold on a moment. This scenario does *not* factor inflation into the equation, which is currently running at about 2 percent.

Your real (inflation-adjusted) return is actually only 1 percent.

At a 1 percent inflation-adjusted rate of return, you would actually have only $64,000 at retirement. Not good! That's the low-interest trap at work. And, by the way, we haven't factored taxes into the equation just yet.

Do you want to know a quick way to figure out how long it will take you to double your money? Use the "rule of 72." The rule of 72 says that to find out how many years it would take to double your money (at a given interest rate), you just divide that interest rate into 72.

So at a 3 percent return, it will take you twenty-four years to double your money. At a 6 percent return, however, it would only take you a dozen years to double your savings. Remember, your rate of return is not only critical to retiring in style — it will help you clarify your investment goals and thus help you avoid the low-interest trap.

FROM COUPON CLIPPER TO MULTI-MILLIONAIRE

When it comes to investing in the stock market, there's nothing quite like employing a tried-and-true strategy with a twist. Just ask Robert Edgewood and his family. From modest beginnings in England where he clipped coupons at an investment bank, Robert realized his passion when he became a student of the stock market. Although he picked up an Associate of the Chartered Institute of Bankers (ACIB) designation while in London, he felt that opportunities for his registered-nurse wife and himself lay somewhere else.

"The best decision I ever made was to leave England and seek a better quality of life in Canada." With his wife, Helen, and three children in tow, the 42-year-old Edgewood arrived in Toronto in 1988 hoping to find what he'd been missing in England. But that was not to be, at least not for their first few years in Canada. Life was difficult financially. "I took a clerical job while my wife toughed it out as a temp with a nursing placement agency."

But Robert always had one eye on the stock market. He invested cautiously in single country funds for many years, all the while observing market trends and patterns from a distance. He had a sixth sense he was good at investing and wanted to do it full-time. Finally, in 1998, he broached a touchy subject with his wife: borrowing to invest.

"I decided to get a loan and invest in the market." But not just any loan: a $120,000 line of credit on the house. Aside from some modest savings, it was their only asset. This was the last thing Helen needed to hear, given their uncertain financial future. But Robert was convinced he could make it work. And when he explained his investment strategy to her, she agreed to let him give it a try. "I had $60,000 in savings, but I knew it wasn't enough to make my investment strategy work. So with Helen's blessing I took the line of credit and went to work."

I'd like to issue a very important caveat here: aggressive investment strategies like Robert's should not be attempted by anyone who does not have sophisticated financial expertise, a deep understanding of market volatility and first-hand awareness of his or her own risk tolerance and reaction to volatility. I want to relate Robert's story because it illustrates how successful a buy-and-hold strategy can be, and it shows us how much discipline is needed to *stick with* the plan through the inevitable ups and downs of the market.

ROBERT'S INVESTMENT STRATEGY

Robert's first investment decision involved pipelines: Pembina Pipeline Income Fund (PIF.UN). He put $25,000 into the trust, which at the time was yielding 15 percent. As with most trusts, monthly distributions were paid out at a preferential tax rate.

"I actually felt my investment strategy was a prudent one. I'd done my homework and knew the oil and gas sector was out of favour back in 1998; I felt it was undervalued, and I wanted to invest in it. Oil was about $12 a barrel back then, and trusts were a relatively unknown investment vehicle at the time. Although there was risk involved, I felt the returns justified the risk. I also felt comforted by the fact that oil and gas trusts are backed by tangible assets."

Interest on his line of credit was tax-deductible. And Robert calculated that his monthly interest payments ($25,000 × 6% percent / 12) would be more than covered by the 15 percent yield (the monthly distributions) from the trust.

"I watched my $25,000 investment like a hawk, and after about two months felt comfortable enough to put the balance of the line of credit plus my savings, about $150,000, into a series of oil and gas trusts. Again, the distributions were averaging 15 percent to 18 percent so they more than covered my interest costs. The 8 percent or 9 percent net return provided a nice little income while I waited patiently for the trusts to begin appreciating in value."

It didn't take long. Within a year, oil prices were on the rise from multi-year lows, and Robert's oil-and-gas trust units began to appreciate in value. But as the trusts appreciated, Robert stuck to his plan and minimized churn. Distributions were reinvested and most of the margin available was used. He avoided selling his winners and thus rode them to new highs, and through aggressive use of margin, he turbocharged his rate of return even further. A couple of trusts left the portfolio because of takeovers and were replaced by newly listed trusts as institutional investors continued to shun the sector.

By 1999, Robert's strategy had paid off in spades. He decided to tweak the strategy and focus on picking up lesser known but higher yielding trusts. "There's no question I have an exceptionally high tolerance for risk. But I do my homework and take calculated risks; I don't act impulsively. I didn't get caught up in the technology stock mania, for example. I just wasn't tempted to cash in my trusts and jump into something I knew nothing about."

By 2000, Robert had built a very healthy portfolio. The line of credit was increased to $208,000. "My strategy seemed to be working," he says modestly. The portfolio continued to grow. It wasn't long before he was able to reduce his line of credit to a nominal amount, and now he keeps it available for emergency use — hopefully not for margin calls!

In a very short period of time, Robert Edgewood had become rich. But Robert didn't feel the need to show off. He was quite happy driving the same economy car he'd had for years, and best of all, Helen had stopped worrying about their financial future. Robert stuck to his plan, stayed the course, minimized taxes by buying, monitoring and disciplined himself to continue holding. As a result, he's minimized the realization of capital gains, reinvested monthly distributions and used broker margin to steadily expand his portfolio.

"I'M A FUNDAMENTAL AND VALUE INVESTOR"

"I establish my own value criteria and check out the usual financial ratios, plus cash flow, net asset value and reserve life index. And I'm aware of the risks. If interest rates rise, the value of income trusts will fall. If oil prices decline, the trust values will fall. Mergers and acquisitions must also be taken into account."

Robert knows about asset allocation and diversification, and he agrees they are useful techniques. But Robert has always marched to the beat of a different drummer and, to this point, his journey has been a success.

"Helen and I have separate but very similar portfolios, which are linked for margin purposes. I trade on both. So far, she hasn't complained about my investment techniques."

Instead of being tempted to branch out to other investment vehicles or sectors, he disciplined himself to stay the course. Now, in the year 2005, Robert owns and manages a portfolio with a gross value heading into eight figures and an after-margin value of mid-seven figures. And at 61, he's not done yet. Not by any means.

"My wife and I have a great and supportive relationship. And though I arrive in my 'home office' every weekday by 8:30 a.m., I love what I do and plan to keep on doing it until the last day of my life."

Multi-millionaire at age 60! And probably the owner and manager of a substantial charitable foundation before he becomes a pensioner at 65! Not bad for a former coupon clipper at an English bank. In a future chapter, I'll share Robert's plans for the future, including a potential change in his investment strategy.

INFLATION MAY BE LOW, BUT IT'S STILL CORROSIVE

Despite the lingering after-effects of the 2001 market correction, equity investments are still widely considered to be a wise investment for the future. According to Craig Alexander, Vice President and Deputy Chief Economist at TD Bank Financial Group, Canadian equities are expected to deliver an annual average return of 7.75 percent, or 5.75 percent after inflation, till 2015. He goes on to say that "a well-diversified portfolio including cash, bonds and equities should deliver a total unadjusted return of 6 to 8 percent over the next decade." On average, inflation is expected to reduce your return by 2 percentage points, which is about one-quarter to one-third of the purchasing power of your portfolio.

CANADIAN CPI INFLATION

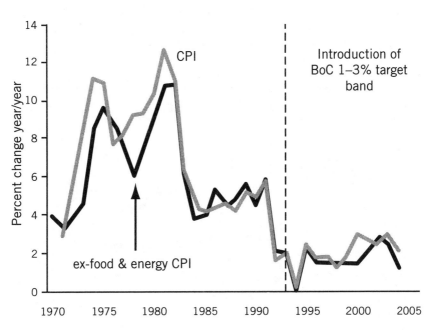

Last year plotted: 2004; Source: Statistics Canada

INFLATION-ADJUSTED BOND YIELDS

Current ten-year bond yields range from 4 percent to 6 percent, but as you can see from the following chart, 2 percent inflation (compounded) eats away at the value of your bond portfolio as well. Nevertheless, if you look closely at the chart, you'll see we're much better off than we were during the mid-1970s. At that time, oil prices and deficits were climbing, inflation was running rampant and for a short period of time, after-tax returns were actually *negative*.

10-YEAR+ GOV'T OF CANADA BOND YIELDS

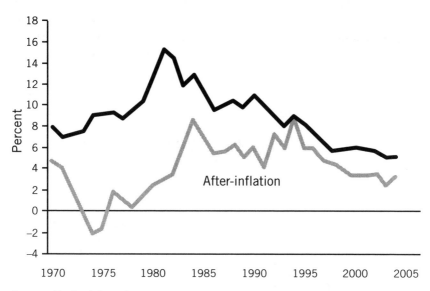

Source: Bank of Canada

A properly diversified portfolio can be constructed that exactly matches your needs and desires if you're willing to take a few moments to evaluate your options. And in my opinion, a key part of your portfolio must be stocks. Again, with interest rates low and matching or slightly above inflation, stocks (combined with fixed-income instruments) offer a long-run return you can't do without. I emphasize, over the long run, because the key with equities is to buy and hold. If you buy and hold good stocks instead of trading them, you'll minimize taxes and maximize your return.

STOCKS FOR THE LONG RUN

What kind of stocks? Stocks for the long run — which also just happens to be the title of a book by renowned Wharton finance professor Jeremy Siegel. *Stocks for the Long Run* tracks economic and market data going as far back as 1802. Yes, there were stock markets back then!

Siegel's basic tenet is that when it comes to stocks and the stock market, "the tried and true always triumph over the bold and new." His advice is to focus less on growth stocks and index mutual funds and more on looking for tried and true stocks that pay high dividends.

Assuming these reinvested dividends are in a tax-deferred account (such as your RRSP), over time you will achieve all the returns you need to build your nest egg.

Siegel explores a number of myths — including the myth that anyone can and should be able to *beat* the market if he or she is willing to learn all they can and then pick the right stocks.

"Poor investment strategy, whether it is for lack of diversification, pursuing hot stocks or attempting to time the market, often stems from the investor's belief that it is necessary to beat the market to do well in the market. Nothing is further from the truth."

In his latest book, *The Future for Investors*, Siegel goes on to say that today's investors must recognize there has been and will continue to be an economic power shift from the West toward China, India and the rest of the developing world. We are facing what he calls the True New Economy. In this environment the smart strategy is to accumulate shares in companies that are reasonably valued and have sustainable earnings, while avoiding the fads and trends that can wreak havoc on an investor's portfolio.

Investments can be fun and exciting, but if we let our emotions take over, we're in for a lot of trouble. It's amazing how many of us don't allow *time* to help us grow our investments. I'm referring to stable investments that offer dividends that can be reinvested to take advantage of the power of compound interest. This must be done to combat the eroding effect of inflation. Most pundits estimate that over the next decade, Canadian equities will deliver an annual average return of slightly less than 8 percent, which means slightly less than 6 percent after inflation.

We'll discuss the impact of inflation and other investment "costs" in more detail later in this chapter and subsequent chapters. But for now, as an investor looking to enlarge your retirement nest egg, it's critical you understand the key factors that influence investments. There are four pillars to investing:

1. Risk.
2. Return.
3. Cost.
4. Time.

All are self-explanatory except perhaps "cost," which refers to taxes, inflation, management fees and transaction expenses. These concepts may be self-explanatory, but they really aren't that simple. Which is why each of them will be explained and explored. For now, let's concentrate on return.

WHAT KIND OF RETURN WILL THE NEXT DECADE BRING?

No one can exactly predict next year's returns, let alone those ten or twenty years from now. But, historically, stocks have outpaced inflation and most other investment instruments, and stock returns tend to gravitate towards the "mean" over time. Just what is the mean or average return? According to Robert Shiller in *Market Volatility*, real stock market returns have averaged approximately 6.3 percent over the past hundred years. Can that kind of performance continue? The obvious answer is yes, but with a clear caveat: Volatility trends indicate that an investor must have a very long time horizon to ensure he gets this kind

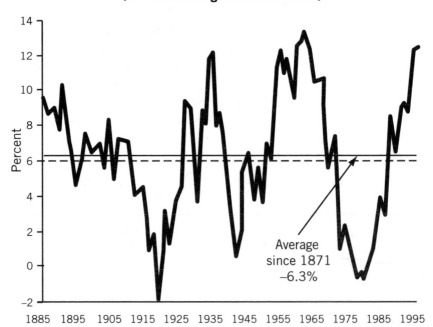

REAL STOCK MARKET RETURNS, 1871–1998
(15-Year Average Annual Returns)

Average
since 1871
–6.3%

Source: The Brookings Institution (Gary Burtless, Senior Fellow, Economic Studies).

of return without incurring undue (short-term) risk. There have been many occasions when the market has returned more than 6 percent, and just as many periods where the market delivered well less than 6 percent. The most recent example of that (1975–1985) lasted over a decade.

In case you were wondering how the various asset classes stack up against each other, as far as returns go, take a look at the following chart. It not only shows comparisons from the past five years, it also provides a forecast of nominal rates of return for the next decade, the years 2006–2015.

Rate of Return by Asset Class

	Cash	Bonds	Cdn. Equities	U.S. Equities	Int'l Equities
	3-mth T-bills	SCM Bonds Index	S&P/TSX	S&P500	EAFE
2000	5.45	10.24	7.41	−9.10	−13.96
2001	1.93	8.08	−12.57	−11.89	−21.21
2002	2.52	8.73	−12.44	−22.10	−15.66
2003	2.92	6.69	26.72	28.68	39.17
2004*	2.17	5.12	10.49	7.32	13.57
2005f	2.50–3.25	2.00–4.5	3.00–6.00	3.00–6.00	4.00–7.00
2006–2015f	4.60	5.75	7.75	8.75	8.00

Returns are the annual percent change from Dec. to Dec. except for Cash which is the average annual yield.
* Year-to-date ending November 16, 2004
Forecasts are by TD Economics
Forecasts for 2006–2015 are the expected average annual return
Source: DRI-Wefa Canada, TD Economics

MISTAKES ARE PRICEY, BUT KNOWLEDGE IS PRICELESS

"There are risks and costs to a program of action. But they are far less than the long-range risks and costs of comfortable inaction."
— John F. Kennedy

George Soros is Chairman of Soros Fund Management LLC. In my opinion, he ranks right up there as a money manager with the likes of Warren Buffett and Peter Lynch. He's not only a billionaire financier, he is a significant philanthropist and a philosopher of note. Despite decades of financial success, he strongly believes in his own fallibility. In fact, his theory of fallibility has become the core of his investment philosophy — and his life.

On the surface, "fallibility" would seem to be a strangely negative word choice for such a positive and successful person. But if we dig a little deeper, we soon understand how this belief supports his financial vision, and realize we can learn a lot about our own investing approach from him. As Soros himself says in his book, *Soros on Soros*, when it comes to investing: "I recognize that I may be wrong. This makes me insecure. My sense of insecurity keeps me alert; always ready to correct my errors. . . . To others, being wrong is a source of shame; to me recognizing my mistakes is a source of pride."

Soros is saying it is okay to be confident, but it is not okay to be cocky. If one of the world's greatest money managers in the world feels this way, shouldn't we learn from him? Whether you've decided to manage your own investments or prefer to have a financial advisor take care of your portfolio, it pays to respect the markets, have a carefully thought out strategy, and stick to it. And, above all, always be aware, in a positive sense, of your own limitations.

THE HAZARDS OF EMOTIONAL INVESTING: PART 1

Investing: It all seems so simple, doesn't it? Well if it was, we'd all be rich. So why do so many of us struggle to grow our savings? Why does all the time we spend trading, investing or just plain worrying about our investments seldom seem to pay off for us with good returns?

The answer lies in our makeup as human beings. No matter how unemotional or logical we say we are, inside each of us is a little voice cautioning us to be careful and avoid taking any risk at all, or conversely, urging us to go hit that home run that will set the family up for life. When it comes to money and investing, the old saw, "the best-laid plans of mice and men often go awry" truly does apply. We may start with a plan, but if things don't go according to plan in the short term or the medium term, how many of us are patient enough to wait? Or if we get bored with our portfolio, how many of us can resist the desire to "tweak" things a bit or maybe even abandon the plan altogether?

In his book, *The Empowered Investor*, Canadian portfolio manager Keith Matthews discusses how emotional investing can sabotage even the brightest and hardest-working investor. Remember, even former

U.S. Federal Reserve Board Chairman Alan Greenspan has often described the markets and investors as being affected by "irrational exuberance." There's even a new field called behavioural finance whose main goal is to study and analyze the irrational tendencies of investors.

Irrational? Not me, you say to yourself. Well, let me give you an example of just how "rational" investors are. We all know the expression, "Buy low and sell high." It's what every smart investor does, right? Well believe it or not, a large percentage of investors do the reverse. They buy high and sell low.

Now why would anyone do that? Are they crazy?

Actually, in a way they're acting rationally, at least from a *non*-investing point of view. Here's what I mean. Human beings are social animals, and as such they're subject to the herd instinct. Investors jump on the "buy" bandwagon when a stock is popular and rising, which pushes demand up. Since supply remains the same, the stock price has to rise. It's simple economics. But the faster the price rises, the more people begin to talk it up on ROBTV and CNBC. The more "noticed" it becomes to the average investor, the more people begin to jump on the bandwagon, and a bubble may begin to form. The last big bandwagon jump was onto those "darling" dot-com stocks of the late-1990s NASDAQ.

At the time, the prevailing attitude was in some ways not totally irrational. People felt the Internet was here to stay (which it certainly is), that exponential growth would continue to remain exponential (which it didn't) and that the management of these dot-com companies could do no wrong (which they certainly could). In other words, as momentum grew, it became a self-fulfilling prophecy. People "knew" they had to jump aboard this once-in-a-lifetime tech-stock phenomenon "right now," or it would be too late.

Okay, that explains the "buy high" trend. What about its counterpart, the "sell low" trap? Investors have a tendency to dump a stock (maybe the same one they bought too high!) when the price begins to fall; if it's hit by bad news or if it falls off dramatically, it gets talked up by mainstream news sources, and then the law of supply and demand really begins to take over. Investors begin to jump off the bandwagon by the truckload, and if the stock price doesn't recover quickly, it leads to a run on (sometimes) perfectly good stocks. The "Nifty Fifty" stocks of the early 1970s are a prime example.

THOSE WHO IGNORE HISTORY ARE DOOMED TO REPEAT IT

In the early '70s, institutional investors became infatuated with the Nifty Fifty — a small group of brand name companies whose stocks (we were told) should always be bought and never sold, regardless of price. These included Avon, Disney, McDonald's, Polaroid and Xerox. Each was a leader in its field with a strong balance sheet, high profit rates and double-digit growth rates. But as Jeff Fesenmaier and Gary Smith point out in an abstract entitled *The Nifty-Fifty Re-Revisited*:

> But is such a company's stock worth any price, no matter how high? In late 1972, Xerox traded for 49 times earnings, Avon for 65 times earnings, Polaroid for 91 times earnings. When the stock market crashed in 1973, the Nifty Fifty defied gravity for a while, held up by institutional enthusiasm that created a two-tiered market of the richly priced Nifty Fifty and the depressed rest. Then, in the memorable words of a *Forbes* columnist, the Nifty Fifty were taken out and shot one by one. From their 1972–1973 highs to their 1974 lows, Xerox fell 71 percent, Avon 86 percent and Polaroid 91 percent.

They concluded that if an investor had decided to "grin and bear it" with these severely overpriced stocks, and held on to them for thirty years, they would have recouped their losses. However, an investor who bought these stocks at their peak in 1972 "would have had 50 percent less wealth at the end of 2001 than an investor who bought the S&P 500."

It's important to realize, as the above story highlights, that bandwagon thinking isn't just the preserve of the retail investor. Even during the tech boom of the late 1990s, a lot of fund managers were guilty of following the herd, and sometimes stampeding in front of it. If a fund manager has cash sitting idle, there's always internal and external pressure to put it to work, to be "fully invested." And that's what happened a few years ago. That's why bandwagon behaviour always seems so logical *at the time*. Of course, 20/20 hindsight always gives us a better perspective.

Many people invest by the seat of their pants, by gut feel, through broker research, via newsletters or friends' stock tips. But some even develop their own proprietary "system" for picking winners and losers. To me, this sounds a lot like going to the track and playing the horses. Every chronic gambler I ever heard of had a "system." I don't know any who consistently made money, and yet they keep going. Why? Because gambling is fun, it's exciting and it's social. And it's more than that. It offers the addictive lure of the big payoff.

THE HUNDRED BILLION DOLLAR MAN

Warren Buffett is arguably the world's greatest investor. He's been investing for more than forty years, and his Berkshire Hathaway funds are now worth over $100 billion!

What can we learn from Buffett about investing? He's made his billions by doing three things: ignoring stock market fads, uncovering intrinsically "undervalued" businesses to invest in and, once invested, staying the course. But the number one lesson we can learn from him is: Avoid the herd.

In a pre-bubble 1999 Salon.com piece, business writer Larry Kanter wrote, "[Buffett's] approach is simple, even quaint. Ignoring both macroeconomic trends and Wall Street fashions, he looks for undervalued companies with low overhead costs, high growth potential, strong market share and low price-to-earning ratios, and then waits for the rest of the world to catch up."

And if you look at his track record, he seldom sells when the world does catch up. In other words, Buffett sticks to his knitting, boring as that may appear. But his knitting — investing in and sticking with what he considers to be undervalued businesses, old-style companies like insurance, razor blades and soft drinks — has paid off. His fund has grown at a phenomenal 24 percent compounded rate since inception in 1965.

It takes more than a smart mind and a plan to achieve this kind of wealth. It takes enormous patience and discipline, because the human tendency is to always want a better return this year than last. Or if we had a bad year, to deny making any mistakes and then go out and make a bigger one. For whatever reason, Buffett has the discipline, and he has it in spades.

Warren Buffett has opinions on many different subjects, and one of them is near and dear to my heart. At the time of writing, Buffett and his business partner, Charles Munger, believe a residential real estate bubble may be forming in the United States, especially in certain parts of California and in the suburbs around Washington, D.C. Here's Buffet: "I recently sold a house in Laguna for $3.5 million. It was on about 2,000 square feet of land, maybe a twentieth of an acre, and the house might cost about $500,000 if you wanted to replace it. So the land sold for something like $60 million an acre."

And here's what Munger has to say: "I know someone who lives next door to what you would actually call a fairly modest house that just sold for $17 million. There are some very extreme housing price bubbles going on."

The above quotes were taken from an interview by Jason Zweig in the May 2005 issue of *CNNMoney*. In the same magazine (September 2004) writer Amy Feldman gives us another reality check. She says that over the long run, housing prices have risen at only about 1 percentage point more than inflation. In other words, our expectations for future growth should be trimmed down considerably.

The *Bank Credit Analyst*'s Managing Editor, Martin Barnes, looks at housing prices another way. Speaking at the Canadian Annual Derivatives Conference in 2005, he said, "It's not simply that house prices are high and people are taking out crazy mortgages. Instead, the housing sector has become too big for its britches, with its highest share of GDP in fifty years, at 36 percent of all private investment in the U.S. It's robbing resources from other sectors where they might be better deployed, such as increasing productive potential through new plants and equipment."

Fortune magazine's *Retirement Guide 2005* highlights another interesting fact about house prices: They are not (and never have been) factored into the Consumer Price Index (CPI).

> ... [CPI] does not calculate changes in housing costs by the sales prices. Instead it uses a figure that estimates what homeowners would get if they rented out their homes. In 2004, national housing prices rose more than 11 percent, but the CPI calculates that they rose about 2 percent. Bill Gross, founder and managing director of PIMCO, an investment company that has more than $464 billion under management, estimated in late 2004 that real inflation could be a full percentage point higher than the CPI. That means, for example, that Social Security payments, which are linked to the CPI, may lag real-life expenses.

What about the situation in Canada? It's too early to tell, but if interest rates stay low and mortgage firms continue letting people buy a house for no money down, there's not much reason for renters to rent and every reason for them to buy — which will continue to put substantial upward pressure on house prices. In a *Maclean's* article by Katherine Macklem, Royal Bank economist Allan Seychuk is quoted as saying, "Housing starts continue to defy gravity."

What's most interesting of all is this article was written back in September 2002.

Am I suggesting you sell your house or invest everything you have in Berkshire Hathaway? Not at all. No one — not even Buffett — is infallible.

BROADEN YOUR INVESTING HORIZONS

What I'm trying to suggest is that it pays to diversify, to avoid depending on one asset for your nest egg, even a million-dollar house. And it pays to have an objective second opinion, even if you're a self-directed type of investor. I'm a big advocate of having at least *some* of your investment portfolio managed by a professional advisor. Control most of it yourself if you like, but always have an advisor in your back pocket. That way, you're less likely to lose focus, wander off the beaten path and find yourself tripped up by speculation and/or penny stock tips. More on that later.

Now having said all of the above, I believe do-it-yourself investors do a *lot* of things right. It's possible to gain incredible knowledge of companies and the markets if you're willing to do your homework. Professional fund investors admit that individual investors can outperform them from time to time — if they know what they're doing, have a plan and stick to it. And I do believe we as individuals need to take control of our investments. There are early warning signals on the retirement horizon, especially related to rising pension and health care costs, and we would do well to arm ourselves now in case they come to fruition. In an August 2005 *Financial Times* article by Andrew Balls, outgoing U.S. Federal Reserve Board Chairman Alan Greenspan sounded a little more anxious than usual.

> Mr. Greenspan said that "fear of change" had also stopped the U.S. from dealing with long-term fiscal reform, notably the failure to deal with Social Security reform. In the past he has warned that the ageing of the U.S. population, and associated rises in pension and health costs, will mean there have to be big tax increases in the absence of early reforms.

Okay, so what's the bottom line? We need to take care of our investments and make them work hard for us. That shouldn't be so difficult, should it? It shouldn't be, but again remember we are emotional human beings who are at our best employing our knowledge and expertise and skill sets in our day jobs. Come on, let's admit it: Many of you think of investing as a "sidelight." Emotions can be a very powerful *positive* force. But when it comes to investing, all it takes is one emotion-driven misstep — even one that was supposedly well thought out — to erode a nest egg that may have taken years to build up.

Everything would be fine in the investing world if it wasn't for the existence of something called risk. In the next few pages, I'm going to illustrate just how risk feeds into our emotions and alters our supposed risk-tolerance levels. In fact, risk can set the stage for some remarkable decision-making blunders, as I'll demonstrate by sharing the story of George the dentist investor with you. But first we need to grapple with this thing called risk.

RISK VS. RETURN: YOU CAN'T HAVE YOUR CAKE AND EAT IT TOO

A general rule of investing is that the higher the potential return, the higher the risk. This is known as the "risk/return trade-off," and is illustrated in the chart below.

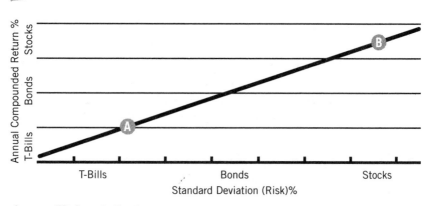

Source: TD Canada Trust

An investor with a lower risk tolerance, such as Investor A, would prefer to invest at a lower point on the risk/return line. Investor B, with a higher tolerance for risk, would invest at a higher point on the risk/return line in the pursuit of a higher potential return. In mutual fund investing, volatility (the degree to which a fund fluctuates in price) and return will depend on market trends, the individual investments held in the fund and the investment strategy used by the manager.

Speaking of individual investments, the following illustration may help you better understand the risk factors associated with various investment classes.

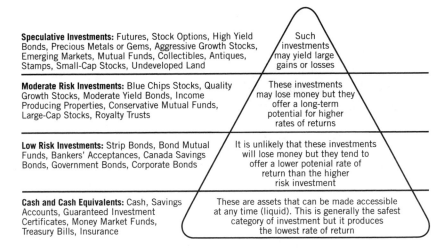

Speculative Investments: Futures, Stock Options, High Yield Bonds, Precious Metals or Gems, Aggressive Growth Stocks, Emerging Markets, Mutual Funds, Collectibles, Antiques, Stamps, Small-Cap Stocks, Undeveloped Land — Such investments may yield large gains or losses

Moderate Risk Investments: Blue Chips Stocks, Quality Growth Stocks, Moderate Yield Bonds, Income Producing Properties, Conservative Mutual Funds, Large-Cap Stocks, Royalty Trusts — These investments may lose money but they offer a long-term potential for higher rates of returns

Low Risk Investments: Strip Bonds, Bond Mutual Funds, Bankers' Acceptances, Canada Savings Bonds, Government Bonds, Corporate Bonds — It is unlikely that these investments will lose money but they tend to offer a lower potenial rate of return than the higher risk investment

Cash and Cash Equivalents: Cash, Savings Accounts, Guaranteed Investment Certificates, Money Market Funds, Treasury Bills, Insurance — These are assets that can be made accessible at any time (liquid). This is generally the safest category of investment but it produces the lowest rate of return

Source: Investor Education Fund

The triangle arranges the most common investment options according to risk-reward. The higher the investment is located in the triangle, the higher the potential reward and the higher the risk. Since cash and cash equivalents offer minimal risk and low return, they are located at the bottom of the triangle. Futures and stock options are naturally at the top of the triangle. Bonds and stocks are in between.

It's important to realize, however, that the types of investments listed under each part of the triangle are only a guide and risk may vary according to economic conditions. The classification of a stock as low-, moderate- or high-risk depends on your point of view and risk tolerance. Thorough research is the best way to construct a portfolio.

AS MUCH AS 90 PERCENT OF PORTFOLIO RETURN IS THE RESULT OF ASSET ALLOCATION

Let's drill a little deeper into the heart of risk management and the investment process: asset allocation. Studies show that up to 90 percent of portfolio return is the result of asset allocation, which is why asset allocation is the primary determinant of both risk and return in many portfolios.

Asset allocation is just a fancy way of referring to the optimal mix of cash, fixed income and equity you should have in your portfolio. The optimal mix depends on factors like your age, the number of years remaining until you expect to retire and your risk tolerance. The following two points *cannot* be emphasized enough.

1) The primary determinant of return is the mix of different asset *classes* that you own.
2) A secondary determinant is the mix of specific *investments* that you hold within these different asset classes

The graph below highlights the results of a landmark study comparing returns of ninety-one large U.S. pension plans over the 1974–1983 period.

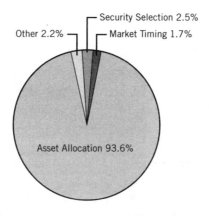

Source: Brinson, Hood and Beebower, *Financial Analysts Journal*, January/February 1995.

As you can see, the vast majority (93 percent) of portfolio performance is due to asset allocation. Clearly, being in the "right" asset class at the right time is *the* most critical component of investment performance.

HOW "RISKY" ASSETS CAN ACTUALLY MAKE YOUR PORTFOLIO SAFER

The graph below helps to illustrate how this can happen. Portfolio A is composed entirely of bonds and over time has experienced both low growth and low risk. Portfolio C, by comparison, is composed of both stocks and bonds. It has experienced higher growth and *lower* risk than Portfolio A. Investments within different asset classes react to market forces in different ways. A diversified asset mix of equity and bond investments in a portfolio can offer more potential return than a 100 percent bond portfolio without increasing the risk level. That's why it's so important to hold a mix of different asset classes that is appropriate for your investment objectives.

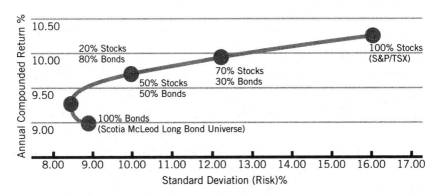

Source: TD Canada Trust Web site/Standard & Poor's Micropal, Inc.

ASSET ALLOCATION AND PORTFOLIO RISK

Risk is a complex subject. Fortunately, the perception of risk — and our ability to manage it — changes with knowledge. Research has proven that adding a variety of investments to a portfolio can increase returns and decrease overall risk. Insurance expert Scott Sanderson of J&H Marsh & McLennan points out in an article entitled, "Combining Hazard and Financial Risk," that: "Risk is not inherently a bad thing. While it may keep management awake at night, profit would not be possible without it. The art of business is to capture the profit portion of risk while managing and minimizing the undesirable elements."

Finding the right balance between risk and return — your place on the "efficient frontier," as it's called in modern portfolio theory — is a critical step in overcoming the aversion to risk that so many of us harbour. Your optimal asset mix should always give you the best return for the amount of risk you are willing to take.

ASSET ALLOCATION VS. DIVERSIFICATION

Investors are sometimes confused about the difference between "asset allocation" and "diversification." The purpose of asset allocation is to help you find and construct an investment portfolio that minimizes risk and maximizes return through optimal diversification among different asset classes such as stocks, bonds and cash equivalents. Diversification is simply the next step in the process. It means spreading your money among different (preferably low-correlated) investments *within* each of the above asset classes. Alone, each one can reduce your portfolio risk, but most experts agree asset allocation and diversification work best in tandem.

Diversification—up to a point

Proper diversification among asset classes means finding assets that do not positively correlate with each other. This reduces your risk and reduces volatility. A well-diversified asset portfolio is one in which your financial *asset* investments don't all go in the same direction at the same time. A well-diversified stock portfolio (part of your overall asset portfolio) is one in which your *stocks* provide you with the right mix of stability, growth and dividend income.

Diversifying the investments of your portfolio reduces risk, but only up to a point. It's possible to have too much of a good thing; that is, to have too many value stocks or too many growth stocks — or too many mutual funds. Then you risk becoming *over*-diversified.

Let's take the mutual fund scenario. Each fund you buy should provide you with an asset or an investment style you don't already have. Duplication won't get you any closer to your efficient frontier.

John Bogle takes this concept one step further. In his excellent book, *Common Sense on Mutual Funds*, he points out that:

> A single ready-made balanced index fund — holding 65 percent stocks and 35 percent bonds...can meet the needs of many investors. A pair of stock and bond index funds with a tailor-made balance — a higher or lower ratio of stocks — can meet the needs of many more. But what is the optimal number of

funds for investors who elect to use actively managed funds?...
Too large a number can easily result in over-diversification.

If you start to over-diversify, you'll end up with the performance of
an index fund but you'll be paying the higher costs associated with managed funds. Worst of all, you may get more short-term volatility, so it'll
be riskier than the index.

You can see his main point from the following table, which was
developed from Morningstar Canada. The risks associated with owning
only two or three of these funds are not much greater than owning ten
or twenty-five actively managed funds.

REDUCING RISK BY OWNING MULTIPLE FUNDS

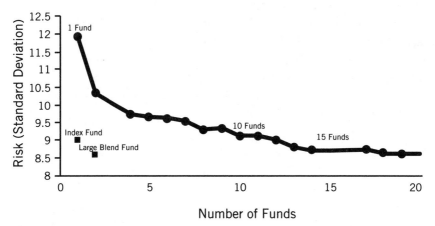

Source: Morningstar Research Inc.

Too much diversification can be dangerous

Backing up Bogle's contention is an exhaustive study of thousands of
stock portfolios that was conducted by Robert Hagstrom and published
in his book, *The Warren Buffett Portfolio*. The portfolios tested ranged in
size from those holding just 15 stocks to those holding 250 stocks.
Hagstrom's study revealed that out of the three thousand 15-stock portfolios tested, a solid 808 beat the market. This compared favourably to
all the other sized portfolios. Out of three thousand 50-stock portfolios,
only 549 beat the market. Out of three thousand 100-stock portfolios,
only 337 beat the market. And out of three thousand 250-stock portfolios, a mere 63 beat the market.

The bottom line? If you're trying to diversify, make sure your investments have low correlation. That is, when the market is volatile, they don't all move in the same direction.

HOW DOES CORRELATION WORK?

I'm so glad you asked. If two asset classes move in step with each other, either up or down, they're said to be perfectly correlated. They have a correlation of +1. On the other hand, if the correlation is completely random (unrelated) then these two assets would have 0 correlation. Finally, and most important of all, if two asset classes move exactly opposite to each other, they are said to be perfectly *negatively* correlated, or have a correlation of –1. In reality, few assets have perfect negative correlation, but many have *enough* negative correlation to make them very useful in smoothing the ups and downs in your portfolio.

Below is an illustration of the degree of correlation between various asset classes and the S&P 500 stock index.

Correlation of various asset classes

CORRELATION TO THE S&P 500 INDEX FROM 1982–2002

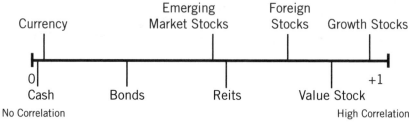

Source: Investopedia.com

As you can see on the left side of the chart, there's virtually no correlation between "cash" and the S&P 500 stock index, since cash and money market funds are traditionally unaffected by market swings. On the right side of the spectrum, however, you'll notice there's a very high (nearly 1:1) correlation between "growth stocks" and the S&P 500. No surprise here, since the S&P index is heavily composed of growth stocks.

Stocks historically offer higher return, but higher risk. Bonds and stock prices generally have low positive correlations, which when combined can reduce overall portfolio volatility. Diversification is effective when investments have low correlation. But remember this: Never let low correlation become so important that you forget to pick good stocks and/or mutual funds. If risk is your primary concern but you need to be invested in the stock market, consider an index fund.

GLOBAL DIVERSIFICATION

If proper diversification is good for your portfolio's health, global diversification is even better. As the chart below shows, investing only in U.S. stocks versus international stocks increases risk substantially.

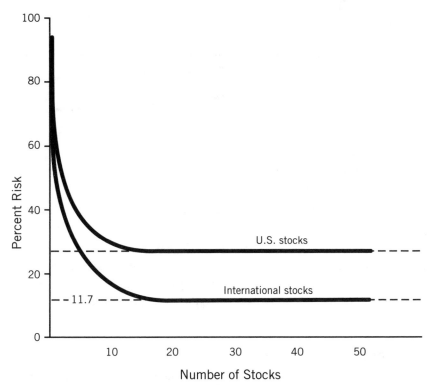

Number of Stocks

In addition, recent research has proven that investing by industry or sector as well as by region reduces risk even more, as the following chart shows.

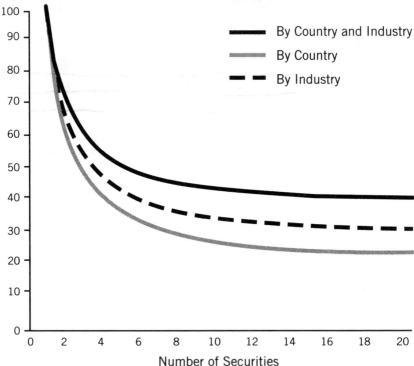

PAST THREE YEARS ENDING 30 AUGUST 2002
Portfolio Variance (% of Average Stock Variance)

Number of Securities

Source: Copyright 2003, CFA Institute. Reproduced and republished from
Equity Value in a Global Context with permission from CFA Institute. Based on
data from the *Financial Times*, MSCI World Index and UBS Research.

A WORLD OF OPPORTUNITY

Canada makes up about 2 percent of the total world market capitalization. That means if you limit your investments to Canada alone, you
may miss out on many opportunities within global markets. Global
investments provide currency diversification, access to sectors that are
not broadly available in Canada and the potential to earn a greater
return by investing in foreign stock and bond markets. A combination
of global and domestic investments can increase potential return while
reducing risk.

CANADA REPRESENTS ONLY 2% OF THE GLOBAL MARKET

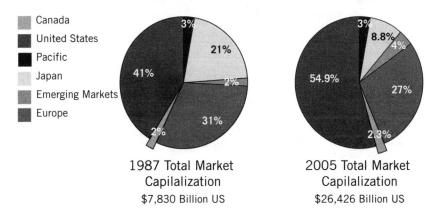

1987 Total Market Capilalization
$7,830 Billion US

2005 Total Market Capilalization
$26,426 Billion US

Outside of a retirement savings plan (RSP) or a retirement income fund (RIF), you can invest as much of your portfolio as you want, globally. Likewise, inside your RSP or RIF, the Canada Revenue Agency (CRA) has changed the rules to allow you to have 100 percent of your portfolio invested in so-called foreign content to help you take advantage of many of the investment opportunities the world has to offer.

IT'S JUST A MATTER OF TIME

In all asset classes, returns can fluctuate extensively. As the chart below illustrates, even the return of a conservative investment such as a treasury

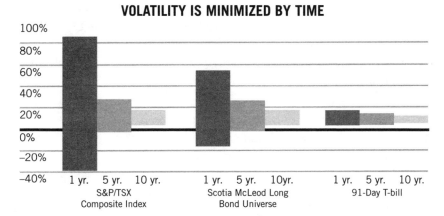

VOLATILITY IS MINIMIZED BY TIME

Percent return January 1960 to December 2002.
Source: TD Canada Trust.

bill can fluctuate up and down. Over longer periods of time, however, returns tend to even out, reducing risk. The chart shows how returns spike up and down considerably during a one-year term. But over a ten-year period, for example, returns tend to stabilize (or, as economists like to say, revert to the mean).

Staying invested for the long term always reduces risk while increasing the compounding potential of every investment you hold. Past performance may not be repeated

When it comes to the concept of time, Professor Jeremy Siegel weighs in with these comments that are excerpted from an interview in the November 1998 *Pennsylvania Gazette*:

"Here is where I think our profession has led Wall Street wrong. When we measure risk, what holding period do we assume? Almost universally, annual returns. It's only appropriate for the investor who, one year from now, is going to liquidate all of their assets. I would dare say that probably no one in this room in twelve months has clients who are going to liquidate all of their financial assets."

REBALANCING YOUR PORTFOLIO

Another way to minimize risk is through periodic rebalancing. As stock and market prices move over time, your portfolio will usually require fine-tuning to restore the asset allocation to its original mix. This usually means selling part of the better performers that now occupy too large a percentage of the portfolio, and reallocating those funds into the under-performers to bring their numbers back up. Studies back up the logic of doing this. You usually have a choice between having the rebalancing done automatically via a computer program, or you can do it yourself manually. One caveat: There is some time involved in analyzing, computing and adjusting the percentages.

In the mid-1990s, Morningstar.com did a study to determine the impact rebalancing had on portfolio return and volatility. They found that rebalancing mattered, but it also required paring back the winners, which triggers capital gains and paying potentially big bucks to the Canada Revenue Agency (CRA). So for investors with taxable accounts, random rebalancing can actually eat away at returns.

With this in mind, there are ways to keep rebalancing costs to a minimum. One way is to put your *new* (hopefully annual) investment contributions directly into the poorer performing portions of your portfolio. If the new money you're adding is sizeable enough, rather than having to sell top performers and realize capital gains tax, you can simply top up the other portions of your portfolio by purchasing additional equity positions or fixed-income securities. The tax consequences of investing will be covered in more detail in Chapter 7.

MAKING THE CASE FOR INDEX FUNDS

There are substantial cost savings associated with passively managed index funds, as opposed to actively managed funds. According to Bogle, the lowest cost publicly available index funds operate at annual expense ratios of less than 0.002 percent. That's because portfolio turnover is very low and, thus, minimal brokerage commissions, transaction costs and potentially lower realized taxes on capital gains inside the fund.

For detailed information about the risks, liquidity and potential returns of various securities see the Canadian Securities Administrators' (CSA) Guide to Various Types of Securities (see Appendices 4–6).

FINDING YOUR OPTIMAL (RISK-ADJUSTED) RETURN

Everyone I know would like a higher return on their portfolio. Historically, investing returns from equities have outperformed those from fixed income. So why wouldn't — no, *shouldn't*— we put all our money into stocks? Because historically, we also know something about investor psychology. And it's all about risk.

If you were to drill a little deeper and ask your friends if they could sleep at night knowing the vast majority of their retirement portfolio was in stocks, I bet most of them (unless they're college students or inveterate risk takers) would say "No way!" And if you were to tell them that over selected multi-year periods, the stock market has endured *negative* growth, maybe even the risk takers would back off a little.

Most good investment advisors stress the concept of risk-adjusted returns, rather than highest returns. And the optimal return comes through optimal asset allocation. But your needs change as your time-line changes. Unless you're close to retirement, your portfolio should be a long-term investment. That is, you should not expect to liquidate it, in whole or in part, for at least ten years. But as you get closer to retirement, your tolerance for risk should naturally decline. If it doesn't, I can tell you from experience you're adding unnecessary risk to your financial future. And the government won't be there to bail you out.

For these reasons, finding the right (risk-adjusted) asset allocation is critical for all investors, and it is *especially* critical if you are near to or approaching retirement.

CONSTRUCTING A PORTFOLIO YOU CAN LIVE WITH

According to Bob Gorman, Vice President with TD Bank Financial Group, when deciding on your appropriate asset allocation, you should start with what he calls a base case. For example, take a look at the general asset mix of a conservative institutional portfolio like a pension fund, which often has the following asset allocation:

55–60 percent in equities
40–45 percent in bonds

Then "tweak" your asset allocation to match your individual risk and return objectives, and your needs and goals. For example, if you have a long time horizon, you could increase the equity portion for potentially higher returns. If your time horizon is uncertain (let's say you may be thinking of retiring early) then you might decrease the equity portion to lower your portfolio risk.

Pension funds are cautious in outlook, but also have a longer investment horizon which dictates their asset allocation. So start from this point, determine what risk/return combination is acceptable and appropriate for you, and then adjust accordingly as needs and circumstances warrant.

Your portfolio is in many ways a living, breathing thing. It is certainly dynamic, because if you were to study it closely, you would notice its balance is changing all the time — hopefully, more upward than downward. But individual components can grow or shrink in relative terms, knocking your asset mix out of whack. Which is why you should review your portfolio and rebalance it on a periodic basis to maintain your original asset mix.

YOUR ASSET MIX VARIES ACCORDING TO YOUR AGE AND INVESTMENT HORIZON

Remember Lisa and Bill from Chapter 2? Let's see what their nest egg numbers turned out to be based on the calculations and assumptions we made in Chapter 2. Then we'll see where they might fit from an asset allocation viewpoint. The following charts are to help you focus on your optimal asset mix; they are not a hard and fast rule for doing so. Besides, there are many other factors to consider besides time (age, needs, tangible assets, etc.), which is why the following is just a starting point for your own analysis.

RRSP PORTFOLIO RETURNS

The asset allocation inside your portfolio is a major factor in determining your expected return. As you can see from the chart below, the most conservative portfolio type — an income-oriented portfolio — is likely to produce the lowest return (6 percent), but it is also the lowest risk. The most aggressive portfolio —"maximum equity growth"— produces the highest return (7.6 percent) and the highest risk. These estimates of future returns are provided by TD Economics, and while they're based on a variety of market and economic factors, the returns are provided solely as a guide to help in your investment decision-making process.

RRSP Portfolio Returns

Portfolio	Asset % share of portfolio					
	Cash	Income	Cdn Equity	U.S. Equity	Int'l Equity	% of Return
Income	20	50	9	12	9	**6.0**
Income & Moderate Growth	10	45	12	19	14	**6.4**
Balanced Growth	5	35	15	26	19	**6.7**
Aggressive Growth	0	20	19	35	26	**7.2**
Maximum Equity Growth	0	0	22	44	34	**7.6**

Source: TD Economics, October 2005.

LISA (AGE 50)

If you recall, Lisa earns a 6.00 percent return on her "conservative growth" portfolio, on her savings of $50,000. Compounded over fifteen years to retirement at age 65, her nest egg would grow to $119,827.91.

Now, if Lisa also contributed $5,000 per year in her RRSP every year for fifteen years to retirement, her total nest egg would grow to $243,191.01.

Lisa's Conservative Growth Portfolio

30%
Equity

70%
Fixed Income

Source: TD Waterhouse Canada Inc.

Constructing a portfolio for Lisa (age 50)

Lisa's optimal asset allocation might be 70 percent in fixed income, 30 percent in equities. Based on TD Waterhouse Financial Planning asset allocations, a potential asset allocation could be 20 percent in cash, 50 percent in fixed income, 9 percent in Canadian equities, 12 percent in U.S. equities and the remaining 9 percent in international equities.

Note that the terms "cash" and "money market" can refer to any short-term, fixed-income investment. Money in a savings account and certificates of deposit (CDs) are examples. The main goal of a conservative portfolio strategy is to maintain the real value of the portfolio, that is, to protect the value of the portfolio against inflation. Lisa's portfolio that you see here would yield a high amount of current income, and would also yield some long-term capital growth potential from investment in high-quality equities.

BILL (AGE 40)

Bill, aged 40, earns 6.73 percent on his "balanced" portfolio, on his savings of $50,000. Compounded over twenty-five years to his retirement, his nest egg would grow to $254,760.88. If Bill also contributed $5,000 per year in his RRSP every year for twenty-five years to his retirement, he would have an additional $324,727.03, and his total nest egg would be $579,487.91. Clearly, there is a big difference in Bill's nest egg versus Lisa's which proves how important it is to begin investing for retirement as early as possible.

Constructing a portfolio for Bill (age 40)

A more balanced portfolio is meant for individuals with a longer time horizon and at least average risk tolerance. An optimal asset allocation for Bill might consist of approximately 60% equities and 40% bonds.

Bill's Balanced Growth Portfolio

Source: TD Waterhouse Canada Inc.

Broken down further, an optimal asset allocation model for Bill might be 5 percent in cash, 35 percent in fixed income, 15 percent in Canadian equities, 26 percent in U.S. equities and 19 percent in international equities. Bill's optimal portfolio would provide growth of capital and some current income by investing 60 percent of its assets in a diversified portfolio of domestic and international equity funds and 40 percent in fixed income, money market funds and cash, respectively. The portfolio manages cash flows to maintain the stated asset allocation.

RETIREMENT FUNDS DON'T GROW FROM COOKIE-CUTTER FORMULAS

Please note, whether you're 20 or 60 or anywhere in between, no one-size portfolio fits all. And that's especially true when it comes to retirement. Retirement planning is not a cookie-cutter process. Every one of us has different needs and timeframes, which is why it's always a good idea to consult with an investment advisor. He or she will help you analyze your financial needs, construct a portfolio with you, and keep you on track.

THE HAZARDS OF EMOTIONAL INVESTING: PART 2

"To invest successfully does not require a stratospheric I.Q., unusual business insights or inside information. What's needed is a sound intellectual framework for making decisions and the ability to keep emotions from corroding the framework."

So says Warren Buffett, the master of self-disciplined investing. But not every investor is like him, unfortunately. In fact, the majority of investors — and not just beginners — are impulsive and driven by emotions. Here is one investor's cautionary tale:

George is a charming dentist I know who loved to tell his friends about the successes he was having in the stock market. Now George was an extremely intelligent fellow, and in the mid-1990s he decided to invest his life savings (GICs worth about $150,000) in the stock market. The reason was simple, according to George:

I wanted to get a better return on my money. I hired a broker to advise me, but after a while I decided to go out on my own. I felt my portfolio was too conservative and the returns didn't match my expectations. Once I was out on my own, I did my research and due diligence, and soon learned how critical price-earnings ratios were in determining the price and relative value of stocks. I discovered that a company's stock PEG (the P/E ratio to growth rate) was an even more significant factor.

For example, if a company has been growing at 15 percent a year for the past five years, and it is forecast to continue to grow at 15 percent next year, its earnings growth is thus 15 percent. Now if its stock is trading at a P/E of 30 times earnings, then it would have a PEG (price to earnings growth) of 2.

George checked the P/E ratios of major brand name companies like Coca-Cola and Procter & Gamble. Their P/Es were around 25 times earnings, and their earnings were increasing at maybe 10 percent to 12 percent a year. So that meant they had PEGs of roughly 2 to 1.

But then George made his most important discovery of all.

"Reading through the *Standard & Poor's 1995 Stock Market Encyclopedia*, I discovered there were a group of large, fast growing companies such as Intel, Microsoft and Cisco, which were trading at what I felt were incredibly reasonable P/E ratios, something in the order of 30 times earnings. And they all seemed to be in the technology sector."

It wasn't their P/Es that were so incredible, however. It was their price to earnings growth: their PEGs. Unlike Coke and P&G, which were growing at 10 percent to 12 percent a year, Intel, Microsoft and Cisco were growing at an astounding 25 percent to 40 percent! Best of all, these growth rates appeared to be sustainable. In other words, their PEGs (unlike most large S&P companies) were in many cases less than 1!

That meant they were not only the fastest growing, they were selling at the cheapest price. According to George:

"The only remaining question mark in my mind was whether the tech sector as a whole really had legs, or was it a one-shot wonder. This was 1995, remember. When I realized that the personal computer was going to be around for a while, I knew the PC was going to drive all the well-managed tech stocks — at least for the foreseeable future."

And so George's really big adventure began.

He invested in a select group of so-called "big technology" stocks and slowly watched his fortunes rise. But as the '90s drew to a close, the tech sector's popularity began to go mainstream. It was shooting up like a rocket. George was so thrilled at this turn of events that he quit drilling teeth and began to trade on the NASDAQ full time. In fact, he became so absorbed he began to work his investments fourteen to sixteen hours a day. He became an expert on trading Long-Term Equity Anticipation Securities (LEAPs), and then began to trade short-term calls.

A TALE OF TWO MINDS

Despite spending a good chunk of his annual stock earnings to support his new lifestyle, George had become a millionaire by February 2000. But he was beginning to get concerned about how quickly the financial markets had moved. Many of his "unsophisticated" friends were now in the market, and most of them seemed to be buying tech stocks. George had a nagging feeling all was not right.

He phoned his accountant and asked him if he thought there was a bubble brewing in the NASDAQ. His accountant, Tobias, said he had no idea, but he offered George some sage advice. If George was worried, why not sell half of his holdings and keep the rest? George became even more anxious when he heard this, and asked what the tax liability would be if he sold *all* his holdings and pocketed the seven figures in cash. Tobias told him the grim news. As an active trader, George would probably owe about a half million dollars or more in taxes!

George was horrified. The government would take a huge chunk of his hard-earned money for doing nothing. Outrageous! His accountant coolly advised him that "you only pay big taxes when you've earned big income. That's not such a bad thing, is it?"

George just stared at him, trying to control his emotions, and finally said he'd sleep on it. He would decide what to do in the morning. As he tossed and turned that night, George's thought process went along these lines.

First, he decided if he was so anxious about a bubble in tech stocks, maybe a lot of others were that anxious too. So why panic, along with the herd?

Second, the rest of the market was up big as well, and yet no one except the contrarians was talking about a bubble, especially in the more sedate S&P 500 index or the even stodgier Dow Industrials.

Third, if the bubble burst, how far would his "blue chip" tech stocks fall? They were quality companies with quality prospects. Maybe they'd drop 20 percent, or at worst 30 percent. Based on that scenario, selling might be a huge mistake.

SO WHAT DID GEORGE DO?

He did what a lot of self-confident investors would do in similar circumstances. He held onto all his stocks and braced himself for the inevitable correction. It came all right — but neither George nor anyone else was expecting how big it would be.

A downward adjustment of 60 percent to 80 percent was not in anyone's cards. But George was leveraged through margin and stock options, and so he rode the NASDAQ all the way down to the bottom. He soon ran out of money to support the lifestyle to which he had become accustomed, and went back to his day job, older and wiser.

Why did I bring up this cautionary tale? Because I want to show you that even a serious and dedicated investor can let emotion profoundly cloud his or her decision-making process. In this particular case, it centred on George's stubborn refusal to pay taxes to the government. That stubbornness cost him his hard-earned portfolio. But for someone less sophisticated than George, it could just as easily have turned into a different story: riding a basket of speculative and illiquid stocks all the way into personal bankruptcy.

THE 7 PERCENT SOLUTION

When it comes to the stock market, ex-Fidelity Magellan fund manager Peter Lynch has a knack for putting things in perspective. In an interview on the Fidelity.com Web site, he says: "The stock market is a volatile animal.... Historically we have a decline of 10 percent or more about once every two years...[but] corporate earnings drive stock prices. If you look at the five hundred companies in the S&P 500, despite ten recessions since World War II, earnings have grown 7 percent annually. That's a pretty good track record."

Seven percent? It certainly is! In the movie *The Seven-Per-Cent Solution*, the great detective Sherlock Holmes is cured of a certain bad habit by none other than Sigmund Freud. In the world of investing, many of us need to be cured of a different addiction: the desire to beat the market. In many ways, the year 2000 market meltdown may have done just that — at least for the medium term.

Duncan Hood, a financial consultant at MoneySense.ca, wrote an interesting article for that publication in which he talked about the big losses he personally suffered in early 2002. He decided to invest heavily in Bombardier after it was hit by massive selling following the 9/11 tragedy, believing it was sharply undervalued. He was crushed when the stock subsequently declined further, but he came out of the experience, he says, having learned three important lessons:

Lesson No. 1: It's really, really hard to beat the market, at least consistently. There are an awful lot of smart, hardworking people on the Street who spend every moment of their working days sniffing for investment opportunities and developing ulcers in the process. If you think you've spotted a sure bet, you should pause and ask yourself what you know that those pros don't. I wish I'd done that before falling in love with my Bombardier theory.

Lesson No. 2: Those folks who talk about the virtues of diversifying your assets may have a point after all. I will never again bet money that I can't afford to lose on a single stock. In fact, I've

become a big fan of the Couch Potato portfolio described on
Moneysense.ca. This simple strategy splits your money among
the major asset classes and ensures that no downturn in a single
sector can ever devastate your portfolio.

Which brings me to Lesson No. 3: Successful investing is all
about psychology. Your own psychology, to be precise. I never
worried about diversification before my Bombardier experience
because it seemed too boring, too mundane, too middle class —
and besides, I was sure I was right. For me, investing was about
the excitement of trying to outwit the market and score big. It
wasn't about playing it safe. These days I've struck a compromise
with my inner gambler. I put 80 percent of my money into a
properly balanced, diversified portfolio. The other 20 percent is
my beat-the-market money.

If you have the time and the money and the smarts, perhaps you can
compete with the workaholic investment gurus on the Street like Buffet
and Soros and Trump. But most of us have jobs and careers and other
interests, so the odds are stacked against us from the very beginning.
Here's how stock picking guru Peter Lynch responded when interviewed
about his track record of investment success by Louis Rukeyser of *Wall
Street Week*:

> *Rukeyser*: "What did you do that the other fellows [fund man-
> agers] didn't do?"
> *Lynch*: "Well, I'm not sure what the other people were doing, but
> what I've tried to do is I've worked as hard as I could. I've visited
> over 200 companies every year."

In other words, the harder Lynch worked, the luckier he became.
Keep in mind, Lynch was a stock picker; he had no expertise in bonds
and was not a bond trader. But what he said raises some important questions. If one of the smartest money managers on the continent felt it was
important to personally visit *every* company he was looking to invest in,
do you feel you can do enough research to keep up? Do you really have
the time to visit a couple of hundred companies? And if you did, how
easy do you think it would it be to set up meetings with top manage-

ment? And if you managed all that, would you even know the right questions to ask?

Some wise person said investing is simple, but it's not easy.

BONDS VS. STOCKS

There are pros and cons to every investment vehicle and every investment portfolio. Bonds make more sense if you are nearing retirement age, need a steady income stream and don't want to risk a sudden drop in your portfolio. If you're nowhere near retirement age, you may want to invest more heavily in stocks. It all comes down to one's age, needs, income level, experience and risk tolerance.

When asked about choosing bonds versus equities, Warren Buffett cautioned people about their expectations: "If you had to make a choice between long-term bonds at around 4.5 percent and equities for the next twenty years, I would certainly prefer equities. But if people think they can earn more than 6–7 percent a year, they're making a big mistake. I don't think we're in bubble-type valuations in equities — or anywhere close to bargain valuations."

Buffett went on to say: "If you told me I had to go away for twenty years, I would rather take an index fund over long-term bonds. You'll get a chance to do something extremely intelligent with your money in the next few years. But right now there doesn't seem to be a clear enough direction to conclude anything dramatic."

TOP TEN INVESTMENT MISTAKES

I've covered a lot of ground in this chapter. So as a reminder of some of the concepts I discussed with you, I've made a list of the top ten mistakes investors make. I've compiled the list from various sources, including: Jim Yih's column in MoneySense.ca, (Yih is author of *Mutual Fundamentals*, plus *Seven Strategies to Guarantee Your Investments*); Ted Cadsby's "The 10 Biggest Investing Mistakes Canadians Make and How to Avoid Them" (Cadsby is President, CIBC Securities); and Merrill Lynch's special investor education Web site at http://www.ml.com.

Mistake #1: Putting all your eggs in one basket

My counsel to you throughout this chapter has been to minimize risk by adopting asset allocation and adding optimal diversification to your portfolio.

Mistake #2: Putting all your money in safe, income-generating investments

Canada Savings Bonds and GICs should be used to park your money, not to invest it. Their safety is offset by their low yields. These yields will compound, but they will be eaten away by the compounding power of inflation.

Mistake #3: Chasing performance

All you have to do is remember the emerging markets fad in the early '90s followed by the tech stocks craze of the late '90s. Don't let it happen again.

Mistake #4: Procrastinating

Procrastination turns attainable goals into impossible ones. The best time to start investing was yesterday, but today is always better than tomorrow.

Mistake #5: Failure to adopt asset allocation

A long timeframe, asset allocation and diversification should offset much of your portfolio risk while improving returns. According to a Merrill Lynch study, investment advisors believe the failure to observe basic investing fundamentals like asset allocation or rebalancing are the biggest mistakes their clients make.

Mistake #6: Misjudging your risk tolerance

Many investors have overly optimistic assumptions about their investments and accept more risk than they should because of this. The longer you can stay invested, the less you risk (as defined by volatility). But just how long do you have to be invested? If you think it's until retirement, you're mistaken. It's actually longer. Your retirement assets must support you throughout retirement, which means some equity exposure well beyond retirement is necessary for most of us.

Mistake #7: Timing the market

Knowing when and which sector, market or investment will outperform is impossible, just as predicting the future is impossible. The best solution is to buy good securities and hold on to them.

Mistake #8: Not knowing what you own

This is particularly true in regards to mutual funds. Know what is in each fund.

Mistake #9: Underestimating the impact of compounding, taxes and inflation

The power of compounding should never be overlooked. A 10 percent annual return in a sheltered RRSP becomes a 12.2 percent gain after only five years. Unnecessary taxes can eat away at your compounded returns (see Chapter 7). And so can inflation — even the low inflation we are experiencing now.

Mistake #10: Not setting quantifiable, realistic goals

To ensure success, develop and write down short (less than twelve months), mid-range (one to five years) and long-range (over five years) goals. Quantify these goals and then devise a plan to attain them. If you don't quantify these goals, you can't assess the success of your investment strategy.

Now that we've discussed ways to minimize risk while generating the kinds of *returns* you'll want and need for your retirement, let's look at the many different investment *tools* available that can make it happen.

CHAPTER
FIVE

"Okay. You've got 17.5 percent in T-bills amortized over the fiscal year, 8 percent in stocks and bonds. Carry the 9, divide by the Gross National Product... fortunately, funeral bouquets are deductible."
—JIM CARREY, *THE MASK*

ARM (Part 2)
ARM YOURSELF WITH THE *INVESTMENT* *TOOLS* YOU NEED

Now that you've picked up some understanding of risk and return, it's time to show you the tools of the investment trade. If you feel you already understand your investment options, by all means skip this chapter. But if you want to learn the difference between wraps and hedge funds, or whether REITs are as safe an investment as an index fund — or maybe even your house — please read on.

THE RIGHT STUFF: ASSET TYPES
While there are literally tens of thousands of investment products to choose from, the process can be simplified if you understand one thing. Just about every kind of investment you can possibly buy falls into one of four asset classes. They are:

1) **Cash (and cash equivalents)**
These include treasury bills, savings bonds and money market funds.

2) **Fixed Income**
These include guaranteed investment certificates (GICs); government and corporate bonds, mortgage-backed securities, bond and mortgage mutual funds.

3) Equities

These include stocks (common, preferred, foreign and domestic), equity mutual funds and income trusts, including real estate investment trusts (REITs)

4) Tangible assets

These include real estate, oil and gas properties, precious metals, and art and collectibles. There are also hybrid assets such as convertible debt, GICs and REITs, but these convertibles are usually a combination of income and equities. For the purposes of this book, we will be talking mainly about the traditional financial asset classes — cash, fixed income and equity. Real estate, in the form of your house, is an issue we will discuss later. But collectibles, precious metals and the like are outside my area of expertise, and deserve separate study.

LOW RISK, HIGH RISK AND EVERYTHING IN BETWEEN

Let's look at the most common investment options available to you. They are:

- Canada Savings Bonds, GICs and term deposits
- Money market securities
- Government and provincial bonds
- Mortgage-backed securities (MBS) and asset-backed securities (ABS)
- Bond and mortgage mutual funds
- Corporate bonds
- Index funds and exchange traded funds (ETFs)
- Equity mutual funds
- Wrap programs
- Hedge funds
- Stocks: common, preferred, foreign, small-cap, mid-cap, large-cap, income trusts
- Derivatives (options)

CANADA SAVINGS BONDS AND GICS

"You can't go wrong with Canada Savings Bonds," goes the old expression. The same logic applies to GICs — they're like cash in many ways, in that they're very safe, do not lose their value (unless you take the ravages of inflation into account) and in the case of Canada Savings Bonds

(CSBs), can be cashed at any time without penalty, and with accumulated interest. GICs have fixed terms and come in numerous forms with countless options including interest rate protection, where rates escalate each year of the investment so you're protected if rates go down. Most GICs are now insured by the Canada Deposit Insurance Corporation (CDIC) for up to $100,000.

There are no fees to purchase CSBs, and the minimum regular interest bond purchase is a very reasonable $100, while the compound interest bond's minimum is $300. A CSB will not rise or fall in value with interest rates, as most other bonds do. This is because CSBs, despite their name, are not really bonds at all, and thus are not traded on a market.

GICs and CSBs can and should be a part of anyone's portfolio, but if you are relying on them to generate any significant retirement money, good luck! The current yield (as of October 2005) on a one-year CSB is 1.55 percent, while the Canada Premium Bond (CPB), is 2.29 percent (if held for the three years). You have a choice of regular interest and compound interest bonds. Canada Premium Bonds were recently introduced for long-term savers. They offer higher interest rates than CSBs, but they can only be cashed once a year.

MONEY MARKET SECURITIES

Money market products are short-term investment instruments that are highly liquid and come with terms ranging from one day to one year. They include: Government of Canada T-bills, government-guaranteed commercial paper, provincial T-bills, promissory notes, banker's acceptances/bearer deposit notes and commercial paper. It's important to note that like a zero coupon bond, they're sold at a discount to par value in order to provide a yield to maturity. Money market products are fully eligible for self-directed RRSPs and RRIFs.

GICs usually offer higher yields than treasury bills, which are issued by the federal and provincial governments. But GICs are locked in, as opposed to T-bills which can be sold on the market. However, T-bills are usually only available in large certificate denominations such as $10,000 or more.

GOVERNMENT AND CORPORATE BONDS

Government of Canada bonds offer attractive returns and are fully guaranteed by the federal government. They are available for terms of as little as one day to as long as thirty years, and like T-bills, are essentially risk-free if held to maturity. They are considered the safest Canadian investment available with a term over one year. They pay a guaranteed, fixed level of interest income until maturity, at which time the full face value is repaid. They are fully marketable, which means they can be sold at market value at any time. You may purchase Government of Canada bonds denominated in Canadian or U.S. dollars, as well as Euros, pounds sterling and New Zealand and Australian dollars.

Corporate bonds offer a higher yield compared to government bonds, but there is a reason. They are not secured by the government and they are usually not secured by any of the company's collateral either. They are originally sold at a price close to par value, which is usually $100. Corporate bondholders must assume interest rate risk and also *credit* risk, because there is a chance that the corporate issuer will default on its debt obligations. Do your homework and assess credit risk before you invest in corporate bonds by checking the bond ratings with the Dominion Bond Rating Service or Standard & Poor's.

SOME FIXED INCOME PRODUCTS
- Government bonds (federal, provincial and municipal)
- Strip bonds
- Mortgage-backed securities
- Real return bonds
- U.S. foreign pay bonds
- Step-up bonds

These are ideal if you have an investment time horizon of longer than 18 months and want a higher rate of return than that provided by regular deposit notes.

Key features include:

1. Low minimum investment amounts
2. Higher rate of return than traditional savings options (e.g., GICs)
3. Low risk: Depending on the type of security, they may be secured by the federal, provincial or municipal government
4. Flexible terms to maturity
5. High liquidity: May be sold at any time prior to maturity at current market prices
6. Fully RSP- and RIF-eligible

THE BOND PERCENTAGE OF YOUR PORTFOLIO

The percentage of your portfolio that should be allocated to fixed-income securities will depend on your particular needs. Fixed-income not only provides predictable income and principal preservation but is also critical in diversifying an investment portfolio and reducing overall risk. As you get closer to retirement, the bond allocation should increase. This will increase the predictability and security of your portfolio while providing income to meet your cash flow needs.

If you're saving for a short-term expenditure, such as a car or house, you should also have a heavy weighting in liquid fixed-income investments. Within the fixed-income component of the portfolio investors must also decide how to divide up their funds between government (federal, provincial, municipal), corporate, asset-backed securities, foreign bonds and structured notes. Again, how much to allocate to each type of product will depend on your needs, including:

- Age
- When you expect to need this money
- What your income needs are
- Whether or not this will be a primary source of income
- Risk tolerance
- Overall wealth
- Outlook for interest rates and the market

HIGH-YIELD INVESTING (JUNK BONDS)

A "junk" bond is any bond with a rating below BBB. Knowledgeable investors seeking higher investment returns may want to explore high-yield bonds. High-yield bonds carry greater risk but offer higher potential returns than investment-grade bonds. The issuer's ability to pay interest and repay principal at maturity is less than certain and its ability to withstand poor economic or market conditions may be weak.

Due to the inherent risks in these bonds, they generally trade at a discount to par and thus offer attractive yields. It is imperative that you do your due diligence when investing in this class of bonds. As an example, Air Canada had their bond ratings slashed to "junk" status, which led to a precipitous decline in their price. Many investors purchased these bonds in the hope that the government would bail the company out if Air Canada declared bankruptcy. In the end the government didn't bail them out and investors lost millions. So, if you're looking for regular income and safety of capital, you should limit your investment in fixed-income products to investment-grade bonds.

RISK/RETURN FALLS BETWEEN INVESTMENT-GRADE BONDS AND EQUITIES

Many experts believe that high-yield bonds should be considered as a separate asset class because of their distinct risk and return characteristics. High-yield bonds have attributes of both fixed-income and equity investments. They resemble fixed-income investments in that their promised return is equal to their yield, and their prices move inversely with interest rates. However, they also resemble equity, because their ratings — and hence their prices — depend to a large degree on the financial performance of the issuing firm.

Because of their unique characteristics, high-yield bond returns are not closely correlated with those of investment grade bonds or equities. Therefore, you can further diversify your portfolio and boost your expected return by adding high-yield bonds to your mix of cash, fixed-income and equity investments. SEI Financial Services, a U.S.-based defined benefit pension fund manager, recommends investors allocate 10 percent to 30 percent of their total fixed-income portfolio to high-yield investments.

If you have funds to invest for the longer term and can accept some risk, you should consider adding high-yield bonds to your balanced portfolios. Many experienced investors believe that the increased pick up in yield is much greater than is actually warranted by the added risk of a high-yield bond. To reduce your exposure to default risk, you should consider investing in at least three or four different bond issuers from unrelated industries.

MORTGAGE-BACKED SECURITIES

A mortgage-backed security (MBS) is a bond whose cash flows are backed by the underlying mortgages within the bond structure. When you invest in a mortgage-backed security you are indirectly lending money to a homebuyer. The mortgage payments from the individual mortgages are used to pay your principal and interest on the MBS.

An asset-backed security is similar to an MBS, except that instead of a mortgage, these securities are backed by such diverse asset classes as retail and wholesale auto loans, credit card receivables, computer leases, equipment leases, conventional residential mortgages and personal lines of credit.

BOND AND MORTGAGE MUTUAL FUNDS

Short-term bond funds and mortgage funds carry a small degree of risk, but you can increase your yield by investing in them. These funds invest in short-term bonds or mortgage securities, generally with maturities of less than five years. One of the cheapest in terms of the management expense ratio (MER) is the iUnits Government of Canada 5-Year Bond Fund, which tracks five-year Government of Canada bonds.

As MoneySense.ca points out: a one-percentage-point increase in interest rates will reduce the market value of your short-term bond or mortgage fund by a little less than 5 percent. But happily, if interest rates fall a percentage point, your principal investment can rise about 5 percent, due to the inverse relationship between interest rates and bond prices. The bottom line is, if you stick with your fund for the long term, your chances of losing any principal are negligible, because you continue to receive interest payments even when the value of the fund falls.

INCOME TRUSTS

Income trusts have become very popular in Canadian capital markets in recent years. Income trusts are high-yielding equities that are essentially flow-through vehicles designed to minimize corporate taxes. They provide the most efficient distribution of a company's free cash flow to its owners (unitholders). The income trust name was coined because they were designed to hold income-producing assets in trust for investors, and they pay out most of their profits as distributions. Cash flow payments are usually made monthly in the form of interest, dividends or return of capital (and are taxed in the hands of unitholders). In the case of the return of capital component, such distributions are tax-deferred until the unit is sold, thus decreasing the adjusted cost base of the units.

The income trust universe is comprised of the following major categories:

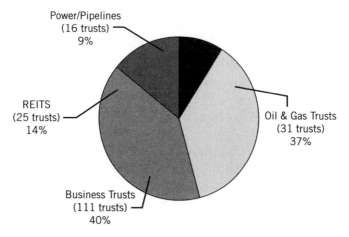

Income Trust Universe, $120.9 Mkt Cap

Power/Pipelines (16 trusts) 9%

REITS (25 trusts) 14%

Oil & Gas Trusts (31 trusts) 37%

Business Trusts (111 trusts) 40%

Note: Number of trusts in brackets

Source: TD Newcrest, August 6, 2005.

A report by TD Newcrest calculated a strong (96 percent) correlation between historical income trust and equity performance — supporting the view that income trusts are equities. In Canada, the income trust market was launched in the oil and gas industry with the creation of Enerplus in 1986. The real estate industry quickly followed, with the conversion of RioCan in 1993, launching the REIT market. As of August 2005, its total market capitalization is over $120 billion, which represents about 12 percent of the Toronto Stock Exchange (TSX) market composite.

When analyzing a trust for investment purposes, always look at the business first. The industry, company and management fundamentals must be strong, as must the actual income fund structure (stability, interest rate sensitivity, etc.). Unlike common equity where investors usually focus on earnings, investors in income trusts must look at the cash available to sustain the monthly distributions. The key here is distributable cash, which is essentially free cash flow after deducting maintenance or sustaining capital expenditures.

Income trust risks

Because income trusts tend to be heavily invested in real estate, oil and gas, pipelines and other infrastructure areas, they're not well diversified. In addition, revenue is passed on to unitholders, rather than reinvested in the business, which potentially sacrifices growth. Trusts do not guarantee their returns, so if the business starts to lose money, the trust can reduce or even eliminate distributions.

If tax laws relating to trusts are challenged and changed, this could negatively impact trust values. Although performance has been exceptional over the past few years, there's no guarantee that this can continue. It's especially important to note that income trusts can be affected by changes in interest rates. Risk is always reduced through knowledge, which is why it's critical for you to read the financial statements and do all the necessary research if you intend to invest in this area.

REITS

REITs have recently surged in popularity among investors. A real estate investment trust is a trust that pools the capital of investors to invest in various forms of real estate, usually income-producing assets that are structured to generate regular distributions of cash. REITs seek out investment opportunities and actively manage real estate assets. It's important to remember that if you buy a REIT you're not *directly* investing in real estate property, but instead own REIT units that are publicly traded. Although their goal is generally to generate income, they remain equity investments, and as such there's no guarantee they'll produce the projected cash flow.

REITs: Are they as safe as your house?

Thanks to the booming value of residential real estate, your house may be one of your best performing investments. But what about the real estate in your portfolio? In 2004, REITs experienced unprecedented volatility. This year, the question on investors' minds is whether this asset class can continue to generate healthy returns. The major concern—and the primary reason for last year's volatility—is interest rates. REITs are sensitive to rising rates because rate hikes make other interest-generating investments more attractive and decrease the appeal of REITs and income trusts. This, in turn, pushes down prices.

Higher rates can also affect REITs' underlying businesses. Because interest rates remain historically low, some REITs may have a highly leveraged property portfolio. As rates rise, more of the income from that portfolio may have to go toward servicing debt, potentially reducing payouts to investors.

When considering a REIT, apply the same scrutiny as you would with any other type of investment. Consider the performance track record, the sector in which it invests, individual holdings, business fundamentals and the capabilities of management. REITs do not all react in the same way to economic fundamentals. For example, those specializing in office buildings could be performing well in a booming economy while a tourism slump could hurt hotel-based REITs.

To decrease the risk of investing in any one particular REIT, you might consider diversifying among income trusts. Another option is to choose a mutual fund that focuses on REITs or an income-oriented fund that features income trusts along with dividend-paying shares and/or bonds.

(Excerpted from TD Waterhouse *Investor Insights*)

EQUITY MUTUAL FUNDS

A mutual fund pools money from many individuals and invests it according to stated objectives. Professional managers make investment decisions on behalf of fund investors, buying and selling securities such as stocks, bonds and money market investments. Some of the key benefits of equity mutual funds are:

Diversification: Because mutual funds typically hold fifty to a hundred different investments, they offer a degree of diversification that would be difficult to achieve on your own.

Professional management: Actively managed mutual funds also give you the benefit of professional investment managers who devote themselves exclusively to tracking the markets and implementing a consistent investment strategy.

Flexibility: Mutual funds can help you meet a variety of investment goals, from shorter term goals like establishing an emergency fund, to longer term objectives like education savings and retirement income.

There are thousands of equity mutual funds available, but the key categories are:

- Index funds
- Balanced funds
- Sector funds
- Global equity funds
- U.S. equity funds
- Canadian equity funds

Some mutual funds hold only stocks or bonds, while others may hold both stocks and bonds and an assortment of other assets such as income trusts and REITs. It's important to note that a mutual fund is an investment product that can contain a number of asset classes within it, but it is not itself an asset class. The fund manager's investments must by regulation remain within the stated investment objectives of the mutual fund. Some funds, for instance, invest predominantly in blue-chip stocks, while others concentrate on small-cap stocks or government bonds. If you can imagine an investment objective, there's a good chance you'll find a mutual fund to match it. The breadth and scope of mutual funds is truly impressive.

FUND MANAGEMENT: ACTIVE VS. PASSIVE

Mutual fund management comes in two broad varieties: active and passive. Active managers buy and sell securities within the fund with the objective of enhancing the return to unitholders beyond that generated by the underlying market. Passive managers, on the other hand, arrange their investments to mirror a market index. Although they will not beat the market, it's unlikely they'll fall much below it.

Open-end funds — the kind most investors are familiar with — issue units to buyers continuously and handle the buying and selling of their units themselves. This is in contrast to closed-end funds, which issue a fixed ("closed") number of shares that trade on a stock exchange. As it happens, closed-end funds usually invest in a pool of actively managed securities specific to a particular country. These funds can have more risk than open-end funds because their price does not directly relate to the value of the underlying securities. With closed-end funds, there is often a discount or a premium on the underlying securities, whereas with open-end funds, the price is always directly matched to the value of the securities within the fund.

Conventional open-end mutual funds have become very popular with investors because they offer a simple, easy-to-buy product with professional management and excellent diversification. With one single investment, you spread your risk over a multitude of other investments that have been screened by specialized managers.

They allow you to automatically reinvest your dividends without cost. They're independently audited and well regulated, and their returns are posted publicly and are widely available.

FUND COSTS

Mutual funds charge management fees, and incur capital gains, dividend and interest income taxes that must be passed on to you. They also incur sales and marketing expenses.

Fund management fees

A fund manager evaluates potential investments, monitors ongoing ones, buys and sells, and keeps enough cash in the fund to pay for redemptions. In addition to paying the manager for these services, the fund has to pay GST, the expenses of communicating with unitholders, legal and auditing costs, custodial fees and, depending on the fund, a trailer commission to a financial advisor or fund distributor. These expenses, divided by the dollar value of the fund, give you the management expense ratio (MER). The MER is deducted from fund returns before the returns are quoted.

Fund taxes

In the process of buying and selling and owning securities to increase the fund's returns, the fund manager generates capital gains and collects dividends and interest that are passed on to you and on which you must pay tax.

Some funds are more tax-efficient than others because their managers do less buying and selling in the process of managing the underlying portfolio. The most tax-efficient funds of all are index funds (see page 108). An index fund reproduces the content and proportion of a given index and changes its holdings only when the corresponding index itself makes a change. This extremely low level of trading within the fund means fewer capital gains are realized and subsequently passed on to the unitholders.

Fund sales charges

Deferred sales charge (DSC): If you buy a mutual fund through an advisor who offers value-added guidance and works on commission, you will most likely receive a deferred sales charge (DSC). This means you don't pay a sales commission until you sell your fund, and perhaps not at all, depending on a few conditions. First of all, you must normally take your money out of the fund company altogether to be charged a DSC fee. If you switch to another DSC fund within the same fund company, you will generally not incur a sales charge. The best news of all is the sales charge declines each year you own the fund, eventually diminishing to nothing after about six to eight years, depending on the fund company. DSC funds also typically allow free redemptions of 10 percent of your holdings every year.

Front-end load (FEL): Front-end load funds charge a sales commission at the time of purchase. In my opinion, they should be avoided as the commission immediately erodes the principal amount of your investment, and thus retards the amount of compounding you can expect to achieve over the long term. However, FELs are sometimes favoured by investors with large amounts to invest, as the commission can be negotiable and the MER may sometimes be lower.

Low load: Low-load funds are a variation on DSC funds. Like DSC funds, there is no sales commission up front and you pay a redemption fee if you redeem the fund within a certain period. But unlike conventional DSC funds, the redemption fee is fixed and low, and applies only for a short period of time, about two or three years. After that, redemptions do not incur a sales charge.

Level load: Level loads are a relatively new sales charge option that adds the sales charge to the MER. They are not to be confused with no-load funds, because they have an ongoing sales charge that is tucked into a larger MER. The sales charge is constant, or "level," and does not decline over time.

No load: No-load mutual funds are the kind sold by banks and fund companies who sell directly to investors. These funds do not have a sales charge attached when you buy or when you sell them, though some companies charge a small transaction fee when you sell a fund.

Trailer fees: Regardless of the kind of load a mutual fund carries, the fund pays a "trailer fee" to the financial advisor as compensation for ongoing service. Certain classes of mutual funds don't pay trailer fees. These are typically known as F-class funds and are sold exclusively through fee-based advisors. F-class funds pay neither sales commissions nor trailer fees, which leaves their MERs lower, but the investor pays a fee directly to the advisor who is structuring a portfolio with these funds.

MUTUAL FUNDS ARE NOT CDIC-INSURED

Because mutual funds are sold through banks and other financial institutions, people sometimes believe that mutual funds are covered by deposit insurance from the Canada Deposit Insurance Corporation (CDIC). This is not true. Savings account deposits and GICs are insured to a specified limit by CDIC, but mutual funds are not covered.

However, there are safeguards you should be aware of. A mutual fund holds the fund's assets in trust with a custodian on behalf of the unitholders, and the assets are audited annually by an independent auditor. In addition, the fund companies themselves must comply with strict industry regulations.

MANAGEMENT STYLES

Like all investment managers, mutual fund managers tend to display a specific style that describes how they approach and select their investments. Many managers say their approach is a blend of different styles, but they almost always favour one or the other.

Top-down managers: A top-down manager looks at broad economic trends and indicators, watches for sectors or industries in ascendance and then looks for companies within those industries or sectors that will profit from the larger economic trends. The emphasis is on the broader economy rather than the individual company.

Bottom-up managers: Bottom-up managers focus on the fundamentals of a company rather than on the larger economic picture. They invest in solid businesses, thinking that a good business will continue to do well, come what may.

Value managers: Value managers look for intrinsically undervalued companies — ones that are out of favour but nevertheless solid businesses. Value investors generally look for companies whose P/E ratios are well below market average.

Growth managers: Growth managers look for companies likely to have large revenue or earnings increases. They are willing to pay higher prices for these companies because they believe the stock price will go up as revenue and earnings increase. At some point, this escalation ends, so it's wise to balance a growth fund with a value fund, though the balance doesn't have to be even. Bull markets generally reward a growth style until, of course, the bears take over.

Sector rotation managers: Managers with this investment style try to anticipate the next big sector. They can move from gold to financials to transportation and back to gold or whatever sector looks promising. Sector funds typically carry greater risk and at times can be very volatile.

DIVIDEND REINVESTMENT PLANS (DRIPs)
One of the many advantages to buying a mutual fund over an equity or bond is that when a distribution is paid, there is an option to reinvest the distribution back into units of the same fund at no cost. This allows mutual fund investors to stay *fully* invested and avoids having small cash balances build up in their accounts.

SYSTEMATIC INVESTMENT PLANS (SIPs)
A systematic investment plan (SIP) allows an investor to regularly purchase a set dollar amount of a mutual fund on a specific day each period.

SEGREGATED FUNDS/GUARANTEED INVESTMENT FUNDS (GIFs)
A segregated fund is essentially the insurance industry's equivalent of a mutual fund. Segregated mutual funds are insurance products that have been gaining popularity in recent years. Instead of buying units of a

fund, the client purchases an insurance contract. The underlying mutual fund assets determine the performance of the fund. It is important to note that a segregated fund (contract) can only be issued by an insurance company.

Segregated funds invest in a pool of funds or a portfolio of funds. They offer maturity and death benefit guarantees, and potential creditor protection and probate fee savings, but there is usually a higher MER than mutual funds because of the associated insurance costs.

INDEX FUNDS

An index fund is a mutual fund or exchange-traded fund (ETF) with a clearly defined set of rules that enable them to invest in the basket of securities that are included in stock market indexes, as opposed to individual stocks. The fund does not have to follow a well-known index. The basic concept behind index funds (and ETFs) is that they are the best way to reflect something economists call the "efficient market hypothesis" (EMH). Without getting too technical, the efficient market hypothesis, which is widely accepted by economists, states that an individual stock price reflects the sum total of contemporary investor knowledge. It is, therefore, the "right" price for the moment. *National Review Online* writer James K. Glassman sums up the concept pretty well:

> Stock movements in the future simply cannot be known from the perspective of the present; they perform a "random walk." If EMH is correct, you can't beat the market consistently through superior intellect. Stock pickers who appear to be brilliant, or have a hot hand, are actually just lucky (just as someone at a roulette table who makes a winning bet on number 29 three times in a row is lucky). EMH posits that managers of diversified portfolios have roughly the same chance of winning, so a smart investor should refrain from being enticed by the funds that are doing well right now and simply buy those with the lowest expenses — which tend to be index funds that use computer programs to mimic the markets.

ETFS

Exchange-traded funds (ETFs) are similar to index mutual funds, but they have one big advantage: instead of being priced once, at the close of each trading day, ETFs trade intraday, just like stocks. They're generally designed to follow a recognized benchmark such as the S&P 500 or the S&P/TSX Composite Index, but may be specifically tailored to follow a certain sector or industry (e.g., financial services or information technology).

They offer a number of benefits including lower management fees (MERs) than those charged by comparable index mutual funds. Each trade is assessed a commission (just as a comparable equity trade would be). You receive full portfolio transparency, which means all the fund holdings and concentrations are easily observed, whereas the full holdings of a mutual fund are reported less frequently. Finally, margin purchases and short-selling are possible (most mutual funds can be purchased on margin but they cannot be used for short-selling). Some common ETFs include iUnits, which are traded on the Toronto Stock Exchange (TSX), and Standard & Poor's Depository Receipts (SPDRs) which are traded on the American Stock and Options Exchange (AMEX).

STOCKS: PART 1

Preferred vs. common stock

Preferred shareholders often receive a higher dividend than that of common shareholders. Preferred shareholders have a prior right to claim assets ahead of common shareholders, but behind creditors. Preferred shares are generally more expensive for a company to issue. Like common stock, they have no maturity date, but unlike common, most preferred shares do not carry voting privileges. Preferred stock may have a redemption schedule; however, it is seldom in the best interests of a company to redeem them.

The "value" of a share

What would you like it to be? I don't mean to be cynical, but contrary to popular belief (at least among less experienced investors) stock prices are not actually determined by some complex mathematical formula. Each share of a company you own in your portfolio represents a fractional ownership of that business. But the price of those shares is determined by the laws of supply and demand.

The mathematical value of a share is based on the discounted (present) value of future cash flows from the company that originally issued the share, taking into account any dividends that may also be paid out over the course of the shareholding period.

The trouble is, no one knows for sure what those future cash flows will be. Charles Biderman, in his book *Trim Tabs Investing*, states that any relationship between the stock price and the underlying value of the business is usually coincidental.

Over the long run, a company's share price is driven by the earnings of the company, and its consistency in delivering those earnings. To get a sense of whether a stock is over- or undervalued, long-term investors usually compare its price to revenue, earnings, cash flow and other criteria. But fundamentals are just one method of valuation, and evaluation. There are many other ways to value a stock.

The market is governed by the free flow of public information and the securities prices in that market reflect that information. This is what's called the efficient market hypothesis (EMH). Those in favour of EMH say there are no undervalued or overvalued securities; fund managers and traders who buy and sell on fundamentals are simply incapable of producing superior returns because when new information is released, it is fully and immediately incorporated into the stock's price.

The "rational" investor

Many old-school economists believe in the existence and predictable behaviour of the so-called rational investor. Nobel Prize–winning economist Joseph Stiglitz is not one of those. In his December 20, 2002, article for *The Guardian* he wrote:

> John Maynard Keynes long ago described the stock market as based not on rational individuals struggling to uncover market fundamentals, but as a beauty contest in which the winner is the one who guesses best what the judges will say.... Different market participants have different (and imperfect) information, and these asymmetries in information have a profound impact on how an economy functions.... Adam Smith's "invisible hand"— the idea that free markets lead to efficiency as if guided by

unseen forces — is invisible, at least in part, because it is not there.

Warren Buffet is another who rejects the rationale behind the efficient market hypothesis. He's been widely quoted as saying that if the market was efficient, professional investors like himself would be out of business. Whatever view of the markets you choose to take, there certainly seems to be plenty of evidence that — at least in the short term — markets are highly inefficient. Stock prices got temporarily out of whack during the "Nifty Fifty" craze of the early 1970s and again during the manic tech sector phase in the 1990s.

More important than investor behaviour (in the long run) is the current and future rate of inflation. Because it dictates how much a future dollar of earnings will *actually* be worth down the road, it explains why today's low-interest-rate, low-inflation environment is such a plus for stocks. It may also explain why P/E ratios have expanded — just like they did in the low-interest-rate, low-inflation 1960s. But ultimately stock prices rise or fall according to the current and future *earnings* of the company. In the go-go 1960s, a lot of companies were earning the money to justify their lofty P/Es; but in the 1970s the oil crisis and high interest rates changed everything.

Although it's impossible to nail down what future dividends or cash flows will be, analysts work hard at estimating future value by other means: comparing relative values of comparable stocks in the same or similar industries, assessing past and future profit-growth rates, reviewing historical return on equity, present and future sales growth, quality of management, their ability to find and maintain a competitive niche and, finally, their ability to create efficiencies and manage their costs.

STOCKS: PART 2—SMALL-CAPS, MID-CAPS, LARGE-CAPS

There's a lot of talk these days about where to find growth opportunities. Some advocate investing heavily in small-capitalization stocks. Others prefer the "safety" of large-cap, blue-chip stocks. And others go by sector or by geographical region.

It's important to understand what market capitalization is, and how it can potentially help — and hurt you. A stock's "market cap" is a public company's total market value. Market cap is very important because most of the major market indices are weighted according to the market cap of the stocks listed within.

Market cap example (BCE)

Market cap is calculated by multiplying the total number of shares outstanding by the price per share. For example, Bell Canada Enterprises Inc. market cap is calculated this way:

> There are 926 million BCE (common) shares outstanding. The share price is, at the time of writing, $29 per share. So, 926 million shares × $29 per share = approximately $25 billion dollars (give or take a few million, but who's counting when you get that high?).

What does market cap mean for you as an investor? Asset allocation by market cap is a critical variable for many fund managers. Some mutual funds are broadly diversified, while others target an asset class or a specific sector of the economy, such as international bonds or science and technology stocks. There are large-cap funds, small-cap funds and everything in between. Brokerages vary on exact definitions, but the current approximate classes of market capitalization (at least in the United States) are:

Market cap of

Mega-cap	$200 billion and greater
Big/Large-cap	$10 billion to $200 billion
Mid-cap	billion to $10 billion
Small-cap	million to $2 billion
Micro-cap	million to $300 million
Nano-cap	$50 million

Source: Investopedia.com.

Keep in mind, the above numbers are rough estimates — actual brokerage and fund managers' numbers will vary somewhat. To get an idea of Canadian market caps, it may help to take a look at the table below.

The 10 biggest Canadian Companies by Market Cap

Ticker	Name	Current Market Cap	Change Year to Date Percent	Last Price
1) RY	Royal Bank of Canada	53,609.69MLN	+28.794	82.75
2) ECA	Encana Corp	50,381.04MLN	+72.222	58.90
3) MFC	Manulife Financial Corp	48,053.20MLN	+8.899	60.33
4) BNS	Bank of Nova Scotia	41,484.89MLN	+2.408	41.68

5) TD	Toronto-Dominion Bank	39,799.38MLN	+12.300	56.06
6) IMO	Imperial Oil Ltd.	36,442.23MLN	+51.370	107.70
7) SHC	Shell Canada Ltd.	28,877.19MLN	+31.266	35.00
8) SU	Suncor Energy Inc.	28,530.46MLN	+41.217	62.42
9) BMO	Bank of Montreal	28,357.12MLN	–1.939	56.64
10) BCE	BCE Inc.	27,528.60MLN	+2.697	29.70

Source: Bloomberg, October 18, 2005.

STOCKS: PART 3—FUNDAMENTAL VS. TECHNICAL ANALYSIS

There are many ways to analyze stock prices, but investment professionals usually fall into one of two camps: fundamentalists or
technicians. In my opinion, all smart investors should learn the elements of fundamental analysis before considering technical analysis.
Fundamental analysts believe in trying to determine a company's
intrinsic value by looking at the company's strategy, management and
products, along with such fundamental ratios as P/E, cash flow, earnings per share (EPS), etc.

Technical analysis is based on charting, which is a picture version of
a stock's price, how much it is traded and which direction the price is
moving in. Technical analysts do not attempt to measure a security's
intrinsic value but rather use specialized charts to identify trading patterns that can suggest future activity. Technical analysts study specialized
charts, such as tick charts:

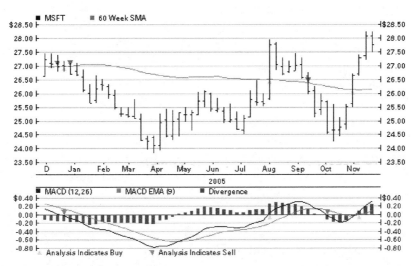

Source: TD Waterhouse Canada Inc.

Technical analysis involves looking at past price changes to try to predict future price movements. People who use this approach believe that the stock's current price is based on all the information available on it, including what traders, investors, portfolio managers and everyone else in the investment world know. So the technical analyst's strategy is to use the price to interpret what the market is saying about the stock so they can take advantage of future changes.

While many technical analysts agree that prices move in trends, they also agree that there are periods when prices do not. This makes charting less predictable than most would like.

Wrap programs

Wraps are designed to bundle or "wrap" assorted fees and services into one comprehensive program for one flat fee based on the size of your account. These programs give you asset allocation, automatic portfolio rebalancing and regular reporting with no ancillary charges. Wraps come in three varieties — mutual fund wrap accounts, pooled wrap programs and segregated wrap accounts — each targeted to successively higher minimum account sizes.

1. Mutual fund wraps: These accounts are offered by mutual fund companies, financial planning firms and banks. They typically require you to fill out a questionnaire that explores your investment objectives, investment horizon and risk tolerance. Based on this information, you are steered to one of a series of model portfolios composed of selected mutual funds. This portfolio will be automatically rebalanced to your original asset allocation at least annually for no charge, but you pay a small fee to be in the program, in addition to the normally unreduced MERs on the underlying funds. Minimum investments can be in the $5,000 range.

You cannot bring your own investments into this program, nor can you customize your mutual fund holdings, although of course you are free to buy whatever you like outside the program. You must own one of the model portfolios without alteration. On the other hand, many investors find the professional management, ongoing review and automatic rebalancing services useful, since this allows the portfolio to run with virtually no supervision from the investor.

2. Pooled wraps: A pooled fund is a proprietary mutual fund run by investment managers for their clients and is not available to the general investing public. Pooled funds typically have lower MERs than retail mutual funds because they pay no distribution costs, commissions, trailers or other similar costs associated with retail mutual funds, but they also have high minimum investment requirements, often around $50,000 or more. You may or may not have to select from model portfolios, depending on the nature of the program. Most pooled programs automatically rebalance to your original asset allocation free of charge.

You must watch your total, all-in costs. Sometimes brokerage charges for trading done to manage the pools are charged to you over and above the flat fee. Fees are generally tiered and decline as account size increases. They may also be tax-deductible because investment counsel fees not relating to registered accounts are generally tax-deductible.

A huge variety of pooled wrap programs is available. As with all investments and programs, it is important to read the fine print and know exactly what is included in the wrap fee. Sometimes it is not as all-inclusive as you might think. In addition to the tax deductibility of investment counsel fees, some pooled programs offer other tax savings. Conventional mutual funds distribute tax liabilities equally to all investors regardless of how long any investor has owned the fund.

If you buy a fund at the end of December, you will get the same tax bill for the gains in that fund as if you had owned it from the previous January, whether or not you benefited from any of those gains yourself. Some pooled programs have sophisticated software that tracks and allocates an investor's individual tax liabilities so, rather than just equally dividing a pool's liabilities among all the investors in that pool, these programs track the time investors have spent in the pool and allot the tax liability accordingly.

3. Segregated wraps: A third kind of wrap program uses individual securities instead of pooled funds or mutual funds. This is frequently called a segregated program because individual securities are, in theory, segregated from a pool and individually owned. In fact, these programs are frequently managed as pools, but specialized software apportions the securities from the pools to individual investors. You may or may not have the option of including your own investments in the program.

Typical minimum investments in these programs run about $150,000. Fees may also include a maximum number of trades.

HEDGE FUNDS

Originally, hedge funds were established as a way to reduce market volatility. By selling the right mix of stocks "short," and buying other stocks "long," the fund attempted to balance out its long and short positions in order to minimize losses due to big market swings.

Hedge funds, and hedge fund definitions, have evolved. Today the term generally refers to a private investment pool that is subject to fewer regulations than traditional mutual funds, and uses alternative, sometimes highly sophisticated methods of investing with the intent of minimizing risk, boosting return, or a combination of the two. Today's hedge funds employ a number of strategies including: Long/Short Equity, Convertible Arbitrage, Equity Market Neutral and Event Driven.

What exactly is a hedge fund?
A hedge fund is a private investment pool that is subject to fewer regulations than traditional mutual funds and which often employs highly sophisticated methods of investing to minimize risk or boost return—or a combination of the two.

Initially, the minimum investment for these products was about $1 million per investor. With the rapid expansion of the hedge fund market over the last few years, minimums have fallen to as low as $100,000. If you qualify as an "accredited investor," your minimum can be as low as $25,000. To qualify as an "accredited investor" you must meet a number of criteria. For example, you must have minimum net investable assets of $1,000,000 or a net income of at least $200,000 over the last two years.

Due to the complexity of the strategies that hedge fund managers use, some investors may not understand the basic characteristics of the fund, which can lead to an improper mismatch of a client's risk and return objectives to that of the objectives of the hedge fund. With the growing popularity of the hedge fund industry it is important that you do your due diligence if and when adding a hedge fund to your portfolio.

OPTIONS (DERIVATIVES), CALLS AND PUTS

Derivatives "derive" their value from their relationship to the underlying stock. An option is a contract giving the buyer the right, but not the obligation, to buy or sell an underlying asset at a specific price on or before a certain date. It is also a binding contract with strictly defined terms and properties. There are two types of options: calls and puts.

A call gives the holder the right to buy an asset at a certain price within a specific period of time. Calls are similar to having a long position on a stock. Buyers of calls hope that the stock will increase substantially before the option expires. A put gives the holder the right to sell an asset at a certain price within a specific period of time. Puts are very similar to having a short position on a stock. Buyers of puts hope that the price of the stock will fall before the option expires.

The power of options lies in their versatility. They enable you to adapt or adjust your position according to any situation that arises. Options can be as speculative or as conservative as you want. This means you can do everything from protecting a position from a decline to outright betting on the movement of a security or index. But keep in mind, options have high risk and are targeted at sophisticated investors.

CHAPTER SUMMARY

Your nest egg is composed of one or more of the following assets:

- Cash/equivalents, fixed income, equities and tangible assets. Of these, equities are usually considered to carry the highest risk and can offer the highest return.
- Canada Savings Bonds (CSBs), GICs, term deposits and money market securities are low-yield, low-risk securities. Bond yields vary with the underlying credit risk attached to the issuer. Income trusts, including REITs, are very popular right now because of their flow-through tax advantages, and because of the lack of abundant alternatives in our current low-interest-rate environment.
- Index funds and ETFs minimize risk by diversifying into a large basket of indexed stocks. Their returns are for all intents and purposes pegged to the major market indices they track.
- Hedge funds and derivatives are generally for sophisticated investors who seek ways to minimize risk and/or maximize return. Offsetting puts and calls can minimize volatility; the leverage

obtained when purchasing stock options derives from the value of the underlying stock.

The past two chapters have given you the knowledge and the tools to *grow* your nest egg. In the next chapter, I'd like to show you how to *protect* your hard-earned money. And for most of us, only two kinds of insurance are needed.

CHAPTER
SIX

"All your dreams and your lovers won't protect you,
They're only passing through you in the end."
—NEIL YOUNG, "STAR OF BETHLEHEM"

ARM (Part 3)

ARM YOURSELF WITH THE *INSURANCE* TOOLS YOU NEED

If you're thinking of skipping this chapter, I think you should know something. Contrary to popular belief, insurance isn't just a hedge against personal or property loss. Certain kinds of insurance policies can be terrific tools for deferring taxable income and capital gains until you retire. What kind of policies? I'll give you all the details later in the chapter. But first, I want you to know something else about insurance.

Insurance is not a rip-off, nor is it a necessary evil. Insurance, if purchased for the right reasons, is a true godsend for pensioners, the self-employed, entrepreneurs, employees, executives, even homemakers. You just have to know what you need, and know what you're looking for to fill that need.

Unfortunately, insurance policies can be complicated at times. It's up to you to go to a reputable source, obtain professional advice and get competitive quotes. Do this and you should never have much of a problem.

In this chapter, I want to talk to you about how the right kind and amount of insurance can cost-effectively *protect* the assets you've worked so hard to accumulate or are in the process of accumulating. For example, it does you no good to invest with such high risk that you can't sleep at night. That's what investment hedging and diversification are all about. It also does you no good to expose yourself to loss unnecessarily.

Selecting the right insurance coverage is all about finding the right hedge and the right protection, getting it at an affordable price, and then tucking it safely away so you can concentrate on living your life.

ACCUMULATE, GROW, PROTECT, ENJOY.

I didn't always feel this strongly about getting insurance, but I had a big change of heart one day when I visited one of my parents' friends (who is now a retiree) and saw her tending her lovely garden. I noticed something was missing.

"Margie," I asked, "What happened to the roses you had growing in the corner there?" She looked up at me with a curious expression on her face. "Rose spot got to them. Had to cut them down so it wouldn't travel to my other roses," she replied sadly.

I had no idea what she was talking about (I'm not much of a gardener) until she told me that rose spot is a fungus that incubates in winter and only affects roses. Apparently, the spores are easily spread to new locations by air currents. Why did this happen to Margie, who tends her garden almost religiously every day and who regularly sprays fungicide? She said she'd never planted roses before, and while she made sure to spray them as soon as the warmer weather came, she neglected to spray them *before* the season started. With roses, that's what you must do. She learned her lesson the hard way. She follows a new system now: "Accumulate, grow, protect, enjoy."

So it's always a good idea to give roses advance protection before they even start to grow and bloom. Okay, this got me thinking. I realized that if you don't protect your prized possessions in advance, before there is any visible danger, they may be gone before you know it, just like Margie's roses.

That's what insurance is all about. We must protect our assets if we want to build something (whether it's a garden or our nest egg) so we can enjoy the fruits of our labour. Accumulate, Grow, Protect, Enjoy.

I get it now.

WHEN INDECISION LEADS TO TRAGEDY

Have you ever heard of a movie called *The Garden of the Finzi-Continis*? It was based on a semi-autobiographical novel by Giorgio Bassani. It's about a family of Jewish-Italian aristocrats at the beginning of World War II who must decide whether to leave their beloved house and its beautiful garden, or stay and face the consequences. When the war began, Mussolini had declared Italian Jews *persona non grata*, and it seemed only a matter of time before their property — and their lives — would be expropriated.

What did the family decide to do? They stayed, clinging to hope and ideals that had long passed by. Why do I bring up this story? It's an allegory for indecision and how uncertainty exposes us to unnecessary risk. The movie reminded me about the emotional attachment we form to the things we accumulate over our lifetimes, and how at times of stress we can actually place our possessions and our way of life ahead of our lives.

AN AVERSION TO SELF-PROTECTION

We are always more important than our possessions. You wouldn't know it according to how we buy insurance. In a December 2004 Financial Times.com article, Francis Klonowski, a Certified Financial Planner, says many people lack critical pieces of insurance: life assurance, disability and critical illness insurance. "We buy all sorts of [property] insurance — house, motor — and yet there seems to be a natural aversion to insure something far more valuable: ourselves," he says. He goes on to say:

"You need to ask yourself: how much income or capital would be needed if you died — and by whom? Now ask the same questions in the event of ill health or incapacity. The answers will be different at different life stages — for younger people it may be a question of being unable to work for long periods. For older people, it may be more about the possibility of ill health leading to the need for long-term care."

Depending on whether you own a business or what kind of employment situation you find yourself in, you owe it to yourself to look carefully at your insurance options. Each is tailored to different needs, so not all will apply to your situation. But let's review the most common ones. And by the way, one of the following policies qualifies as a marvellous tax deferral, as I mentioned earlier.

LIFE INSURANCE

Basic life insurance is essential if you have dependents and are not independently wealthy. It's also vital if you're making significant changes to your employment status (i.e., moving from a corporate position with full benefits to a self-employed status without benefits). This type of life insurance is also important if you are purchasing a new home or refinancing an existing home with a higher mortgage balance to protect.

Financial obligations like child support, educational support and spousal support create a need for life insurance. Basic life insurance products are not generally purchased during or after retirement. Instead, more complex saving and tax advantaged concepts are used in this stage of life. Why? Because the main purpose of basic life insurance is to protect your dependent loved ones in the event you die.

Your biggest asset is not your house; it's your ability to earn an income, specifically, multi-year cash flows from future income. This asset is your "human capital," a term introduced by Moshe Milevsky and Aron Gottesman, the authors of *Insurance Logic*. To calculate your potential earnings for life insurance purposes, just take your annual income and multiply it by the number of remaining years that you expect to work. Let's say you're earning $70,000 per year, you're 45 years old, and you expect to stop working when you are 65. In this example, your potential lost income would be $70,000 × 20, which is $1.4 million dollars!

The amount of life insurance you need varies through your life as your financial responsibilities to your loved ones rise and fall. If you are a member of a group plan, your life insurance may be based on a multiple of your salary, perhaps one or two times your salary. But the most accurate way to determine your life insurance needs is to look at your financial responsibilities.

You want to protect those who depend on your income should you die before you reach financial independence. You should consider your mortgage, education for your children, support for a stay-at-home spouse, nursing home care for your parents and other financial responsibilities you have. It's not unreasonable to want all your debts paid off on your death, with enough cash left over to fund the ongoing expenses of your dependants. Two times your salary might do that, but maybe it won't.

BUYING THROUGH A GROUP PLAN

It's easy and usually quite competitive to buy additional insurance through a group plan. The advantage of buying private insurance rather than adding to group coverage is portability. Most group policies allow you to convert to a permanent product when you leave your employer, but the option must be exercised almost immediately and may be a substandard product or outside of your budget constraints. However, personally owned insurance protects you between jobs or through the transition to self-employment. Another place to look for portable supplementary insurance is through your professional association, if you have one. It usually offers tailored insurance packages at competitive rates. Most association coverage is group coverage, not personally owned, however.

Before you dash off to check your coverage, you should give some thought to the kind of life coverage you want. There are really only two kinds of life insurance — term and permanent. Term doesn't build up any cash value over time, while permanent insurance can. Permanent life insurance, including whole life and universal life, is designed to provide insurance protection for the entire lifetime of the insured person. Many people appreciate this kind of security. There are pros and cons to each, however. Which one is right for you will depend on your unique needs and investment objectives. Let me explain.

TERM INSURANCE: "THE NO-FRILLS SOLUTION"

Term insurance covers you for a fixed term, for example, five, ten or twenty years. When you are young or middle-aged, term is *by far* the cheapest kind of life insurance, because there is no investment (forced savings) component built into the premiums. It is truly "no-frills" insurance. I do not recommend that anyone at retirement age or later buy term, as the premiums by then will be prohibitively expensive. Whatever your age, if you buy term insurance, make sure your policy includes what's called a guaranteed renewable clause. This allows you to renew your coverage (if and when the term expires) *without* having to undergo another medical exam, which is very useful to have if your health is deteriorating. (Expect a large premium hike on renewal, though.)

Term often comes with an option that allows you to convert to some form of permanent insurance before age 70, so it can be flexible as well as inexpensive. Term insurance is not recommended for estate planning purposes, since it gets increasingly expensive as you age and generally won't cover anyone beyond age 80. Term-to-100 insurance is the exception, as it covers you for life even if you live beyond 100.

WHOLE LIFE INSURANCE: "GUARANTEED FOR LIFE"

Whole life is permanent insurance with a guaranteed savings component to it. As long as you pay your premiums, the insurance will not expire and your premiums should not go up. Over time, the policy will build up a cash value from which you can borrow to pay premiums or for other uses. If you do borrow from the policy and die before repaying it, your death benefit is reduced by the amount of the loan. You can also obtain the cash value by cancelling the policy, although you'll have to pay taxes on it. Whole life is often used for estate planning purposes, since you can't outlive a permanent insurance policy in good standing. Both the insurance and the savings components are paid out at death, and because they're considered death benefits, they're not taxable.

UNIVERSAL LIFE: "THE TAX SAVER"

Universal life is another form of permanent insurance, which means it doesn't expire and your premiums may not go up. Universal life offers flexibility in how long and when you choose to pay your premiums as well as allowing you to defer tax on the investment component of your policy. A universal life insurance plan combines lifetime protection with a tax-sheltered investment fund. The policy is designed to help your family cope when you're gone, but it can also build you another nest egg for your retirement. Before I talk about the tax savings, it's important to truly understand the main difference between whole life and universal life. Here's an excellent explanation from Investopedia.com that may help you understand the difference.

> Universal life insurance was created to provide more flexibility than whole life insurance by allowing the policy owner to shift money between the insurance and savings components of the policy. Premiums, which are variable, are broken down by the insurance company into insurance and savings, allowing the policy owner to make adjustments based on their individual circumstances. For example, if the savings portion is earning a low return, it can be used instead of external funds to pay the premiums. Unlike whole life insurance, universal life allows the cash value of investments to grow at a variable rate that is adjusted monthly.

Life insurance is a complex subject, and what follows is just an overview. I suggest you talk to your advisor for a full understanding of how universal life may help you defer taxes. Assuming you have contributed the absolute maximum to your RRSP, here's how universal life works.

Part of your premium goes to paying the pure insurance cost (mortality and administrative costs) and part of your premium goes towards a savings component to fund future premiums. The investment or savings portion will grow inside your policy, tax-free. Of course, if you decide to take the cash-surrender value of your policy, you will have to pay taxes at that time, but the savings from tax deferral can be substantial. Here's a simple example of what I mean, as outlined by Milevsky & Gottesman in *Insurance Logic*:

> Imagine that you invest $10,000 at 5 percent interest for thirty years, and the inside buildup is taxed every year at your 50 percent marginal tax rate. Each year you pay taxes on any gains. Do the math yourself and you will find that in thirty years you have $20,975. Now what happens if the buildup is tax-free? In this case, you will have $43,220 before taxes are paid — a gain of $33,220. Then you must pay 50 percent tax on the gain of $33,220, which leaves you with $26,610. Compare the numbers. You have $5,635 ($26,610 – $20,975) more from the tax-free inside buildup.

Because you haven't eroded the growth of your shielded premium by paying taxes every year, you have a bigger nest egg at the end. From an initial premium of $10,000, you've earned an additional $5,635. This works out to about a 50 percent *additional* return. Not bad at all. And if you'd invested $100,000, your return would be staggeringly good. What investment options are "inside" some of these policies? Here's what LifeInsuranceQuote.com has to say on the matter: "... some are designed to provide returns that mirror well known mutual funds and they are managed by mutual funds managers. Examples include Standard and Poor's Index Accounts, Canadian Index Accounts, Canadian and American Equity Index Accounts, Bond Index Accounts, and 1-, 5- and 10-year GIC type accounts."

Noted tax expert Tim Cestnick has this to say about universal life:

> A universal life insurance policy can allow you to accumulate investments inside the policy on a tax-sheltered basis. This idea can make sense for those who would otherwise invest that money in interest-bearing investments outside the policy or a registered plan. It's generally best for those who are a little

older — say, 60 years of age and up. Of course, it's reason enough to buy a policy if you have a need for insurance for other non-investment reasons.

DEATH AND TAXES

Death and taxes, they say, are inescapable, but the insurance industry is able to hold at least one of them at bay. In Canada, the death benefit from virtually all forms of life insurance is non-taxable. That fact makes life insurance with an investment component very attractive because not only does the investment element compound, it is paid out at your death tax-free. You can access this money at any time by cashing in your policy. But keep in mind, the cash value gain in the policy is not a death benefit and thus is taxed as income. Because life insurance premiums are paid for with after-tax money, leaving your money in the plan until your death allows it to avoid tax.

Did you know many permanent life insurance policies will generally pay you a discounted settlement while you are still alive, should you contract a terminal illness? This is arranged by an interest-bearing advance on the policy.

Tip: Watch out for high management fees.

If you want some form of permanent insurance, scrutinize the management fee the insurance company charges for managing the investment portion of your premiums. These can be quite high by mutual fund standards, so you have to weigh the benefits of tax-free compounding with the annual management fee, which, of course, also compounds. In some cases, it can take twenty years for the tax sheltering to overcome the drag of a high management fee. Ask your insurance advisor to show you those numbers before signing on the dotted line and put your fixed income capital inside the universal life policy to optimize your tax savings. In some instances you may be better off buying term insurance and investing the difference in the premiums in some solid mutual funds if you don't feel you need the protection of insurance that is guaranteed to last until you die.

Tip: Buy term, then convert to permanent later.

A viable concept for younger clients is to buy term insurance while young, continue to pay off their debts and maximize RRSPs. Then before the first renewal of a policy, convert to permanent insurance with no medical exam and invest additional money into the tax sheltered policy as an estate planning tool.

Your money will compound tax-free until you pass away, at which point the money can go directly to your beneficiaries, tax-free and without having to go through the estate. Avoiding the estate means avoiding probate fees, too. (See Chapter 8 for more details.)

Tip: Use permanent life insurance as collateral for loans

Depending on the nature of the policy, you can borrow as much as 90 percent of the investment portion of the policy from a bank. You get your cash while the lender waits steadfastly for you to make your exit. You have the option of paying the interest on the loan or accruing it to the loan balance. Many older investors supplement their retirement income this way. However, be aware that this option may not always be available and is only a current understanding between the banking institutions and the Canada Revenue Agency (CRA). Remember that these loans are callable, and if the lender determines that the loan has exceeded its guidelines they may call the loan or ask for additional collateral. If the option of assigning the policy to a financial institution for tax-free loans is not available, alternate options such as policy withdrawals or policy loans will still exist.

Tip: Look at the relative cost of a life insurance portfolio

A topped-up insurance portfolio may appear to have high monthly payments, but it's important to look at the expense as a percentage of your total income. The absolute numbers may strike you as high, but as a proportion of the salary you are trying to protect or replace, a well-designed basic insurance plan should not be a significant percentage of your total salary.

Now let's take a look at two ways you can protect yourself from potential health problems down the road: disability and critical illness insurance. These are two of the most critical yet misunderstood areas in the health insurance arena.

DISABILITY INSURANCE: "PEACE OF MIND"

Disability insurance is expensive because it has a high likelihood of being used. The chances of your becoming disabled are much greater than of your dying prematurely. Yet far more people have life insurance than disability coverage. Most people seem to think disability insurance is a waste of money because "I'll never be disabled," but if you check the table below you'll see the statistics don't back that statement up.

If you're self-employed, disability insurance is a must. It is usually set up to provide about two-thirds of your current before-tax income. You have the choice of paying your premiums with after-tax money, or you can expense it. But if you expense it, your benefits are taxable. If you don't expense the premiums, your benefits are tax-free for as many months or years as you receive them. I strongly suggest you *don't* deduct it from your income because the tax you'll have to pay on your disability income will likely be far greater than the tax you'll save by deducting the premiums. In addition, the disability income you are counting on will not be nearly as much as you think, once income taxes are deducted from your monthly disability cheque.

Here's an example that may help. A commercial illustrator friend of mine who earns $60,000 a year decided to buy disability on the advice of a commercial photographer she knew. She bought a plan that provides her with $3,000 a month in benefits in the event she's disabled. Because she pays the premiums with after-tax cash, she's now set to clear $3,000 a month tax-free until she turns 65 — if she becomes disabled according to the terms of the policy and cannot work. That's $36,000 a year *after* taxes, which is pretty darn close to her net *after-tax income* of $45,000 per year.

Remember to review the terms of your chosen policy carefully. Costs and coverage vary. The cost of disability insurance is also related to the type of "disability" you want to be covered for.

There are three definitions of disability:

- Any occupation
- Regular occupation
- Own occupation

Only highly skilled professionals qualify for the definition of "own occupation." This disability benefit will pay if they could not perform the daily functions of their specific job, but they would also have the option to earn an income in another field without affecting this ongoing payment. For example, a surgeon may no longer be able to operate, thus fulfilling his disability definition, but could go into teaching.

"Regular occupation," on the other hand, means you cannot perform the daily functions of your current job and are not earning an income elsewhere. If a client with this type of coverage were to begin a claim and subsequently take another job, the salary earned from the new occupation would be deducted from his disability payment.

The final type is "any occupation," which means that if you are not able to perform the tasks of any job in which you are reasonably trained by education or experience, you are deemed to be disabled. It is wise to be wary of this last form of coverage as it will only cover extreme cases of disability. Insurers define such jobs as cashier, post office work and telemarketing as the type of jobs that nearly any individual is able to do by education or experience and therefore are able to cancel the benefits payable. It is irrelevant if this job is available or whether the salary is comparable to your pre-disability income.

All disability insurance is designed to replace your after-tax income and is usually limited to replacing a percentage of your income up to a fixed maximum monthly payout until age 65. Other options to look for in disability insurance include the length of the waiting period and options to renew or cancel the coverage. The waiting period is the amount of time you have to wait before your insurance benefits kick in. The longer the waiting period you choose, the less expensive the insurance premiums will be. You will often see policies with waiting periods of ninety days, but if you have enough of a cash cushion put aside, you might consider a six- or even twelve-month waiting period.

MAKE SURE YOU'RE FULLY COVERED

Make sure that your policy is broad enough to cover a wide range of disabilities and illnesses. Understanding some insurance jargon, such as "renewable" or "non-cancellable," will help you better evaluate policy options. For example, a guaranteed renewable policy will never be cancelled, but your premiums may increase. A non-cancellable policy will never be cancelled, nor will your premiums go up, but there is no such thing as a free lunch — the premiums will be higher.

Disability insurance is a highly specialized area, and if you need to top up your coverage, you should consult with a qualified disability insurance specialist. There's no shortage of options, and with them a range of costs, which make this kind of insurance particularly complex. Will your benefits be indexed to inflation? Are common mental illnesses covered? Does it cover vocational rehabilitation expenses? Will you be penalized for returning to work part-time? Can you buy more insurance in the future? Will your premiums be automatically paid if you become disabled?

As long as you're willing to pay for it, there's an insurance option for just about any contingency. But don't pay for "bells and whistles" you don't really need and might not even have known about without a careful reading of the policy.

What about Canada Pension Plan (CPP) and Quebec Pension Plan (QPP) disability payments? They are taxable, but if you are disabled and need to live on the benefits they provide, good luck. The maximum CPP/QPP benefits are pegged at around $1,000 a month, not nearly enough to live on. And the definition of disability is "any" so to qualify, in addition to not being able to work at any job, your affliction must be deemed to be prolonged and severe. What about Worker's Compensation? If you consider yourself lucky to be covered by Worker's Compensation, curb your enthusiasm a little: It only pays benefits if you become disabled while on the job.

WHAT? ME WORRY?!

What are the odds of you becoming disabled? The numbers may surprise you.

Your Age	Likelihood of Long-Term Disability	Average Duration
30	1 in 3	32 months
40	3 in 10	42 months
50	5 in 22	50 months
60	1 in 10	54 months

Source: 1985 Commissioners' Disability Individual Table A.

Group disability issues: If your employer pays for your disability insurance, any benefits you receive from it will be taxed. Hopefully, that scenario will never happen! If you're part of a group plan, and your monthly employment income after tax exceeds your group plan maximum, you'll have a shortfall. Look closely at the income ceiling on your group disability plan; if you find the monthly payment would pose a hardship for your family, you can always buy supplementary disability insurance privately.

As a general rule, you can't insure 100 percent or more of your pre-tax employment income. If you buy a private disability policy before joining a group plan, you can circumvent this restriction, but it doesn't work the other way around. Private disability insurance purchased after you are already in a group plan member will reduce the benefits when your group plan also pays out.

It's still useful to have private insurance, however, because group plans generally have more restrictive definitions of disability and it's quite conceivable that your group plan would not consider you disabled when your private plan might. Before you buy supplemental disability insurance, make sure you determine what will happen to your benefit payments when other disability insurance is in place.

Check out how long your group disability lasts and under what conditions. Group plans will generally pay disability benefits for two years when you can't do your regular job. After that, they may pay only if you are unable to do any job that you are qualified for by training and experience as mentioned previously. A private supplemental plan is most useful when it doesn't have a provision like that.

Often when a private plan is used to supplement a group plan, it is structured to only begin paying after two years of disability. This lowers premiums and ensures you have continuous coverage if the group plan does end after the first two years.

For a very enlightening interview on disability, please go to the following link: http://investmentexecutive.com. Key in the phrase "disability insurance" or look for the article entitled: "A strategy for making the most of disability insurance" (January 2003 interview with Craig Sangster, President of CS Investment Counsel Corp).

Disability insurance may not help you if you're derailed by a serious illness. What if you get cancer or have a stroke or a heart attack, the three most common illnesses to befall Canadians? In addition to lost income, how will you pay for potential health-related expenses like private nursing care, physical therapy, medical equipment, child care and babysitting services, even modifications to your home?

CRITICAL ILLNESS: "FILLING THE GAP"

If the disability statistics didn't shock you, this one from the Heart and Stroke Foundation of Canada almost certainly will: "One in four Canadians will contract a serious illness by the age of 65." Sixty-five hardly seems old anymore, yet a quarter of the people this age have serious health problems. Less than two decades ago, critical illness insurance made its appearance in Canada to fill the gap between disability and life insurance.

This type of insurance will pay a tax-free lump sum if you are diagnosed with — and survive — a variety of major illnesses, such as stroke, cancer, heart attack, Parkinson's, multiple sclerosis, Alzheimer's and specified others. You must survive for a specified period, usually more than thirty days. (With most plans, a full refund of premiums is available should you die within the thirty days.) The benefit money can be used without restriction, and the amount you wish to insure for has a general maximum of $2 million. This amount can be increased in certain circumstances, but premiums tend to keep clients below these maximum thresholds.

Critical illness insurance can be tailored to suit many budgets with terms of 10 years, to age 65, 75 or 100 (permanent). There are also riders that allow clients to take premiums back and cancel the policy at certain policy anniversaries if they have not suffered a critical illness.

Be careful to check what is and isn't covered. While most critical illness policies will cover between nineteen to twenty-four illnesses, a few policies keep rates competitive by covering only the three most common illnesses suffered by Canadians: cancer, heart attack or stroke. According to the Heart and Stroke Foundation and the National Cancer Institute of Canada (2001), approximately 250,000 Canadians are diagnosed with cancer, heart attack or stroke annually. And thanks to improved medical treatments, most of them will survive.

- Over 80 percent of heart attack patients admitted to hospital survive.
- 95 percent of hospitalized heart attack victims survive the first attack.
- 75 percent of men and 77 percent of women who develop cancer survive.
- 75 percent of stroke victims survive the initial event.

Yet, while medical treatments and survival rates have improved, most health plans haven't kept pace with the changing needs of patients. Provincial health plans can't help with personal finances. As highly regarded as our Canadian health care system is, it cannot help critical illness patients recover their financial footing if they are not prepared for the financial consequences of surviving a critical illness. Living with a critical illness can mean major changes to your lifestyle and serious financial challenges if you are not prepared.

Critical illness coverage is not like traditional life insurance or disability insurance because it can provide a living benefit to give you time and money to recover fully from a critical illness — comfortably, at your own pace and without financial worries or lifestyle compromises.

Sometimes thought of as lifestyle insurance, critical illness insurance is also a potential way to finance medical treatment in the United States or alternative therapies not covered by your provincial health care system. The younger you get this insurance, the better, because your family history will probably reveal fewer illnesses. As you age, your family members are more likely to develop an illness that will increase the cost of your insurance or make you ineligible for coverage for those familial illnesses. The ailments covered by critical illness insurance vary from policy to policy, as do rates.

On average, men are less expensive to insure than women of comparable age.

This type of coverage shouldn't be confused with disability insurance. Disability will replace a portion of your income when you can't work. It will not give you money to build a wheelchair ramp, pay for medications or hire a physiotherapist, for instance. A prolonged illness can impose onerous additional expenses on your family and it's quite possible a serious illness will not keep you out of work long enough to collect disability benefits. It may, nevertheless, seriously change your lifestyle.

CRITICAL ILLNESS OR DISABILITY INSURANCE: WHICH IS RIGHT FOR YOU?

Now that you've learned a little about the ins and outs of disability insurance and critical illness insurance, perhaps you're wondering which is right for you. Let's quickly review the key differences between them. Disability plans are designed to give you a monthly income for as long as you are disabled (as defined by the plan) until the age of 65. Critical illness plans are designed to give you a lump sum payment to cover the extraordinary costs of a sudden and unexpected illness. If you already have one of these two plans, I'm not suggesting you go hog wild and spend all kinds of extra money on the other plan as well.

But if you think about it, each one covers a completely different kind of catastrophic event that may happen to you during your life. Disability insurance is limited in that it does not cover illnesses. Critical illness insurance does not cover accidents and other non-illness-related disabling events, nor does it provide a continuous stream of income. So what do you do if you want a certain level of protection and peace of mind, but you don't want to spend a significant chunk of change each year? In my opinion, there is no simple answer; but if there is an answer, it may lie somewhere in the middle.

Purchasing disability and critical illness protection together is certainly a wise choice — even if the coverage you get is lower than what you'd receive if you'd just purchased the one. It gives you a broader degree of protection, and allows more flexibility if a life setback occurs. However, many people are ineligible for disability insurance. Stay-at-home parents, homemakers and caregivers don't qualify because they don't receive "official" income. Then there are singers, actors, models, professional athletes and many others who are ineligible because of the nature of their chosen profession. Conversely, critical illness insurance does not usually cover disabilities such as stress, back strain or other such items that may keep a person from working for a defined amount of time.

To give you an idea of some typical premiums for critical illness, they might range from $50 to $100 per month for young people in good health seeking $50,000 to $100,000 coverage, up to several hundred dollars a month for retirees or near retirees who want to protect a sizeable income stream while they are in their 60s or even 70s. As always, the younger you are and the healthier you are, the lower the premiums will be.

Few of us have so much money floating around that we can pick up all the protection that's out there. But as the Rolling Stones song says, "You can't always get what you want, but if you try sometime, you just might find, you get what you need."

Those with lots of money may choose to have no insurance coverage at all if they will feel no pain in parting with a slice of their nest egg. For the rest of us, if we have to choose between disability protection and critical illness protection, it comes down to two things: lifestyle and personal choice.

MATCH YOUR HEALTH INSURANCE TO YOUR STAGE IN LIFE

How important do I think the right package of life, disability, health and critical illness insurance is for you? If you and/or your family need to be protected in the event of income loss and debt/expense coverage, it's critical. Here are some real-world examples of what I mean. Take a look at a couple of self-employed professionals, one young, one well-established.

Sean

Sean, a young family man, is newly self-employed. Cash flow is a big issue for him, but he wants to know his wife will be left debt-free in the event he passes away. An ideal mix of insurance for him would be some low-cost term insurance to cover his mortgage and his business expenses, including a collateralized line of credit. Then, by adding some "bare bones" disability protection, he would also be able to cover the family's debts and basic expenses in the event he couldn't work.

Florinda

Florinda is well-established in her business, and may even be winding down a little with a view toward retirement. Unlike Sean, cash flow is not an issue for her. But she not only wants her loved ones to be debt-free, she wants to make sure she leaves behind a nest egg that her heirs can enjoy. Florinda would be well served with universal life insurance, which would give her the insurance coverage of term, plus the tax-deferred accumulation potential only universal life can offer. Her disability should probably be upgraded to "own occupation," because as a highly skilled architect (and company owner), the option of "pushing a broom" the rest of her working life is not an option.

Although Florinda is in good health, she wisely takes advantage of critical illness insurance to keep her health options wide open. For example, she can jump to the head of the line and go to the United States or abroad if she needs to pay for urgent treatment of unexpected health woes. It's important to note that critical illness insurance is paid to her just thirty days after diagnosis — even if she's on the mend just a week later!

Sudhir

Sudhir is known as "Mr. Dependable." No matter what the weather or time of the year, he always shows up twenty minutes early for his shift. Sudhir has a large family and is a long-time employee at one of North America's largest auto manufacturing plants. Ninety percent of the people he works with have group insurance (life, disability, health and dental insurance). His group life insurance provides one year's income if he were to pass away, so he needs to top it up with additional private insurance to ensure his family is well taken care of. Sudhir purchases universal life for its investment and tax benefits, but also because he knows he can withdraw some of the amount in an emergency, or borrow against the policy in the event of a sudden loss of income.

We all know that insurance is big business and a profitable one. Warren Buffet's portfolio is heavily weighted with insurance stock. Insurance firms pull in a lot of cash through premiums, but have you ever wondered how much they give back in claims in a given year? If you're thinking, "Not very much," the numbers in the table below may surprise you.

Payouts to Canadian policyholders in 2003

Life insurance	$ 5.2 billion
Annuities	20.1 billion
Health benefit plans	16.4 billion
Policyholder dividends	2.1 billion
Total	$43.8 billion

According to the Canadian Life and Health Insurance Association, benefit payments to Canadian policyholders and annuitants during 2003 totalled $43.8 billion. Benefits were paid out at a rate of $842 million a week, and 99 percent of the payments went to living policyholders, while only 10 percent were paid out as death benefits. Note: These figures include benefit payments under uninsured contracts administered by life insurance companies totalling $5.8 billion.

Source: All text and graphics © Canadian Life and Health Insurance Association Inc.

Insurance: Women more interested than men

A successful insurance executive I know (he has more than two thousand clients) told me that in his experience, women are much more interested in insurance protection than men. It's perhaps no coincidence that women are also more conservative about their financial affairs than men. From a psychological point of view, this may suggest why gamblers, risk takers—and men!—buy less insurance than average. If that is true, as a woman I can honestly say it's *their* loss.

WHAT WOULD YOU DO IF YOUR PARENTS BECAME VERY ILL?

I've talked about various ways you can protect yourself from illness, but there's another important health concern I'd like to raise. Two good friends of mine, a couple who both earn six-figure salaries, were faced with a dilemma: What to do with a parent who had been bedridden for over a year, needed round-the-clock care and showed no signs of getting better.

LONG-TERM CARE

Most people want to live at home as long as possible. Should a debilitating illness strike, making home care necessary for you or your parents, a great deal of the financial burden will be lifted if you have a long-term care insurance policy in place. Long-term care insurance has been available in the United States for decades and now is becoming more widely accepted in Canada. It's important to note that there is little government assistance for this kind of care. You're usually on your own and the costs can be staggering.

"Come in, she said I'll give you shelter from the storm."
— Bob Dylan, "Shelter from the Storm"

According to the United States General Accounting Office in Washington, D.C., individuals and their families, as well as federal, state and local government programs, spent more than $100 billion on long-term care in 2000.

The 21st century will be marked by a dramatic increase in the size of the elderly population as the large baby boom generation ages. While most elderly people are not disabled, the elderly as a whole have the greatest likelihood of needing long-term care. As a result of this population aging, researchers predict that the number of elderly needing long-term care may as much as double in the next twenty-five years. Recent projections of elderly needing long-term care reach between 10 million and 14 million by 2020, and 14 million to 24 million in 2060, compared with about 7 million today.
(Source: General Accounting Office, November 1994.)

The couple I mentioned above had to eat into a major part of their capital to pay for nursing care, averaging $40,000 to $60,000 per year! Could you afford that kind of expense? Long-term care can be tailored to your family's specific needs and requirements. It can also be used should a move to a retirement home or a nursing home be needed. As with most insurance, the younger you are when you get it, the lower the premiums will be — in other words, planning ahead when you're in your 60s, instead of your 70s or 80s, as an American acquaintance of mine did, relieves a lot of future financial strain.

Like other services covered by insurance, long-term care insurance must be purchased before you or your loved one requires the services covered. It's possible — and of course, ultimately desirable — that you'll never benefit from it. In that regard, Investopedia.com notes:

Some financial professionals recommend that only individuals closer to ages 50 to 65 purchase long-term care insurance, as these individuals are more likely to benefit from the purchase of a policy. If you're employed, check with your employer regarding coverage. Many employers provide long-term care insurance for their employees, and some will even extend coverage to parents of their employees. If you are already covered under an employer-sponsored policy, then you may not need to purchase a separate policy until after you retire.

Even if you decide to do nothing right now, it's worth learning as much as you can about long-term care insurance. Call your financial or insurance advisor for details.

A QUICK WORD ABOUT ACCIDENT INSURANCE

In my opinion, there's very little reason for most people to buy accidental death and dismemberment insurance (AD&D). If you want your loved ones to benefit financially if you die or are dismembered, you're much better off buying life insurance or disability insurance. AD&D insurance is very inexpensive. That's right, *in*expensive. But that's not a good thing. Why? Partly because there are so many exclusions, and partly because the odds of the insurance company having to pay out are very slim. In addition, most basic AD&D plans only pay out if you're killed on a common carrier. The premiums are much higher if you want to include private automobiles, which statistics prove is where most traffic accident fatalities occur.

MORE ON TAX SAVINGS WITH INSURANCE

Now you're aware that universal life insurance can be useful in managing your wealth in a tax-advantaged way, I'd like to mention another insurance product that can do the same thing for you: annuities. I'll discuss annuities in more detail in Chapter 8, but for now, here's an easy definition to remember.

An annuity is a contract in which an insurance company promises to make certain regular payments for either a fixed period or until your death in exchange for a lump sum up front. It's a little like buying a bond, only an annuity pays out principal and interest. Because you're not taxed when the principal is returned to you, annuity payments are tax-advantaged to the extent that they give you your own money back.

There are many varieties of annuities. Many guarantee a fixed rate of return, whereas others are variable and depend on the nature of the underlying investments. Annuity rates are linked to interest rates, and when rates are low, as they are now, annuities are not as popular. Universal life insurance is currently a more interesting option, but that may change. Remember what I said earlier: Universal life has a term life insurance component and a tax-sheltered investment component. Although life insurance is usually bought with monthly premiums, you can also buy a universal life policy with an up front cash payment, and you can decide what kind of investment options you want within your policy. Your money grows tax-free and your beneficiaries get the insurance portion of your policy as a tax-free death benefit. The investment portion is also paid out tax-free upon your death.

Something else can be done with a universal life policy that will generate retirement income for you and a tax benefit, too. Financial institutions may actually allow you to borrow against a universal life policy, up to as much as 90 percent of the investment value of the policy. The more you have in fixed investment options, the higher the percentage you can borrow. This borrowed money can finance your retirement. What's the advantage? While you have to pay interest on the borrowed money, you don't have to pay any tax on it. As a result, when you pass away, the bank gets the proceeds of the policy to discharge your loan, but you have received a retirement income for only the cost of interest, not the cost of your marginal tax rate.

In the past three chapters, I've shown you how you can *grow* and *protect* your nest egg. Now it's time to find out how you can *shelter* it through effective tax strategies — and potentially save thousands, or even hundreds of thousands of dollars each year.

C H A P T E R
SEVEN

"*You* can be a millionaire... and never pay taxes! You say,
'Steve, how can *I* be a millionaire... and never pay taxes?' First, get
a million dollars. Now, you say, 'Steve, what do I say to the taxman when
he comes to my door and says, "You have *never* paid taxes?"'
Two simple words. Two simple words in the
English language: '*I forgot*!'"
—STEVE MARTIN, *SATURDAY NIGHT LIVE* MONOLOGUE

ARM (Part 4)
ARM YOURSELF WITH THE
TAX STRATEGIES YOU NEED

If you're asking: "Self, how can I be a millionaire...and *never* pay taxes?" you won't find the answer anywhere in this book. At least you won't find an answer to the "never pay taxes" part. This book is about the real world, and so is this chapter. But here's the good news: unless you already employ a skilled tax accountant, I'm going to show you a number of strategies that may save you more money than you ever dreamed, and keep saving you big money every year of your life. Where do I think taxes fit into your portfolio growth strategy? Right near the top. Unless you're lucky enough to inherit money or win a lottery, you can only accumulate wealth three ways:

1) Increase your income
2) Invest well
3) Save more

And one of the absolutely biggest ways to save is by cutting your tax bill. Yes, that's right. Taxes. I can't stress enough how important, and yet how overlooked, taxes and effective tax planning are when it comes to Canadians and their investments — and their savings, for that matter. The profits you see on your year-end brokerage and bank statements are before-tax returns. That little detail doesn't seem to matter to the average investor, but I can tell you, the tax savvy investor profoundly understands there are returns, and then there are *real* returns.

Depending on your tax bracket and your method of investing and saving, taxes can eat away up to a third or more of your pre-tax profits.

Remember George the dentist from Chapter 4? He was faced with a potentially staggering tax bill on his investments. That's because George was generating investment income, since after he left his dental practice that's where the majority of his income came from.

Although tax planning is such a big-time cost-saver, few Canadians give it a second thought. Oh sure, filing your return and paying taxes is a big deal, don't get me wrong. But if you want to save more of that hard-earned money of yours, you need to think about taxes more than once a year. The payoff for a few minutes with your tax advisor or broker each week or month can be a lifetime worth of extra money in your pocket. And if you want an even bigger payoff, all you have to do is study and employ a few tax strategies that will help you defer taxes effectively and completely legally.

Oh, and by the way, contributing to an RRSP is only *one* of those strategies.

What counts is what you *keep* in your bank account, not how much you "made" according to your brokerage statement. Effective tax planning is a long-term strategy that should become part of your thinking (off and on, at least) all year long, year after year and all the way into the estate planning period of your life.

START THINKING ABOUT AFTER-TAX RETURNS

Kurt Rosentreter is a financial advisor. In an April 2001 article published in Advisor.ca, he says that tax-efficient investing should no longer be reserved for the wealthy:

> Most would leap at the opportunity to pay less tax, as taxes can make up almost 50 percent of their (and our) incomes. But many advisors have yet to grasp tax-smart investing, the process of building and managing a client's investment portfolio according to after-tax returns. Tax-smart investing means thinking about investments the same way one thinks about a paycheque: after-tax. After all, we live our lives out of cash flow, which is after-tax.... I have spent my career advising high-net-worth diems and have found these clients to be long past maximizing RRSPs and have accumulated significant taxable wealth where saving tax within the investment portfolio matters.

TEN SURE-FIRE STRATEGIES TO SAVE TAX DOLLARS

Rather than make you wade through 101 tax tips, I've prioritized what I think are the ten top ways to save money on your taxes. These strategies for the most part apply to everyone. They are:

Strategy #1:   "Buy and hold" to defer taxes for a lifetime.
Strategy #2:   Maximize your RRSP contributions.
Strategy #3:   Split your income with family members.
Strategy #4:   Invest in your home.
Strategy #5:   Dividends — your secret weapon.
Strategy #6:   Borrow to invest.
Strategy #7:   Maximize your RESP contributions.
Strategy #8:   Maximize tax deductions.
Strategy #9:   Maximize employee benefits.
Strategy #10:   Employ yourself (part- or full-time).

It's important to note that the taxes you save from the above strategies depend on your marginal tax rate, your employment status and your investment strategies. Nevertheless, in combination or alone, these strategies should have a substantial impact on the rate of growth of your retirement portfolio.

Before reviewing these strategies in detail, it's important to understand the tax rates applicable to you and your investments. The following text summarizes, but by no means exhaustively covers the many elements of the Canadian tax rules. I highly recommend consulting with your advisor or accountant for the rates and situations that will apply to your particular financial circumstances.

KNOW YOUR MARGINAL TAX RATE

Proper tax planning means knowing *at all times* where you fall on the marginal tax rate scale. Your marginal tax rate is the amount you'll have to pay on each additional dollar of taxable income you make in a year. Be sure to verify the rates with the Canada Revenue Agency (CRA), as rates may change.

Here's a simple example of what can happen if you don't know your marginal rate. Zack is a young, married, orthopedic surgeon whose taxable income was $115,000 (all salary). Zack lives in B.C. Zack's income falls into a certain (combined) federal and provincial tax bracket, which in 2005 was 40.70 percent because this bracket covers taxable incomes between $92,185 and $115,739. Now, what happens if Zack manages to invest a small amount for the first time? Let's say his investments net him a modest $1,000 in extra income. Suddenly, Zack is thrust into the highest tax bracket.

Zack may be thrilled to have made an extra thousand dollars. But Zack's taxable income has now increased to $116,000, which would put him into the highest tax bracket. From now on, all his future investment income is likely to be taxed at 43.70 percent. Welcome to the harsh reality of marginal taxation, Dr. Zack. The moral of the story? Actually there are four. Always know what taxable income bracket you're in; know how close you are to the next bracket; know what your approximate investment income will be for the year; and act accordingly.

INTEREST, DIVIDENDS AND CAPITAL GAINS: THEY'RE TAXED DIFFERENTLY

Interest income, dividend income and income from capital gains receive different tax treatments. If you want to be a serious investor and maximize your portfolio growth, you should know the differences. Interest income from your bank accounts, CSBs, bond investments and portfolios is taxed at the highest rate — your marginal income tax rate. By the way, this applies whether you actually receive the interest income in cash, or simply accrue it for tax purposes! Unfortunately, every little bit of interest income, whether on simple or compound income investments, must be reported annually, and it doesn't matter whether they're Canada Savings Bonds, long-term GICs or anything else.

Dividends

Dividends from foreign corporations are treated exactly the same as interest income. But dividends paid by Canadian companies receive favourable tax treatment. Why? Because the Canada Revenue Agency (CRA) has already collected tax on the corporate profits used to pay out those dividends, and doesn't want to tax them twice. (All right, some of the people at CRA might *want* to tax them twice, but by law none of them can.)

If you owned dividend-paying equities, a dividend tax credit would be issued to you to be applied against your taxable income. Of course, nothing is that simple when it comes to tax calculations. The dividends you receive from Canadian corporations are actually "grossed up" by 25 percent, and then included on your income tax form as taxable income. Both federal and provincial governments then grant you a tax credit, which is a percentage of the grossed up amount. Depending on your marginal tax rate, this can result in substantial tax savings.

Capital gains

Capital gains are the profits on the sale of assets, like stock and property, adjusted for transaction costs. Capital losses result from losses on the sale of assets, like stock and property, adjusted for transaction costs. Capital losses can be subtracted from capital gains to give you tax relief.

Capital gains are not taxed as heavily as interest income, because since October 17, 2000, only 50 percent of the capital gain, adjusted for costs, is taxed. The gains, netted against any capital losses you might have, are added to your taxable income for that year and taxed at your marginal rate. Unfortunately, there's no longer any provision for a lifetime capital gains exemption except in relation to selling a small business and transferring farms between generations. The good news is, unused losses may be carried back three years and carried forward *indefinitely* against other taxable capital gains. And if you still have undeducted losses at the end of your life, you can deduct them against any type of income. You see, the CRA can sometimes be your friend. However, not all securities qualify for capital gains and tax laws can change, so consult your advisor or the friendly CRA.

Capital gains are a vitally important tax-planning instrument because only 50 percent of capital gains are taxed. Another way of looking at it is, even if you're in the top marginal tax bracket (around 50 percent) profits from the sale of stock are only going to be taxed at 25 percent. Not bad. But not only do capital gains offer the most attractive after-tax return, they are only taxed when realized. This leads me into one of the most important points in this chapter: you can avoid a huge tax bill by choosing your investments wisely, holding them for the long term and deferring any capital gains accruing inside your taxable portfolio.

Please note: The following recommendations expressed are of a general nature and may not be appropriate for all individuals. You should consult with a tax advisor to discuss your individual circumstances.

TAX-SAVING STRATEGY #1: BUY AND HOLD

Who do you think is the most brilliant tax strategist in the world? Maybe you don't know, or maybe you think it's one of those tax hot shots in a big accounting firm like PricewaterhouseCoopers, or Deloitte or KPMG. Good guess, but I think you should guess again. I think the most brilliant tax strategist in the world is the Oracle of Omaha, Warren Buffett.

"Buffett?" you cry in disbelief. "He's an investment guru, not a tax accountant! Come *on*, Pattie, get with the program." Okay, you're right; he's an investor, and a great one, as we noted in Chapter 4. But one of Buffett's most successful investment strategies is to buy and hold for the long term. That dusty old strategy has probably saved his Berkshire Hathaway fund — and his investors — billions of dollars in taxes over the years. That doesn't mean Berkshire avoids paying taxes. On the contrary.

The following is an excerpt from the Chairman's Message in the 2003 Berkshire Hathaway Annual Report.

> Berkshire, on your behalf and mine, will send the Treasury $3.3 billion for tax on its 2003 income, a sum equaling 2 ½ percent of the total income tax paid by all U.S. corporations in fiscal 2003. (In contrast, Berkshire's market valuation is about 1 percent of the value of all American corporations.) Our payment will almost certainly place us among our country's top ten taxpayers.

Buffett isn't necessarily unhappy paying that much tax. Yes, $3 billion is a heck of a lot of money, but it's probably far less than other fund managers might have paid in taxes had they run a similarly constructed fund. It's also important to put the above in context. The current market value for Berkshire Class A shares is about US$134 billion, and a significant portion of Berkshire's securities are fixed income instruments. Unlike stocks that can be held for the long term, fixed-income products cannot escape annual taxation.

Bottom line: When Buffett took control of Berkshire Hathaway in 1965, it traded at $18 per share. It's now trading at $80,000 per share. That's a remarkable annual return on equity of about 25 percent. And he has done it consistently over four decades. This does not mean the fund will return 25 percent next year. But it does mean that if you'd spent a paltry $230 on BRKA shares forty years ago and not sold a share since, you would have sheltered a nice million dollars from taxes. That would be a nice little retirement nest egg, wouldn't it?

What lesson can we learn from Buffett? When it comes to constructing, managing and monitoring our own portfolios, follow the master. Be disciplined and patient and hold for the long term. Buffett minimizes costs and maximizes return three ways:

1) He's got many excellent, long-term performers in his portfolio, so he doesn't sell unless a stock begins to underperform over the long term.
2) He minimizes turnover (buying and selling) because trading incurs transaction costs and triggers capital gains.
3) He automatically reinvests the dividends accruing from his stock holdings.

These three factors turbo-charge the already impressive growth provided by the stocks in his portfolio, and they can do the same for yours by minimizing taxes and maximizing the natural compounding power of your portfolio over time. And time in Buffett's case — and hopefully yours — is measured in decades.

In his book, *Common Sense on Mutual Funds*, John Bogle says that even if taxes eat away at only a small percentage off your portfolio return, they create a huge opportunity cost. Depending on the size of your portfolio, a few lost percentage points compounded over a multi-decade investment period can potentially cost you hundreds of thousands of dollars.

As I mentioned in an earlier chapter, most investment pundits predict the market will return on average 6 percent to 8 percent annually for the foreseeable future. History shows us it's tough enough for the average investor to match the market, let alone beat it. Paying sizeable — and unnecessary — transaction costs and capital gains taxes will almost certainly guarantee you do neither.

Stock pickers "R" (not) us

Turnover in some mutual fund portfolios approach 100 percent annually. You can only imagine the tax damage being done to these funds' returns. The job of a growth fund manager, for example, is to be active in the market by finding the hot stocks and sectors and get in an ongoing quest for market-beating returns. They're usually so focused on their top-line investment mandate that they don't, or can't, worry about the tax implications of the trades they make.

Having praised the Buffett buy-and-hold strategy to the skies, I now must throw off a big caveat: From a stock picking viewpoint, none of us are Warren Edward Buffet. Besides, most of us have day jobs to worry about. Which means we're better off leaving the stock picking to the experts — and not just any experts.

Ideally, you want to search out well-managed, low-turnover, low-fee or no-fee mutual funds. Index funds or exchange-traded funds are ideal choices (revisit Chapter 5 for details). If you choose traditional mutual funds, make sure you know what stocks are in the fund, what the manager's strategy is, what happens to dividends, turnover levels and so forth.

Impact of excessive turnover on a portfolio

In a study by Michael Thorfinnson and Jason Kiss, the after-tax effect of turnover was calculated on an initial $1 million investment in a Canadian equity portfolio. The return was estimated at 12.4 percent over twenty years. For simplicity, no management expenses were incurred and all dividends and realized capital gains were reinvested on an after-tax basis.

As the following graph shows, when portfolio turnover increases, the market value of the portfolio decreases dramatically. When turnover increased to 8.5 percent, the portfolio return dropped 1.2 percent. When portfolio turnover increased to 35 percent and 80 percent, performance declined by 2.5 percent and 3.0 percent, respectively. Those are big percentage declines. As a side note, it is not uncommon for some aggressive mutual funds to experience 100 percent annual turnover or more.

The chart shows the after-tax effect of turnover on an initial $1 million investment in a Canadian equity portfolio invested at 12.4 percent for twenty years. Clearly, as turnover increases, the market value of the portfolio decreases dramatically.

Reviewing the details of your portfolio

The portfolio detail section of your statement identifies the individual assets in your account, the value of your investments at the end of the statement period, the book value or purchase price and account activity

EROSION BY TURNOVER

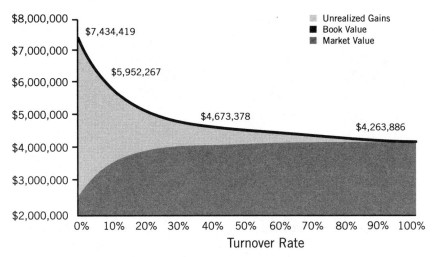

Source: www.tdcanadatrust.com.

showing interest and dividend payments. This information is very useful for tax planning purposes as it allows one to determine the tax implications that will be triggered in the event of a sale of securities.

By carefully reviewing the nature of your investments and the investment income you are receiving, you can become a more savvy, tax-efficient investor. Now let's discuss the ins and outs of RRSPs, a tax break virtually every Canadian taxpayer knows intimately.

TAX-SAVING STRATEGY #2: MAXIMIZE YOUR RRSP CONTRIBUTIONS

What would you say if someone said you could invest thousands of dollars in a portfolio every year and deduct it all from your taxes? Pretty good stuff. Now what would you say if they told you that every penny of income and profits from those investments would be left alone to grow tax-deferred for years to come? Now that's awesome.

Registered retirement savings plans (RRSPs) are probably the greatest gift our government has ever bestowed upon us. RRSPs were introduced way back in 1957 to encourage us to save for our retirement, and millions of Canadians have done just that.

Here's what tax sheltering can do to grow your nest egg. If you started at age 35, and invested $100 a month for thirty years in a taxable portfolio at an average annual rate of return of 10 percent (rate of return breakdown of 2.0 percent dividends, 4.0 percent capital gains and 4.0 percent deferred growth), you would have a nest egg of about $179,550 at age 65 (assuming a tax rate of 23.84 percent).

If you started an RRSP at the exact same age, and contributed just $100 a month for 30 years *inside* the RRSP and received the same average annual rate of return of 10 percent (all tax deferred), you'd have a retirement nest egg of over $187,298. Not a big difference, but you also have to include the tax credit from the RRSP contribution. On the $1,200 annual contribution, the tax credit will be $286 (tax rate of 23.84 percent). If this $286 is invested each year at 10 percent it would grow to $38,975 after twenty-nine years. Therefore for a $100 monthly contribution, you will have $179,550 in a non-registered account compared to $187,298 in a registered account and $38,975 in a non-registered account.

But hold on you say, this is comparing apples and oranges as the registered portfolio would then have to be deregistered and be hit with a huge tax bill, which would result in a smaller after-tax amount than the non-registered account. If you then withdraw the $187,298 in the registered account and redeem the $38,975 in the non-registered account over twenty-five years you will receive $21,207 each year. If you redeemed the $179,550 in the non-registered account over twenty-five years, you would receive $18,798 per year. That's a difference of $2,409 every year if you take advantage of the RRSP.

The following chart illustrates how much difference taxes make to growth in an RRSP fund versus a non-RRSP fund.

RRSPs not only give you an immediate tax deduction each year equal to the RRSP investment contribution you make, they shelter tax on all the interest and capital gains accruing inside the plan from your investments. In short, the government has agreed not to tax your nest egg — and all the growth inside it — until you receive it much later in your life when your tax rates and financial needs may be more modest.

The amount of tax you save depends on your marginal tax rate. As I'll discuss later, marginal tax rates vary from province to province, but you're eligible to contribute to an RRSP as long as you have "earned income" in Canada and pay Canadian taxes. And maybe best of all, you can invest in an RRSP all the way until you turn 69.

THE VALUE OF TAX-FREE GROWTH

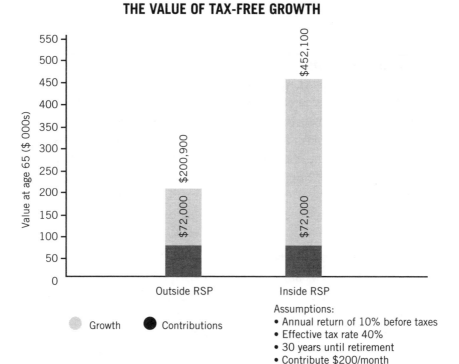

Source: Tim Cestnick, *Winning the Tax Game.*

What the heck is "earned" income?

Earned income for RRSP purposes is determined this way:

- Add your employment earnings, if any
- Add your self-employment earnings, if any
- Add net rental income, if any
- Add royalties, research grants, taxable alimony or maintenance payments
- Add disability payments from CPP or QPP, and supplementary UIC payments
- Subtract specific employment expenses excluding pension contributions (as applicable)
- Subtract business or rental losses (as applicable)

Earned income does not, however, include investment income. A quick tip for retirees: If you buy a rental property, you can still generate additional contribution room for the RSP through the rental income you earn.

Make sure you "earn" the right income

If you're self-employed, make sure you pay yourself enough salary so you can make the maximum RRSP contribution each year. Once your salary figure is established, work out the optimal mix of dividends and bonuses you might want to take out of your company. Why? While bonuses are taxed as personal income just like a salary, you can get a whole year of tax deferral by declaring the bonus toward the end of the calendar year and not paying it out until the following calendar year. Just make sure the bonus is paid out within 180 days of the company's year-end.

"My income? It's pretty simple, old chap!"

Says who? Not Canada's Income Tax Act s4(1):

For the purposes of this Act, a taxpayer's income or loss for a taxation year from an office, employment, business, property or other source, or from sources in a particular place, is the taxpayer's income or loss, as the case may be, computed in accordance with this Act on the assumption that the taxpayer had during the taxation year no income or loss except from that source or no income or loss except from those sources, as the case may be, and was allowed no deductions in computing the taxpayer's income for the taxation year except such deductions as may reasonably be regarded as wholly applicable to that source or to those sources, as the case may be, and except such part of any other deductions as may reasonably be regarded as applicable thereto.

Managed RRSPs

RRSPs come in two main flavours; the first type is called a managed RRSP. A managed RRSP means that someone else takes care of the plan for you, which is ideal for less sophisticated investors or those who don't want to actively manage their investments.

With managed plans, you purchase all of your investments through the same financial institution and no further management is required for as long as you hold each investment. You can hold as many managed RRSPs as you want.

The drawback of managed plans is the allowable investments you can purchase within the RRSP account. Managed RRSPs are allowed the following investments: GICs or term deposits, savings accounts (similar to those you withdraw and deposit from every day) and most mutual funds.

Self-directed RRSPs
Self-directed plans let you manage the plan on your own and choose the investments yourself. These plans allow for more flexibility, as you can hold a wide array of investments including bonds, equities and mutual funds. For example, with a self-directed plan, you can invest your home mortgage. Financial advisors and brokers can help you set up a self-directed RRSP, but make sure you compare the set-up and administration fees they may charge for doing this before making a decision.

Spousal plans
When it comes to RRSPs, a *Canadian Business* magazine article by Debbie Ammeter of Investors Group relates a common mistake couples make. The registered retirement savings plans set out by the Canada Revenue Agency are rarely used to their full potential. Ammeter says many couples fail to use a spousal RRSP account to balance out their retirement incomes:

> Too many couples miss out on a really good income-splitting opportunity while saving for retirement. By investing money in your spouse's name (assuming he or she earns less than you), your tax bill can be drastically reduced. And when it comes time to collect your old-age security payments — which start to be clawed back if you earn more than $59,790 a year — a spousal RRSP account can help keep the government's paws off your money.

If you're married or living together common-law, you can contribute to an RRSP in your spouse's or partner's name and vice versa. Splitting the tax deduction with your spouse enables the higher taxed partner (whether that is you or your spouse) to claim the tax deduction for the contribution, but the RRSP belongs to the lower taxed partner. When the money is finally taken out of the RRSP or the registered retirement income fund (RRIF), the RRSP holder will then receive the retirement income at a (hoped for) lower tax rate.

Rule of thumb: If you are the lower income earner, you should be the RRSP holder, and your spouse (the higher income earner) should take the deduction. That way, if you think you'll have less income in retirement than your spouse will, you'll be paying tax on the income from the plan at a lower rate than your spouse would pay. And your spouse gets a bigger tax deduction at the time of establishing the RRSP, since he or she is in a higher tax bracket.

Another benefit of spousal RRSPs: If your spouse is younger than you are, you can contribute to a spousal RRSP even *after* you've turned 69, for as many years as your spouse is 69 or younger. That is, provided you continue to have earned income.

There are some limits to all this largesse, however. Neither of you can exceed your own personal allowable limit. In other words, if you have an allowable contribution limit of $15,000 and you've already put $10,000 towards your RRSP, you can only put an additional $5,000 into your spousal plan.

Currently, the CRA defines a *spouse* as your husband or wife, a common-law spouse with whom you have lived with for the past twelve months or a partner with whom you have a child who is wholly dependent on you for support and over whom you have custody. A common-law spouse is no longer eligible after ninety days of separation. Same-sex partners are also treated as spouses.

Tax Savings with a Spousal RRSP

	Spouse A	Spouse B	Total
Couple 1 (No Spousal RRSP)			
Retirement income	$40,000	$10,000	$50,000
Less taxes*	$6,395	$0	$6,395
Net income	$33,605	$10,000	$43,605
Average tax rate	16.00%	0%	13%
Couple 2 (Spousal RRSP) ($15,000 of RRSP contribtuion is switched from spouse A to spouse B)			
Retirement income	$25,000	$25,000	$50,000
Less taxes*	$2,803	$2,803	$5,606
Net income	$22,197	$22,197	$44,394
Average tax rate	11%	11%	11%

The above table is based on 2004 Ontario tax rates for 66-year-olds who are eligible for the age exemption and the pension income credit on RRSP income. It includes adjustment for non-refundable tax credits transferred from your spouse, where applicable.

Splitting retirement income more evenly between partners can reduce taxes. In the example above, both couples had $50,000 in total income. But Couple 2 used a spousal RRSP for a $789 annual tax savings over Couple 1 ($6,395–$5,606).

Spousal RRSP accounts can be opened for married spouses, common-law partners and same-sex partners. They're great things, but there's one restriction you should keep in mind. Spousal contributions have to be kept in the account for at least two calendar years following the year the contribution was made before being withdrawn or the withdrawal is attributed to you, the contributor, as income. In that case, you'll have to pay tax on this withdrawal at your marginal rate, which means you'll have gained no tax advantage in the contribution and you'll have lost that contribution room.

What a difference a day makes

If you think you might need to withdraw funds from a spousal RRSP, consider the timing of your contributions carefully. A contribution made on December 31, 2004, with no subsequent contributions, will be available for withdrawal without attribution on January 1, 2007. A contribution made only two days later, on January 2, 2005, would not be available for withdrawal free of attribution until January 1, 2008. A day's difference in contributing can make a whole year's difference in withdrawing without attribution.

Watch out for the attribution rule

It's important when considering a spousal RRSP to understand the impact of the three-year attribution rule. Attribution rules simply mean that any tax breaks you accrue from income splitting can (under certain circumstances) be charged back or *attributed* back to you as taxable income. This rule is designed to prevent a high-income spouse from contributing to a spousal plan, then having the funds almost immediately withdrawn and taxed to the lower income–earning spouse.

If your spouse withdraws from his or her spousal RRSP within three calendar years of your last contribution to any spousal RRSP, the withdrawal is treated as income on your personal tax return. However, if the withdrawal is made more than three years after the contribution, the withdrawal is treated as income on your spouse's tax return. The important thing to note is that the three years are based on calendar years. If your last contribution was made in December 2004, for example, a withdrawal is taxable as your income until January 2007.

The three year rule does *not* apply in the following cases, however:

- You and your spouse are living apart due to marriage breakdown
- The contributing spouse dies in the year a withdrawal is made
- Either spouse becomes a non-resident of Canada for tax purposes
- The money is transferred to an annuity

Note: If you convert your spousal RRSP into a RRIF, watch out: until three years after the last spousal contribution, you're only allowed the minimum withdrawal (unless you want income attribution rules to kick in). Any withdrawals above the minimum will be taxed as income on the contributor's tax return.

Key benefits of RRSPs
- Tax-deductible contributions
- Tax-sheltered investing
- Tax deferral until your retirement (when you'll probably be in a lower tax bracket)
- Income splitting through spousal RRSPs

RRSPs for your kids
If you have kids, they too can invest in an RRSP, provided they have earned income and a Social Insurance Number. But remember, a parent or other adult must set up the RRSP in trust for children under 18, as minors cannot legally enter into contracts.

Maximum RRSP Contributions
Your maximum contribution is the lesser of 18 percent of your earned income or a set amount established by the CRA in a given year. In 2005, the maximum contribution was $16,500; it will be $18,000 in 2006, and rises to $22,000 by 2010.

What about over-contributions?
An over-contribution occurs when you contribute more than your contribution limit. The CRA will allow you to over-contribute up to $2,000

without penalty because they allow for an honest mistake. If you contribute more than the allowable $2,000, you can withdraw the extra without penalty as long as it's withdrawn within the year. But watch out. The CRA is not *infinitely* generous. If your over-contribution remains above $2,000, you'll be penalized 1 percent per month on any outstanding amount above $2,000.

By the way, if you have plenty of taxable investments but not much ready cash to contribute to your RRSP, the CRA also allows you to make a "contribution in kind." As long as it is within your contribution limit, you can transfer assets from a taxable investment portfolio into your RRSP. But a word of caution: If you transfer investments with capital losses into an RRSP, claiming these losses on your tax return will be denied.

Borrowing for an RRSP

An RRSP loan can be used to "catch up" all unused RRSP contribution room at once. The loan, paid off over several years, is a conservative form of leverage — borrowing money to invest. While the interest expense is not deductible, when you invest borrowed funds in an RRSP, you get two big benefits: You immediately get a much larger RRSP growing earlier, and you'll get your tax deduction for the contribution now as opposed to later.

Some caveats: Make sure the interest rate is as favourable as possible (if you hold your investments with the lender, this is usually the case). Be sure that the loan is within your budget, and don't continually borrow to invest in RRSPs. Another tip: When you get your tax refund, make sure to use it to pay down the loan.

Effect of pensions on RRSP contribution limits

If you belong to a pension plan, you'll have a "pension adjustment" (PA). Your PA has to be deducted from your "earned income" to determine your maximum RRSP contribution for the coming year. Your PA reflects the amount of the pension you built up in the pension plan during the year. Don't worry, you'll find the amount on your T4 or T4A slip, and the CRA does the RRSP contribution limit calculations for you: Your RRSP limit is printed on your last year's Notice of Assessment.

Try and avoid early withdrawals

While you can withdraw funds from your RRSP at any time, no matter what age you are, I recommend you don't do it, if at all possible.

Whatever you withdraw will be added to your taxable income in that year. It works this way: The government slaps a withholding tax of 10 percent on withdrawals of $5,000 or less, 20 percent on withdrawals of $5,001 to $15,000, and 30 percent on withdrawals over $15,000. The percentages are even higher in Quebec. But that's not all. Since these held back amounts probably won't cover your full taxes owing, you'll have to make up the difference when you file your tax return. This is how the government "claws back" the RRSP tax deduction they gave you earlier. Yikes!

The ten biggest RRSP mistakes

1. **Don't make contributing to your RRSP a once-a-year event.**
   - For too many people, contributing to an RRSP happens once per year, if at all.
   - Start a regular contribution plan for your RRSP and you will see two benefits: You'll avoid the February rush and, more importantly, your money will start working for you sooner.
2. **Don't let your tax refund go to waste.**
   - Your lump-sum tax refund is a great opportunity to save.
   - Rather than spending your tax refund, consider repaying your loans and credit cards, paying down your mortgage, or if you have the RRSP room, "top up" your contribution.
3. **Don't forget about your long-term financial plan.**
   - Without a financial plan in place, you won't know how much you need to save, for how long or how to invest in your RRSP.
   - By establishing a formal plan and monitoring your progress on a regular basis, you will have a far better chance of reaching your retirement goals.
4. **Don't forget to maximize your RRSP contribution.**
   - Three factors affect the annual amount you can contribute to an RRSP:
     - A dollar limit, which in 2005 was $16,500, or 18 percent of your previous year's earned income, whichever is less.
     - Pension adjustments, if you participate in a pension plan.
     - If you contribute less than your allowable maximum amount, you can "carry forward" the extra deduction room and make a contribution in a following year.

5. **Don't forget to diversify your portfolio.**
   - Studies have shown that more than 90 percent of your portfolio's return is the result of asset allocation and not individual investment selection.
   - By ensuring your investments are allocated across all asset classes (cash, fixed income and equities), it will help to ensure that you always have the best performing asset class in your portfolio.
6. **Don't neglect the importance of designating a beneficiary for your RRSP.**
   - Despite the fact that RRSPs make up the bulk of many people's assets, some still do not designate a beneficiary or take into account the tax consequences when they do name a beneficiary.
   - Under the Income Tax Act, upon death, the assets in an RRSP that are designated to a spouse can be automatically transferred tax-free to their plan, avoiding probate fees and income taxes.
7. **Don't forget to consider income-splitting strategies.**
   - Spousal RRSPs can provide a means of income splitting for couples. They can help defer taxes right away for the contributor and reduce taxes at retirement.
   - Shifting investment income from a higher income earner to the lower income earner can mean less tax payable if the lower income earner is in a lower tax bracket during retirement.
8. **Don't "park" your RRSP contribution indefinitely.**
   - Every year, many Canadians "park" their RRSP contributions in money market funds.
   - These contributions could be missing out on growth potential and the opportunity for a better rate of return if invested elsewhere.
   - Take the time to speak with your financial planner or advisor and re-allocate your investments within your RRSP.
9. **Don't miss an RRSP contribution just because you're temporarily short of money.**
   - Many people may find themselves short of cash at RRSP time, and many may simply give up on contributing all together. Borrowing the money may be the answer.
   - RRSP loans are usually offered at attractive rates and often give you the option of deferring the first payments for up to three months, potentially allowing you to repay all or part of the loan with your tax refund.

10. Don't contribute in-kind securities that have capital losses.

- If you contribute securities into an RRSP, the CRA deems this a disposition (sale) of the securities; if the "sale" is done at a profit, taxes must be paid on the capital gain.
- If you contribute securities to an RRSP that carry a loss, you will lose the ability to net these losses against taxable capital gains at tax time.

TAX-SAVING STRATEGY #3: SPLIT YOUR INCOME WITH FAMILY MEMBERS

Income splitting simply means moving income from one family member (let's say it's you) at a higher tax bracket to one who is in a lower marginal tax bracket (let's say it's your spouse). The split could be with other relations including children, in-laws or a niece or nephew. In addition, you can't just go ahead and split income by waving a finger and saying abracadabra! The CRA will deem you to be evading taxes if you do this without working through and adhering to all the tax aspects of income splitting.

If the CRA thinks you're splitting primarily to avoid paying your full share of taxes, they will deny your request according to a number of attribution rules. As I mentioned earlier, attribution rules mean that any tax breaks you accrue from income splitting can (under certain circumstances) be charged back or *attributed* back to you as taxable income.

The good news is, there are a number of ways to legally get around these rules, and the CRA does not mind as long as the transactions have not been set up for profit. Some of the most common income-splitting strategies include establishing spousal RRSPs (discussed earlier), making loans to family members, buying RESPs and (if you are retired) splitting CPP benefits.

Income splitting also provides advantages when calculating your Old Age Security (OAS) benefit and any potential clawback you might face. The OAS program currently requires a repayment of benefits or clawback when your personal income exceeds $60,806 (as of 2005). The OAS is totally clawed back when your income reaches $98,850. So if you and your spouse can keep your respective income levels below that threshold through income splitting, you can completely avoid the clawback.

Avoid giving the CRA a "splitting" headache

As with spousal RRSPs, the CRA enforces attribution rules to avoid abuse of the income splitting process. Several types of transfers can trigger attribution rules.

- A loan or transfer of assets to a spouse in which no or below market value interest is charged.
- A loan or transfer of assets to a minor child. The exception is capital gains; capital gains can be earned by the minor child without attribution.
- A loan or transfer of assets to a trust where the income beneficiaries include your spouse or minor children. You cannot simply insert a trust into the arrangement and expect to avoid attribution.
- A loan or transfer of assets to a corporation where your spouse or minor children are shareholders of the corporation, unless the corporation is a "Small Business Corporation."
- A loan to an adult child where it is established that one of the primary purposes of the loan was to reduce your tax bill.

When you transfer (as opposed to lend) assets to anyone other than your spouse, you are deemed to have sold those assets at fair market value, which could trigger a tax liability in the year of the transfer. Transfers to your spouse automatically take place at your adjusted cost base, unless you elect otherwise.

According to Grant Thornton LLP, Chartered Accountants, proper and effective income splitting can "save as much as $8,000 per person annually in income taxes."

Income-splitting savings vary according to your marginal tax rates and the differences between those rates. It's always advisable to consult your tax professional before entering into income-splitting arrangements.

More ways to split your income

There are other ways to split income, whether you have children or not. Some of these strategies include:

High income earner pays expenses; low income earner invests

Expenses that could be paid by the high-wage spouse include: income taxes, groceries, mortgage payments, credit card bills and other personal debt payments (i.e., loans taken out that are not for investments). The high-income earner pays the interest on a loan for an investment, but not the principal. Make sure that the form of payment can be directly tied to the high-income earner, such as a personal cheque bearing their name. The idea is to have the high-income earner pay for these costs in order to free up income earned by the low-income spouse so the low-income spouse can invest those dollars. The low-income spouse will pay less tax on any investment earnings.

Split CPP/QPP benefits with your spouse

If your spouse's marginal tax rate is lower than yours and you're close to retirement, splitting your CPP/QPP (taxable) benefits can save you money. If you and your spouse are over 60 and one of you is in a higher tax bracket, you can apply to assign up to one-half of your CPP/QPP benefits to your spouse.

The above points just touch the surface of the income-splitting arena. There are many more possibilities, some very intricate. As a starting point I recommend going to the Certified General Accountants of Ontario Web site (www.cga-ontario.org) for more details.

TAX-SAVING STRATEGY #4: INVEST IN YOUR HOME

For many, our home may be the single largest tax-free investment we ever make. Your principal residence provides a fabulous opportunity to grow a huge part of your nest egg tax-free, because it can be sold at retirement if you decide it's time to shift to a more modest home or apartment. By the way, you can also elect to make your cottage or summer home your principal residence. Why would you do that? One reason it might make sense is if you have substantial capital gains pending in a very old (but well located) cottage.

It's important to be absolutely clear just what a principal residence is. While your principal residence is that place where you regularly reside, you are only exempt from capital gains on the sale of the structure and up to one-half hectare of extra land. Anything beyond that may be taxable. A word of warning: If you buy and sell houses on a frequent basis, these transactions might be deemed "adventures in the nature of trade." It's a good idea to consult with your tax advisor as the profits on the sale of these houses might be considered active business income. You might be prevented from claiming a principal residence exemption, and in a worst-case scenario, you might end up being taxed on the profits at close to a 50 percent rate.

Just a quick aside: Try to always purchase a mortgage with a relatively short amortization period. The longer the amortization period, the more interest you pay and the slower you pay off the principal. Over many decades, this can add up to thousands of dollars in potentially "lost" savings. Over the course of your life, as you trade up to larger houses, the proceeds continue to be reinvested tax-free.

The Home Buyers' Plan

The Canadian government realizes how important a home is to one's retirement planning. That's why they established the Home Buyers' Plan (HBP). It actively encourages young people and first-time buyers to withdraw from their RRSPs without penalty in order to purchase a home.

Here's how the plan works. The HBP allows you to withdraw up to $20,000 from your RRSP ($40,000 per couple) to buy or build a qualifying home for yourself (as a first-time home buyer) or for someone who is related to you and is disabled. The borrower must be a resident of Canada and must pass an eligibility test. Disabled individuals automatically qualify for the HBP. To qualify as a "first-time home buyer," you cannot have owned a home as a principal residence in the preceding four years, and if you're married, you must not be living in a house owned and occupied by your spouse.

Your RRSP withdrawal is not taxed as income and no interest is owed on those funds, provided you repay the amount you withdrew within fifteen years, and pay no less than 1/15th per year. If you repay less than that amount, the difference is added back to your taxable income at your marginal tax rate.

The following conditions also apply to HBPs:

- Your HBP balance on January 1 of the year of the withdrawal must be zero.
- Neither you nor your spouse or common-law partner can own the qualifying home more than thirty days before the withdrawal.
- You must buy or build the qualifying home before October 1 of the year after the year of withdrawal.

You may still be considered a first-time homebuyer if you own a rental property or if you have not recently owned a home, and you can make withdrawals from more than one RRSP as long as you are the annuitant (plan owner) of each RRSP. However, please note: You will not usually be allowed to withdraw funds from a locked-in RRSP.

HBP pros and cons

The primary pro of the Home Buyers' Plan is getting unexpected cash for a down payment when you don't have any other savings. The HBP is also a perfect choice if you want to make a larger down payment than you normally could. A bigger down payment means a smaller mortgage, and a smaller mortgage means you pay less interest over the life of the mortgage. This can be substantial.

The cons include losing growth in your RRSP (since the money is withdrawn from there), and potentially losing more growth in your RRSP than you make up in reduced mortgage payments. However, according to some studies, the reduction in interest paid over the length of your mortgage will almost always be greater than the lost returns in your RRSP. The HBP works as long as the interest rate on your mortgage is higher than the foregone return on your RRSP investments.

In some ways, the HBP/RRSP dilemma is remarkably similar to another dilemma:

"Hmmm. Pay down my mortgage or invest in an RRSP?"

The answer to this question depends on your age and personal priorities; everyone's current and future financial situation is different. The following questions are raised by Terri Williams, President of the Investor Education Fund. They should help give you a starting point for your own analysis.

What is your financial outlook for the future? For example, if you have a child who is expected to go to college or university in five years, would it be helpful for you to be mortgage-free when the first university payment comes in? What kind of pension plan do you have, and have you factored that into your RRSP needs? Do you have a financial plan that shows you how much you will need for your retirement — and are you on track?

What about doing both? Make your RRSP contributions on a regular basis and then take the tax refund it generates and apply it to your mortgage. Or, if your child's education is more of a priority, put the tax refund into a registered education savings plan (RESP) instead (see Strategy #7).

What about finding additional ways to pay off that mortgage faster? Pay your mortgage on a weekly or biweekly basis. The extra payments generated by fifty-two or twenty-six payments instead of twelve goes straight onto your principal — saving you money in interest payments. How about doubling up on a payment every once in a while, as those payments typically come right off your mortgage?

Do you know what interest rate you're paying on your debt? If you're locked into a high interest rate for your mortgage, go to your bank and try to negotiate a new rate. If you're carrying high credit card debt (which have really high interest rates), that might be your first priority over RRSP or RESP or mortgage payments.

TAX-SAVING STRATEGY #5: DIVIDENDS—YOUR SECRET WEAPON
Dividends of Canadian companies are given favourable tax treatment in Canada. The dividend tax credit essentially gives you the first $30,000 or so of dividend income with just a nominal amount of tax charged. After that, applying the gross-up and dividend tax credits to your taxable income will still provide you with a lower effective tax rate than most other forms of investment income. Remember though, that U.S. dividends do not receive the dividend tax credit, and are taxed as though they are "income" in Canada.

How to calculate your dividend tax credit
To calculate your dividend tax credit, you "gross-up" the dividend income you receive by 25 percent — in other words, the amount you have to include in income is 125 percent of the actual dividend you received. The additional 25 percent is referred to as the gross-up. But don't panic. A tax credit is then deducted from your taxes payable. The federal dividend tax credit is calculated as 13.3333 percent of the grossed-up dividend.

Here's a simple example. If you were in one of the lower tax brackets, say 23 percent, the tax you'd owe (before any credits) on a $100 dividend would be $125 × 23 percent = $28.75. But your federal tax credit is 13.3333 percent × $125 = $16.67. Then calculate your provincial credits. In B.C. and Ontario, for example, the provincial tax credit is 5.1 percent of $125 = $6.38. Add your federal and provincial credits together and you get a total credit of $16.67 + $6.38 = $23.05. And since the initial tax owing on the grossed-up dividend was $28.75, after you deduct the credit of $23.05, much of the tax payable is gone. Thank you, Mr. Taxman. And by the way, at the time of writing, the federal government is contemplating legislation to reduce the dividend tax rate.

The power of DRIPs

Dividend reinvestment plans (DRIPs) let you reinvest dividends without paying commissions. Under such plans, dividends are automatically reinvested into new shares without any transaction costs. Many DRIPs also have a "cash investment option" or share purchase plan (SPP) that allow shareholders to purchase shares directly from the company without having to pay commissions to a broker. A few of the plans even give a discount off the market price of the shares.

While the saving in brokerage commissions may seem small, every little bit helps when you are building a retirement nest egg. The longer the investment is held, the more the benefit compounds.

Not all dividend-paying companies in Canada have a DRIP. But more than forty blue-chip Canadian companies do, including all of the major banks and many of the better known names listed on the Toronto Stock Exchange, such as Molson, Noranda, TransCanada Pipelines and BCE.

At least forty-five income trusts also offer DRIPs (in this case, *distribution* reinvestment plans). The list includes many of the popular real estate investment trusts (REITs) and oil and gas royalty trusts.

About half of the DRIPs offer investors the option of putting in more cash to buy more shares or trust units without having to pay brokerage commissions. These cash investment options range from a little as $3,000 annually to as much as $350,000 a year. BCE, for example, limits such cash investments to $20,000 a year. And Riocan REIT and Canadian REIT each apply limits of $25,000 a year.

There's a downside to DRIPs, despite all their benefits. You must keep track of the cost of your investments under a DRIP so as to not pay too much in tax when the securities are sold; every DRIP adds to the adjusted cost base. There's a lot of record-keeping involved, which is why many savvy investors choose to use DRIPs only in their RRSP accounts where the ACB (adjusted cost base) is not relevant.

To participate in a DRIP or SPP, you need to be a shareholder in the company. To do this, most investors will buy an initial stake through a broker and have it registered in their name. The MoneySaver Web site (www.canadianmoneysaver.ca) is an excellent place for investors interested in exchanging shares for the purpose of setting up DRIPs and SPPs.

David Stanley argues that a portfolio of blue-chip, high-dividend Canadian stocks that have both DRIPs and SPPs can serve as an important step in your retirement planning. He quotes Gail Dudack, America's "perennial Mama Bear" on the importance of investing in blue chip, dividend-paying stocks:

> Dividends are a financial commitment from a company. They cannot be paid with smoke and mirrors. And companies that increase their dividend payments are steadily and consistently rewarding shareholders for their loyalty. Equally important, companies with a track record of paying dividends and increasing dividend payments are making a clear statement about the confidence they have in their earnings potential, real cash flow and the viability of their long-term business plan. It is action instead of words.

Stanley goes on to show how his own portfolio has performed. The following table gives the results of his long term DRIP program.

Stock	SYM	Date	% change	Days	Yield	Real Yield
Altria	MO	26-Aug-96	134.49	3016	5.02	11.77
BCE Inc	BCE	14-Jul-95	54.13	3425	4.17	6.43
Can Reit	REF.UN	05-Dec-01	83.38	1089	7.15	13.11
Dofasco	DFS	20-Jul-95	222.76	3419	3.13	9.99
Emera	EMA	15-Sep-98	47.20	2266	4.78	7.04
Enbridge	ENB	06-Jul-95	411.71	3433	3.27	16.72
IBM	IBM	02-Jun-98	157.63	2371	0.76	1.96

Stock	SYM	Date	% change	Days	Yield	Real Yield
Johnson & Johnson	JNJ	08-Oct-97	37.78	2608	1.89	2.60
National Bank	NA	30-Oct-96	356.32	2951	3.24	14.80
Terasen	TER	30-Oct-96	269.36	2951	3.11	11.49
T-D Bank*	TD	22-Jun-95	229.35	3447	3.01	9.91
Transalta	TA	06-Jul-95	185.73	3433	5.54	9.04
Average			182.49	2867	3.76	9.57

* Only began a DRIP in 2002, no SPP.
Source: Investopedia.com

DRIP performance: David Stanley's long-term DRIP portfolio
Stanley explains the basis for his portfolio:

The real benefit for someone planning for retirement is that they are now receiving about a 9.6 percent return on their original investment by doing nothing but reinvesting the dividends. Not a nickel came out of my pocket after the initial purchase, although I could have added more if I wanted, and commission-free via the SPP. Sure, taxes must be paid on those dividends yearly, but at a rate much lower than interest income, and the investor gets to enjoy the benefits of compounding.

The power of dividends
If you think dividend-paying companies are boring, low-return investment vehicles, think again. For decades, savvy investors have been using dividend-focused strategies to buy shares in household names such as Coca-Cola, Johnson & Johnson, Kellogg's and General Electric.

The following chart, courtesy of Investopedia.com, tracks Johnson & Johnson's adjusted share price over twenty years (adjusted share price accounts for both splits and dividends) to demonstrate just how powerful an appreciating share price can be in conjunction with a steadily increasing dividend. The split-adjusted share price for JNJ at the beginning of 1983 was $0.09; in mid-2004, the stock traded for a split-adjusted price of around $55!

ADJUSTED SHARE PRICE FOR JNJ

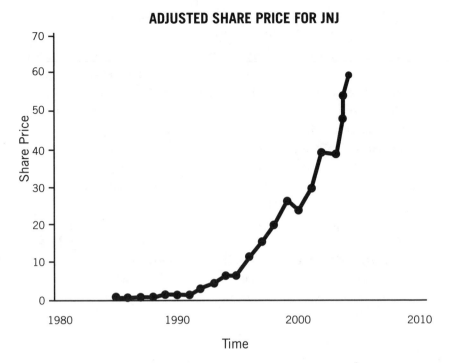

The payoff

Reinvesting dividends of blue-chip Canadian companies means you automatically purchase more shares in companies that are doing well enough to pay dividends in the first place. By reinvesting dividends that are paid regularly, you are also able to take advantage of dollar cost averaging, and you are incurring taxes on the investment income at an exceptionally favourable rate. Choose your stocks wisely and, who knows, your returns may begin to approximate those of Johnson & Johnson.

TAX-SAVING STRATEGY #6: BORROW TO INVEST

Loans taken out to earn investment income are tax-deductible. In some situations, it can be in your best interest if you borrow to invest rather than using existing savings. One caveat: Please don't borrow to invest unless you are debt-free, have maximized your RRSPs and are in a high marginal tax bracket. Otherwise, the drawbacks outweigh the benefits. But many Canadians who have maxed out their RRSP contributions are looking for tax-deductible investment options outside their RRSPs.

Investment loans are similar to borrowing money for any large purchase, but with one big difference: When you borrow to invest, you're (usually) not investing in a depreciating asset like a car or furniture or appliances. You expect your investment to *appreciate* over time, and thus be worth more when you sell it. That's the power of leverage. But leverage works both ways, so when it comes to the investments you borrow for, it's imperative that you make wise choices.

It's natural to assume that if you borrow money at 7 percent, you need the investment to return 7 percent to break even. But, since interest payments are generally tax-deductible, the break-even return is generally lower than the interest rate you're paying on the loan.

Example: Assuming the interest is 100 percent deductible and let's say you're marginal tax rate is 45 percent. If you borrowed $100,000 at 7 percent, you'd only need an annual return of 4.97 percent to be better off with a leverage strategy than with a non-leverage strategy. (This is assuming a 10-year investment period, 100 percent deductibility, 33 percent taxable portion of return and a 30 percent tax rate on investment income.)

TAX-SAVING STRATEGY #7: MAXIMIZE YOUR RESP CONTRIBUTIONS

The cost of a post-secondary education continues to rise. According to Human Resources Development Canada, by 2020 the anticipated cost of four years (away from home) at a typical Canadian university may be in excess of $103,800.

Although the expense may seem a little overwhelming, there are ways parents and grandparents can make the most of the savings they may wish to set aside for a student's education.

A common strategy to help ensure you can provide adequately for a child's education is to set up a registered education savings plan (RESP).

Registered education savings plans

RESPs were created by the federal government to encourage Canadians to save for a child's education while offering certain tax benefits. Contributions of up to $4,000 can be made for each beneficiary every year to a lifetime maximum of $42,000.

Types of RESPs

- **Single plans:** Under a single beneficiary plan, the subscriber (contributor) can name one beneficiary. The beneficiary named does not have to be related to the subscriber by blood or adoption, which means that anyone can start a plan for a child and make regular contributions.
- **Family plans:** A family beneficiary plan is similar to a single beneficiary plan, except that subscribers can name more than one beneficiary to the plan, provided they are all related to the subscriber by blood or adoption. The family plan provides the flexibility of sharing the assets within the RESP among the beneficiaries. For example, if you have four children named as beneficiaries and only two pursue post-secondary education, the RESP funds may be transferred to those two children within the plan without penalty.

The Canadian Education Savings Grant (CESG)

Contributions made to an RESP are eligible to receive a grant from the federal government. The Canada Education Savings Grant (CESG) provides RESP account holders with a grant of up to 20 percent on the first $2,000 contributed to the plan every year for each beneficiary under the age of 18. That works out to a maximum annual grant of $400 per beneficiary for a total lifetime grant of $7,200.

There is also an additional CES grant which is based on income. With an income less than $35,000, an additional 20 percent of the first $500 in contributions per year is given, and for income between $35,000 to $70,000 an additional 10 percent of the first $500 in contributions per year. Canada Learning Bonds are also available to all Canadians with newborns. The Canada Learning Bond, part of the Canada Education Savings Act, allows qualified families to earn up to $3,000 per child born after 2003 before they are old enough to pursue post-secondary studies.

The benefits of tax deferral

While contributions to RESPs are not tax-deductible for the contributor, income earned on the RESP investments remains tax-deferred until withdrawn. Withdrawals by the beneficiary are taxed in the beneficiary's hands.

Certain restrictions apply to a beneficiary aged 16 or 17. Remember, CESGs are linked to individual beneficiaries, so in a family plan, a maximum of $7,200 per beneficiary can be paid out in CESGs. Since you decide the allocation of payments, if one beneficiary doesn't attend post-secondary school, other beneficiaries can share in the plan, as well as any CESGs as long as the $7,200 limit mentioned above is adhered to. Any excess CESGs over the $7,200 limit must be repaid to the federal government.

RESP considerations

Age differences between children
If there is a significant age difference between your children, you may want to consider separate RESPs to avoid the risk of the family plan having to be wound up before the youngest child has completed his/her education.

Designating a successor
In the event of your death, the plan can be continued on your behalf by your heirs, executors, administrators or other legal representatives, if outlined in your will.

However, if your will does not specify a successor, current tax law allows any other person making contributions to the plan to become the new subscriber upon your death. As the new subscriber, they may claim a refund on the capital contribution, leaving only the accumulated income and CESG for the child. If your intention is for the capital in the plan to be used by the beneficiary, then you may want to designate the successor in your will.

Take advantage of tax-deferred growth

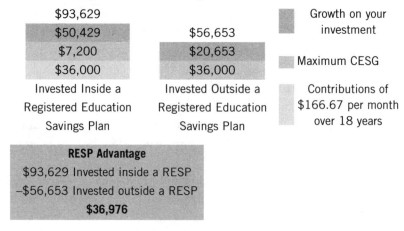

This example assumes an annual effective rate of return of 8 percent; that the CESG is 20 percent of the contribution to a maximum of $400 per year per child is paid quarterly; and that the investment income received outside the RESP is taxed at a marginal tax rate of 40 percent. Rate of return shown is used to illustrate the effects of the compound growth rate and is not intended to reflect future values of an investment or returns on investments.

The lifespan of an RESP

Contributions can be made to an RESP for twenty-one years (twenty-five years for single plans) from the date the RESP is opened; the RESP must be collapsed by December 31st of the twenty-fifth year (thirtieth year for single plans) following the year the plan was opened.

In the majority of cases, this time limit isn't a problem. However, if your child takes a "break" between high school and post-secondary education, you may be forced to collapse the plan before realizing the full benefit from the funds held within the plan. Any funds that remain in the RESP after the twenty-five-year limit will be subject to withdrawal penalties. See Appendix 3 for an RESP calculator.

TAX-SAVING STRATEGY #8: MAXIMIZE TAX DEDUCTIONS

Too many Canadian taxpayers don't take advantage of many of the tax-reduction opportunities available to them. Remember, the value of a tax deduction is equal to your marginal tax rate, and the higher your income, the higher your marginal tax rate. In order to be put in the lowest tax bracket possible, you must try to reduce your taxable income as much as possible.

Besides RRSPs, key deductions include: medical expenses, charitable donations, pension contributions, union and professional dues, child care expenses, moving expenses, support payments, interest expense (for business or investing), auto expenses, travel expenses, meals and entertainment (for business meetings) and supplies and equipment to perform your job.

Give yourself a break

Besides the satisfaction you'll get from seeing your charitable donations put to good use, your donations can also help trim your tax bill. But not all donations are created equal. Ensure that your donation provides maximum benefit for both your selected charity and your own tax situation. There are also different strategies to consider, depending on whether your donation is made during your lifetime or as part of your estate.

Limits

Believe it or not, the CRA allows you to claim a tax credit on donations of up to 75 percent of your net income, plus 25 percent of most taxable gains arising from gifts of securities or property. Certain gifts "in kind" (such as capital or depreciable property, ecologically sensitive lands or certified cultural property) allow the limit to be increased to 100 percent of net income.

Gifts in cash or kind

A cash gift is probably the most common form of charitable giving. It can be something as simple as dropping a few coins in a box, or writing a cheque to a foundation. On the positive side, it is easy to measure the value of your donation and the tax effect it will have. It also gives the charity maximum flexibility — they can choose to invest your donation, or spend it immediately. Unfortunately, it is usually the least tax-efficient way to donate. When you make a receipted cash gift to a charity, you receive a tax credit for approximately 25 percent on donations given up to $200 and approximately 50 percent on donations made above $200.

A gift "in kind" is a non-cash gift, like publicly traded securities. Note that for tax purposes, your gift is recorded at fair market value. If your gift has appreciated in value, you are considered to have divested it and result in higher taxes from the capital gain. See Chapter 9 for a detailed example of donating securities.

Life insurance

Make sure you have enough insurance to preserve your estate. Donating money to charity through life insurance is a useful estate planning tool. Basically, this involves transferring the ownership of your life insurance policy (such as a whole or universal life policy) to the charity, as well as making the charity the beneficiary. It is the cash surrender value, if any, of the insurance policy that is eligible for credit as a charitable donation.

Once the policy has been donated, any additional premiums paid to the insurance company for the policy by the donor are considered a charitable donation, earning you further tax credits. (You must donate the policy itself: Just making the charity a beneficiary does not provide any tax benefits.) When giving insurance, you should first consider the needs of your heirs. Make sure you have enough insurance to allow them to preserve your estate before considering a policy donation to charity.

Charitable remainder trusts

If you own an income-generating property such as real estate, you can set up a charitable remainder trust. This is a trust that gives the property to the charity, but ensures that you continue to receive the property's income for the rest of your life. The gift is recorded at fair market value (which means you might trigger a capital gain, as if you were donating a security and recaptured depreciation, if any), giving you an immediate tax credit while ensuring you receive an income during your lifetime.

The valuation of the gift can be complicated. If no reasonable value can be ascertained, then the donation will be ineligible for a tax credit. Other downsides are the professional fees required to set up such a trust, and the need for the trust to fill out a tax return each year. The benefit to the charity is that it receives the property immediately, and need not worry about a will being contested. The CRA is currently reviewing the policy on these trusts. For a full discussion of trusts, see Chapter 9.

Type of Donation	Credit	Tax Considerations
Cash	50%	None
Securities	50%	Capital gains at 25% if security is donated, at 50% if security is sold and cash donated. The limit of donations you can claim each year is 75% of your "net income" plus 25% of the taxable capital gains arising from donations of capital property.
Property	50%	Capital gains tax if property has appreciated in value and recaptured depreciation, if any. Consider a charitable remainder trust if you need the income in your lifetime but wish to ensure transfer of asset on your death.
Insurance	50%	Make sure your estate is protected. Policy must be donated—making the charity the beneficiary creates no tax advantage for you or your estate. Any additional premium payments are considered a donation.

Child care expenses

Child tax benefits help defray some of the cost of raising children, and low-income parents have this topped up by the National Child Benefit Supplement (about $172 per month per family). But some child care expenses can also be deducted. Examples are daycare, boarding school, hockey school and summer camp fees. Deductions apply only as long as both spouses are working, or where one spouse is attending school for all or part of the tax year. Deductions also apply if you're the parent in a single-parent family.

The maximum deduction is $7,000 per child under 7 and $4,000 for each child over 7 and under 16. If you have any children with disabilities, you can deduct up to $10,000, but the deductions cannot exceed two-thirds of your earned income.

Medical expenses

Non-reimbursed medical expenses can be claimed as a non-refundable tax credit. A complex calculation determines the federal and provincial portion to the credit. Consult with your tax advisor for the details. Medical expenses may also be claimed for dependants other than a spouse or common-law partner, but the total expenses claimed are again subject to a complex calculation.

Key medical expenses eligible for tax credits include the cost of attendant care for the disabled (up to two-thirds of earned income); full time attendant care for individuals with severe and prolonged mental or physical infirmities; the cost of supervision of an individual eligible for the disability tax credit who is residing in a qualified Canadian group home; any reasonable travel expenses incurred to obtain medical services outside of the vicinity of an individual's home (provided they haven't been reimbursed by a provincial health plan or other source).

There are all kinds of exclusions and conditions (provincially as well as federally) so I would suggest careful study of this area. But there are many hidden benefits. In Quebec, for example, you're entitled to a tax credit for payments made to a dentist, nurse, practitioner, public hospital or licensed private hospital, for medical, dental or paramedical services; and payments for drugs prescribed by a physician or a dentist and obtained from a licensed pharmacist; payments for eyeglasses, contact lenses or other devices for the treatment or correction of a defect of vision, where such items are prescribed by an ophthalmologist or an optometrist.

TAX-SAVING STRATEGY #9: TAKE ADVANTAGE OF EMPLOYEE BENEFITS

Some benefits are taxable and some benefits aren't. In order to claim benefits as one or the other, it's crucial that you maintain accurate records.

Taxable benefits

- Interest-free or low-interest loans
- Travelling expenses of employee's spouse, board and lodging
- Wage loss replacement plans
- Gifts
- Travel benefits
- Premiums under most government health care programs
- Cost of tools
- Personal use of employer's vehicle
- Trips and other prizes
- Rent-free or low-rent housing
- Employee counselling
- Tuition fees
- Subsidized meals

Non-taxable benefits

- Moving expenses
- Premiums under a private health services plan
- Subsidized meals
- Subsidized school services
- Daycare facilities
- Transportation to work
- Discounts on merchandise
- Employer contributions under provincial hospitalization and medical care insurance plans
- Uniforms and clothing for work
- Educational assistance
- Employer-provided recreational facilities
- Club memberships for business purposes

Loans from an employer

Loans are treated differently depending on certain aspects of the loan. If the interest rate on a loan is less than the going commercial rate of interest, then there is a taxable benefit that is equal to the difference between the "prescribed rate of interest" and the actual rate of interest that the loan is for, for the entire year. The prescribed rate is determined by CRA and is based on the 90-day T-bill rate. You'll be taxed on the difference between the prescribed rate of interest and what you're currently paying in interest.

Personal use of a company car

The CRA separates the potential tax benefits of a company car into two parts: standby charges and operating costs.

Standby charges are taxable and must be included in the employee's income, whether the car is leased or purchased. If the car is owned by the company, the benefit is 2 percent of the original cost of the car per month. If the car is leased, the benefit is two-thirds of the lease payment, including maintenance, excess mileage and lease termination charges.

The operating cost portion is also taxable (less any reimbursement by the employee) and includes gas, insurance, repairs, car washes, etc. It's important that the employee does not pay the costs directly (i.e., to the vendor of the services), but instead reimburses the employer if he/she so desires since paying directly would actually raise the employee's tax burden. Reimbursing the employer will reduce the taxable benefit by the amount of the reimbursement.

Instead of providing an employee with a car, your employer may pay an allowance for the use of a car to perform his/her job. Only if this amount is in excess of a reasonable amount is it a taxable benefit. Most of the time, all allowances are taxable, particularly if the employee is already reimbursed for car expenses.

Reimbursement of moving costs

These benefits are not taxable if paid by the employer. If the employee pays these costs, they can be deducted against income as long as the employee's new and old residences are both in Canada and the new residence is located at least 40 kilometres closer to the new work location and income earned during the year (or subsequent year) equals or exceeds the moving costs. Costs that can be deducted include: travel, transportation and storage, board and lodging (as long as it's less than sixteen days), lease cancellation costs, legal costs, as well as land transfer taxes. If these costs are paid by the employer, they, too, are not a taxable benefit.

Insurance premiums

If private health insurance premiums are paid by your employer, they are not taxable in your hands. The employer should try to be the sole contributor since the employer receives a deduction and the employee pays no tax. The tax treatment of life insurance depends on the type of life insurance that you have: Group Term Life insurance benefits are taxable. Split Dollar Life insurance benefits are fully taxable if the employer pays a large portion of the premium relative to the employer's interest in the policy.

Club memberships, meals and entertainment expenses

Club memberships are taxable if the membership does not pertain to the business (i.e., fitness club). If the membership directly assists the conduct of business, then it is not a taxable benefit. Meal and entertainment expenses that do not pertain to business are taxable while meal and entertainment expenses that do pertain to business aren't taxable.

Retiring allowances for employees

Payment in recognition of long service, loss of employment or for things such as accumulated unused sick days is often paid in a lump sum. To defer this fully taxable income, transfer the amount to your RRSP within sixty days of the end of the year. Fortunately, this transfer will not affect your contribution limits

TAX-SAVING STRATEGY #10: EMPLOY YOURSELF, PART-TIME OR FULL-TIME

If you're an employee with a family to support, the thought of becoming self-employed may be more than a little scary. But I have some good news for you. You can ease into it by doing it part-time on the side, see all the benefits and decide if it's for you before making the leap. And believe me, there are benefits galore!

Part-timers

Expenses related to your home business such as computer costs, partial auto expenses, even some of your mortgage interest and property taxes can be deducted. For example, if your home office takes up 10 percent of your total floor space, you can deduct 10 percent of your home maintenance costs, such as heating, electricity and cleaning materials. Any expenses that are directly related to the business, such as supplies and travel, are also deductible. Your home office can be a segregated area, or a room in your home that is devoted entirely to your business.

If you can negotiate it with your employer, try to hire an assistant. Employees are allowed to claim deductions for salary or wages paid to an assistant, provided you needed an assistant and were required to pay for one by your employer. Of course, your lower-income spouse would be perfect as that assistant, letting you split income and save tax in the process.

If you're a renter you can claim a portion of your monthly rent, and deduct a share of the utilities, insurance or home maintenance allotted to the area of the house set aside for business use. The claim you make is based on a percentage equal to the percentage of your home that is reserved for business. Just remember, the CRA won't allow you to use these items to create a loss that could be deducted against other sources of income, however.

Full-time business owners

Many of the same deductions — and more — apply to full-time business owners. If you're a sole proprietor or partner in a business you can pay a salary to a family member (e.g., a spouse) and then deduct their salary against your business income. The spouse must then pay tax on this amount. For this strategy to work, your spouse must be in a lower tax bracket than you and the salary must be reasonable for the services that were rendered.

According to Caroline Cakebread, a Toronto financial writer, you should pay yourself the basic minimum claim of $8,148 since you pay no personal income tax up to this amount. But beyond that, if the personal tax rate is higher, you might be wise to keep the income in the company. If the corporate tax rate is higher, pay income out as a salary to yourself. When it comes to taking money out of the business, Cakebread says there are bad ways and good (tax-efficient) ways. For example:

Salary is the best way to draw a steady flow of cash. A salary also lets you make RRSP, EI and CPP contributions.

Bonuses can drop you and your firm into a lower tax bracket, whether you're paying yourself or your employees.

Dividends are taxed at a discount to your marginal rate, but your business is also taxed on them before they're paid out.

IPPs: Individual pension plans are an effective way to take money out of the business and put it into a defined-benefit pension plan. Contributions are tax-deductible to you and your company, and are creditor-proof.

RCAs: Retirement compensation arrangements are seldom your best option, but are attractive if you're nearing retirement and planning to settle abroad.

Your business shouldn't be your only investment option

"If you think your business is the only retirement investment you need, you may want to reconsider. There's a natural tendency for small business owners to invest their disposable income back into the business, instead of buying RRSPs," says Kathryn Del Greco, an investment advisor at TD Waterhouse Canada. "Their belief is that their best asset is their own ability to generate wealth. They generally own a home and their company and feel that those assets will be enough for their retirement."

Source: *Globe and Mail*, February 8, 2005.

The benefits of incorporating

If you're self-employed, or planning to become self-employed, you should know the pros and cons of sole proprietorship and incorporating. And I can tell you, there are many more pros than cons, because the government rewards risk-takers who have the potential to create jobs.

Tax advantages of incorporating

Incorporating can also have numerous tax and estate planning advantages for those currently operating as proprietors or partners. For one thing, incorporated businesses can retain earnings and issue bonuses and dividends. These corporate characteristics allow a margin of tax deferral on your personal income taxes, and sometimes an out-and-out tax savings. By keeping income in your corporation, you defer paying personal income tax on it until you take that money into your personal income. Being able to issue bonuses and dividends means you can push your personal receipt of declared bonuses or dividends into another calendar year and thereby defer income tax on that money for a whole year.

In addition to these advantages, the first $275,000 to $300,000 of active business income earned through what the CRA deems a "Canadian-controlled private corporation" is taxed at very favourable rates. The federal corporate tax rate on the first $300,000 is 13.12 percent, compared with the regular federal corporate tax rate in 2005 of 22.12 percent. Provincial rates vary but are also considerably reduced, though they may not apply to a full $300,000. Generally, your combined federal and provincial tax rate will be around 18 percent on the first $200,000 and 26 percent to 38 percent on income from $200,000 to $300,000 or thereabouts, depending on your province's cut off.

According to Tim Cestnick, it generally makes sense to bring your company's taxable income down to the small-business limit ($275,000 in 2005, and $300,000 after 2005). Active business income up to this limit is taxed at a Canada-wide average of just 18.6 percent.

The capital gains exemption still exists—but only for small business

The biggest tax advantage of incorporation is the alluring $500,000 capital gains exemption, which is allowed on the eventual sale of a "qualified small business corporation." The definition of a qualified small business corporation is very precise because the government wants to make sure it is giving this exemption to real businesses and not just to corporate entities. The definition sets restrictions on share ownership and the use of assets within the corporation. It also makes conditions on the use of assets and the ownership of the shares for two years prior to the sale of the corporation.

According to GlobeAdvisor.com, some corporations may *not* qualify for the small business tax rate. They are:

- Investment holding companies,
- Specified investment businesses (SIBs)
- Personal service businesses (PSBs)

An investment holding company is a company that is set up to hold the owner's investments. A specified investment business is a business established with the sole purpose of earning income from property such as interest, dividends, real estate, etc. Unless such a business has greater than five full-time employees, it will not qualify for the small business rate. A personal service business is a service organization in which the owner would likely be regarded as an employee if not for the existence of the corporation designation.

The full $500,000 will not be available to you if you have a cumulative net investment loss account (CNIL). Broadly speaking, investment costs such as investment loan interest, rental property losses and tax shelter write-offs that exceed your investment income can be deducted from your income. These net expenses must be paid back before you can access your capital gains exemption.

The top ten "most queried" list (according to the CRA)

Having shown you some of the many tax breaks available to you, if you're willing to do your homework and look closely at the Tax Act, I want to express the following caveat. The CRA looks closely at certain items on your return, and expense deductions rank right up there. Tim Cestnick compiled the following from an informal poll of tax specialists at his former accounting firm, Deloitte. He says the top ten most often questioned items by the Canada Revenue Agency for 2004 were:

1) **Capital gains and losses.** The CRA often asks for details supporting the calculation of your capital gains and losses. Pay particular attention to your adjusted cost base (ACB). Is it correct? For example, income trusts often distribute returns of capital, which should reduce your ACB.

2) **Allowable business investment losses.** According to Deloitte, this one is automatic. Losses on the shares of, or loans to, small business corporations will trigger a form letter from the CRA asking for more details. Make sure you have supporting information handy.

3) **Carrying charges.** Expenses incurred to earn investment income such as interest and investment counsel fees may be deductible. But keep supporting documentation available. Be aware that the CRA is stepping up its look at interest expenses to ensure you truly have an expectation of profit from your investments.

4) **Foreign tax credits.** Many Canadians claim foreign tax credits for taxes paid on foreign investment or employment income. The CRA has become much more active in the past year in questioning entitlement to claim these credits.

5) **Province of residence.** This was never an issue in the past, but the provinces have stepped up their questioning in this area. Increased interprovincial tax planning at the personal, trust or corporate levels has led some provinces to try to protect their revenue base.

6) **Charitable donations.** The donation tax credit has become the new tax shelter for many promoters. It's no surprise, then, that the CRA looks closely at donations other than cash, and cash donations over $25,000. The CRA wants to weed out abusive donation schemes.

7) **Employment expenses.** Most employees are not eligible to claim employment expenses. So, the CRA is taking a close look when employment expenses are claimed. Be sure you have supporting documentation such as a signed T2200 form and receipts.

8) **Child care expenses.** Knowingly or not, parents often claim expenses that don't qualify. The principal purpose of the expenses must be child care. So, athletic coaching, music lessons and tutoring don't normally qualify. The key is to ensure you understand what qualifies, and only claim those amounts.

9) **Mining, oil and gas expenses.** It's not uncommon for these items to be reported incorrectly for tax purposes. And so the CRA will often ask for information related to flow-through shares and similar investments.

10) **Tuition and education expenses.** The CRA often requests more information as to tuition and education amounts. Be sure your child has the T2202A form to support the amounts claimed. Also, make sure the amounts are claimed on your child's return first if he or she has sufficient income.

TAX-SAVING STRATEGY #10: EMPLOY A LITTLE COMIC RELIEF

Death and taxes. Which is worse? It's a close call, but I think we all know the answer. Taxes, like death, are an essential part of life. While it isn't a good idea to make fun of death, there's nothing wrong with poking fun at the writers of the Tax Act, and their long-winded explanations of basic concepts like income (see the quote from the Act at the front of this chapter).

Taxes are hard work, even for the experts. That's why I think a little comic relief is helpful, especially if you want to get the most out of your hardworking accountant. And by the way, even if *you* don't appreciate accounting humour, I'm pretty sure he or she will, especially at tax time. So without further ado, here is a Canadianized version of David Letterman's Top Ten (Dumb) Tax Tips:

Letterman's Top Ten (Dumb) Tax Tips (*Canadianized version*)

10. Send tax return to NRA instead of CRA, since NRA never pays taxes.
9. Answer every question with: "Wouldn't *you* like to know?"
8. Hide all money in mattress; on return write "No money hidden in mattress."
7. If you've just eaten, don't do taxes for at least half an hour.
6. Hire yourself as an employee, fire yourself, sue yourself for discrimination, deduct court costs.
5. Report $1 billion income so CRA will think you're some sort of big shot.

4. For "charitable contributions," list $9 you spent on last
   Kevin Costner movie.
3. Fill out the Simplified Return because it only has two lines.
2. Find out those two lines are: 1) "How much money did you
   make?" and 2) "Send it to us."
1. List your imaginary friend as a dependent.
Source: CBS.COM © MMV, CBS Broadcasting Inc.

There. Don't you feel better already? If you aren't laughing just yet, maybe this *CA Magazine* article via Ernst & Young will help get you going. It's all about those wacky sales taxes (the dreaded GST and PST):

1. In Ontario, the rental of a boat is taxable. If the boat is rented with an operator, it is not taxable. If it's rented with a guide, it is taxable. If the boat is rented with a guide who is also the operator, it is not taxable.

2. In Ontario, a vehicle emissions test is not taxable if the vehicle passes the test. If, however, the vehicle fails the test and repairs are made to bring it in line with the appropriate emissions standards, the emission test is taxable.

3. While GST legislation zero-rates (taxes at 0 percent) many goods and services, "ice lollies" are specifically excluded.

4. GST applies to a flight to Saint Pierre and Miquelon or Alaska, but not a flight to Hawaii.

5. GST applies to juice drinks with less than 25 percent juice. If the drink has more than 25 percent juice, GST applies only if the drink is less than 600 mL.

6. GST on deli-counter items depends on whether they are sold hot or cold. If they are served cold to be reheated by the customer, they are zero-rated. If they are sold warm, GST must be collected on their sale.

7. Railway men's watches continue to be exempt from the federal excise tax on watches.

8. You do not pay Ontario retail sales tax on a cup of coffee from a coffee shop. If you buy a pop at the café it is taxable; but if you buy a sandwich with a pop and it costs less than $4, it's not taxable.

9. GST applies to snack items such as muffins or doughnuts, but not if you purchase a half-dozen or more at a time.

10. Boxes of breakfast cereal that contain a premium or bonus item are not subject to Ontario retail sales tax, provided the item is not liquor, wine or beer.

Are you feeling better? I know I am. We've discussed a lot of tax issues in this chapter because it's important to save as much money as you can. So rather than foregoing your latte or pint of beer at the corner pub, why not forego paying unnecessary tax money to the taxman?

We've seen many of the ways you can *grow* your money, *protect* your money and *shelter* your money from tax. Let's enter a new arena, a place where you still have ways to grow, protect and shelter your savings and investments. It's time to leave the tax arena and enter a whole new world — an emotional, often fragile place where all is new again, where questions are raised and many questions are answered: your *transition* into retirement.

CHAPTER
EIGHT

"I had a good day yesterday, worked on aboriginal rights,
and it seemed like a good day to have a last day.... I had a good day.
It was a great walk in the snow. I went to judo, felt very
combative, and here I am."
—PIERRE ELLIOTT TRUDEAU ANNOUNCING HIS
RETIREMENT, MARCH 12, 1984.

TRANSITION
MOVE SEAMLESSLY INTO RETIREMENT

It's daylight, but your bedroom is quiet. Neither the alarm clock nor your spouse has stirred, the neighbour's dogs aren't howling for their morning constitutional and the paper boy has yet to fire his little bomb at your door.

You bounce out of bed and head for the den as the scent from the lilac tree floats in through the half-open window.

You log on and check your office e-mails, just like you have at the beginning of every working day for as long as you can remember. It's what you do, even before you brush your teeth or take a shower or make coffee.

But this time your colleagues haven't sent you any early morning messages. This time there's not a whiff of gossip from Leslie or anyone else about last night's client party. Even Frank's regular-as-clockwork early morning joke has disappeared into the ether.

You sigh with disappointment, but only for a moment. It's time to get ready for the day. But wait a moment. What day *is* it? It must be Saturday...yeah...that explains it. You scroll over your computer clock and stare in amazement: *Friday*, May 25, 6:53 a.m.

Friday!?

You wipe the sleep from your eyes and shake your head; and then the realization hits you like a brick to the solar plexus.

And as you stand there absorbing the blow, the morning paper *slams* against the front door like a cannonball and you start to shake like a child in your pajamas even though you're 54 years old.

Because you know.

196 LIVE WELL, RETIRE WELL

Once, and for all time, you know.
You...are...*RETIRED.*

RELAX. YOU'RE NOT ALONE.

The above is exactly what my friend Winston went through today. How do I know? Because when I phoned him to congratulate him on his new-found freedom, he told me. Winston is definitely type A. Always busy, always restless, always on the go. His middle management job had defined his life in more ways than he might ever admit. But then Winston was "given" early retirement, and today and the next several todays are going to be a whopper of a transition for him — and for others like him.

How you handle the transition period goes a long way to determining how you handle the rest of your retirement. But you know what? How you lived your life *before* your transition has an equally important bearing. Some people are always onto new things, filling their lives with new experiences. I'm convinced many of these people are born with the innate ability to multi-task. And this ability pays off in spades when you retire. Simone can tell you directly.

A LIFE WELL-LIVED

Simone Marciano has always been a positive person. Maybe that's why volunteering has always been in her blood. When she was 8 years old, she'd make the rounds with her aunt who volunteered at a local hospital. One day, when she was thinking about stopping, her aunt told her, "Hey, they like you being here." And Simone was hooked from that day forward.

Today, in her 70s, she's created a unique lifestyle for herself. A mother of three and a grandmother of six, her life is filled with people, activities and worthwhile accomplishments. This is her story:

> When I was married with small children, we moved from
> England to Nigeria. My husband was an engineer and had a very
> rewarding job. Money was never a big motivator for me, but
> being active was. Even in those days, after I took the kids to
> school, I did things like manage an architect's office and worked
> for a minister. Then, when we went back to England, I started a
> clothing business which catered to high-end clientele. Though

the money was very good, I decided to sell the business to pursue other interests.

I volunteered to help patients at an orthopaedic hospital and I guess they liked the work I was doing because they offered me a paid job within six months. I found myself working with a patient one day, a young man whose head injury had left him literally speechless. His condition really had an impact on me because I decided to learn all I could about speech pathology. One thing led to another and I ended up volunteering at the Stroke Centre.

We travelled again, and I arrived in Canada twenty-five years ago. To get out of the funk that uprooting (yet again) had put me in, I decided to help out at the Speech and Stroke Centre in Toronto. It was run by a marvellous woman named Pat Arato, who would go on to win the Order of Ontario and the Order of Canada for her speech therapy work.

For the last twenty years of my "non-retired" life, I worked in occupational and speech therapy at Riverdale Hospital. I loved it. But then I was notified that I would be given mandatory retirement the following year, at age 70. I'd never thought about retirement. Ever. So now I began a big soul-searching period. I knew I wanted to see my family more, although none of them lived anywhere near Toronto. But making big trips to England and Quebec City and Colorado wasn't going to be enough for me. I needed some kind of a weekly routine.

I HAVEN'T DISCOVERED WHAT BOREDOM IS, AND I HOPE I NEVER WILL

I sat down and made a list of the things I was interested in doing. When I was finished, I decided I'd try to do all of them. It wasn't going to be that easy because I didn't have a lot of money now. But here are the things on my list that I do and will continue to do:

1) travel (to visit family)
2) music (concerts and instruction)
3) theatre classes
4) exercise/fitness
5) writing classes
6) book club

7) continuing education

8) volunteer work

It's funny how life goes. It's never predictable, thank God. Otherwise I'd be bored to the heavens. To help me in the transition to retirement, the world of music magically came calling. My passion for music and people somehow connected me with the Toronto Symphony Volunteer Committee. Today, I get involved in fundraising and also get to assist some wonderful musicians with special programmes. The Adopt a Player program is a great example. TSO musicians go to local schools and inspire children to create their own music with whatever musical instruments are available at the school. Another big thrill for me was to discover, for the first time in my life, that I had pretty good organization skills. This has really come in handy because I now chair committees, write agendas, make projections and do all kinds of things I never even knew about when I was younger.

FINANCES? MY RRIF TAKES CARE OF ME

My life isn't all volunteer work, though. I have a wide circle of friends and study meditation, Tai Chi and Qi Gong. I really couldn't be happier. As far as my finances go, money is not a motivator for me, but money is very important in retirement. I know you need a plan, so I hired a financial advisor many years ago. I have a very small pension, plus CPP and OAS, my RRSPs which are now collapsed, and an inheritance from my mother. My advisor put everything he could into a RIFF, with a percentage in medium and higher risk securities, and a percentage in low-risk securities. I live off the interest income.

I honestly don't know the exact size of my nest egg, but it's a few hundred thousand dollars. I haven't touched the principal and I don't want to if at all possible, but you never know. I'm a cancer survivor, so if that happens — and I hope it never does!— I want to make sure I have enough money for a full-time nurse to look after me. That's about the extent of my money worries. I have no other real worries; the transition to retirement has been good so far. I haven't discovered what boredom is, and I hope I never will.

RETIREMENT IS ABOUT MUCH MORE THAN MONEY

Simone is a shining example of why you don't need money to be happy. But as my friend Winston's reaction showed, when you make the transition into retirement, the biggest issues you're likely to face are emotional. For many, transition is freedom and a chance to explore and awaken the spirit. For others, transition is about watching your identity slip away; it's about finding a new identity to replace the one you lost or think you're losing.

If my recent conversations with Canadians are anything to go by, more men than women are suffering and will suffer from the "retirement blues." It may have to do with self-image differences. Health experts say men tend to be far more concerned with being competitive, powerful and successful. The single-mindedness that can be so useful in a job can be a detriment after work has ended. Women, on the other hand, are more used to multi-tasking and are less likely to define themselves by their jobs, whether they are mothers and homemakers or career women. For some men, retirement may be seen as a "step down" in life, but I know my friend Winston isn't one of them. He'll do just fine because he's a positive, active and adaptable person. He also has one other advantage: the support of a loving family and friends.

PICTURE TRANSITION AS AN OPPORTUNITY

Personal coach and motivational speaker Gary Billings says, "the transition from first adulthood to second adulthood is something akin to moving from infancy to adolescence." But I think there's a big difference. Unlike most adolescents, we have the experience and ability to actively *prepare* for our transition. If you picture your retirement as an opportunity for growth, wisdom, knowledge and discovery, it will become so. But you must visualize it in your mind's eye, and do so *in complete detail*, for it to imprint itself as a reality. If you have trouble picturing your retirement, why not revisit Chapter 3 and follow the mental imagery process outlined there.

BLOCK OUT YOUR LITTLE VOICE

As I also discussed in Chapter 3, almost every one of us has some kind of an inner voice that pre-judges the actions we are about to take, whether they involve our relationships, careers, sports, finances or any aspect of our lives. It's a waste of time trying to eliminate the little voice inside us, because it will never entirely go away. To be successful, we need to find ways to minimize its impact. The best way to do that is to recognize and acknowledge its presence when we hear it, and then block it out. Again, if you have doubts about your ability to be as positive as you can about the changes you're going to make, why not revisit Chapter 3 and follow the process outlined there.

THE TRANSITION CHALLENGE

If you're a hard-driving person who doesn't have a retirement plan, transition can be hard. It's tough to turn off the spigot when retirement hits the shut-off valve. According to the Financial Planning Association, the people most likely to have difficulty with transition are those with:

- A single-minded commitment to, or identification with, their work
- Limited interests beyond their careers
- Social lives that are closely integrated with their working lives
- Challenging, high-visibility jobs
- Feelings of incompleteness because career goals have not been met
- Inadequate financial security
- Few friends
- Incomplete relationships at home
- No established retirement goals or expectations
- Retirement forced on them before they are mentally prepared

DEVELOPING YOUR TRANSITION OPTIONS

The last two points in the list above are the most critical. Why? Because they're the ones over which we have the most control. If you haven't established any retirement goals or expectations, it's a problem you can fix. And if retirement is forced on you before you are mentally prepared, that, too, is an issue which you can also address in advance.

No one ever said change is easy. But change can be the most enjoyable and exhilarating experience in one's life — if approached the right way. Creating a transition plan involves being strong, facing reality head on and learning how to assess your retirement options as objectively as possible. The key to success in life — and retirement — is to invest in yourself and those who are close to you. You've probably done that unconsciously all your life, so why stop now? You know, there are quite a few options when you transition into retirement. Here are my top eight.

Strategy #1: Keep your options open

A phased-in retirement program works well for many people. Negotiation with your current employer is key and can involve using your current skills to continue to work full-time, part-time or on contract.

Strategy #2: Reinvent yourself

How about that long-awaited career shift? Now's the time. You can work in another capacity for your current employer or another employer through full-time, temporary or freelance work.

Strategy #3: Help those in need

The opportunity to perform full-time or part-time volunteer work has never been greater, especially now as the Boomer generation enters their retirement years. As long as you remain healthy and energetic, the possibilities are endless.

Strategy #4: Take the plunge

Providing you have a reasonably sized nest egg, why not start a business using the skills you've picked up over a lifetime of hard work? You'd be surprised at what a skills assessment test might reveal.

Strategy #5: Open your mind

The beginning of your retirement period is the perfect time to throw yourself into continuing education courses or make extensive travel plans. Either one will open your mind to an infinite number of possibilities; opportunities that you probably never even considered when you were working full-time.

Strategy #6: Live it up!

Begin or continue a full and active social life with family and friends. A caveat: be prepared for your family to rely on you much more and see you in a different light. Now that you're retired you're supposedly available morning noon and night. But if you don't want to become a sacrificial lamb, it's your job — not anyone else's — to keep them abreast of your *own* plans, needs and desires.

There's nothing wrong with indulging in or catching up on all the hobbies or sports or pastimes you never had time for before. Whether it's golf or tennis or curling or fly fishing or the book club or bridge or any of dozens of other activities, now's the time to do it. Enjoy.

Strategy #7: Delay Retirement

If money issues are clouding your retirement picture, you may want to consider delaying your retirement by a few years. Below is an illustrative chart showing how much your retirement fund can grow if you postpone in increments of two years or more. The example given is based on $100,000 invested at age 40, with $6,000 saved per year. Your individual situation will of course vary.

DELAYING RETIREMENT

$100,000 invested at age 40; $6,000 saved per year;
7% annual return, compounded quarterly
Source: TD Canada Trust

Strategy #8: Give up

Yes. You can always get depressed and do nothing. Yecchh! I included this option because it *is* an option. My guess is, if you're reading this book it's not an option you intend to take up. But it's sure a good way to make yourself and those around you completely miserable. Just remember, having or developing a positive attitude is the critical first step to achieving peace of mind and retirement success.

Now let's take a look at the *financial* aspects of transition, because twenty or thirty years or more is a long time to try to live without an adequate and predictable income. A mid-50s professional couple I know is about to leap into the great mystery known as retirement, but they aren't worried. They've been planning their leap for years. Here is their story.

JOHN AND MARIANNE: SLOW AND STEADY WINS THE RACE

The couple that invests together stays together. John and Marianne Wilkins wouldn't have it any other way. Although only in their mid-50s, they're transitioning into full retirement mode in just a few more months. Actually, John has been slowing down ever since he had a bypass back in 2001 and was advised by his doctor to get out of high-stress matrimonial work. John is a matrimonial, wills and estate lawyer (sole practitioner) and his wife Marianne is an accountant. Through hard work and a frugal lifestyle they've managed to accumulate nearly $2 million for retirement. And their nest egg continues to compound at a very healthy rate.

The Wilkins built their retirement fund the old fashioned way: through RRSPs, asset allocation, portfolio diversification and by eliminating debt. Their story is a shining confirmation of the power and leverage of tried and true investment techniques. In that sense, they are the polar opposite of Robert Edgewood, the coupon clipper who became a multi-millionaire. Remember his story in Chapter 4? Unlike Robert, the Wilkins haven't the inclination to mount a highly concentrated attack on one sector of the market. Even in retirement, they'll remain "investment worriers" with a low tolerance for risk.

Here's how their investment story unfolded. Shortly after John and Marianne married in 1990, Marianne agreed to leave her accounting job and help John directly with his legal practice. She was paid a good, income-splitting salary, "but we both worked long hours, six days a week under high pressure, and had few if any holidays," says Marianne. For the next ten years (until 2001) they worked so hard they hardly had time to spend any of the money they were making.

But the pressure was mounting on John — the emotionally draining matrimonial side of his practice was taking its toll. Then came the heart bypass, followed by his doctor's dire warning to take time off. Instead of doing that, however, they decided to meet with their investment advisor and asked him a simple but very important question.

"Do we have enough money to take early retirement?"

The answer was yes. The Wilkins decided to set some financial goals. They started the process by selling their house in a desirable part of Toronto called the Beaches, and kept Marianne's house, which was situated in a nice Mississauga neighbourhood. For a long time, they had been investing in money market instruments which had minimal after-tax and after-inflation returns. So they enrolled in an investment course and began to invest in stocks and bonds. Their goal was to have around $50,000 a year in retirement income.

They were lucky to start investing *after* the 2001 market correction, and by the beginning of 2005 had begun investing heavily (three hours a day). The split on their retirement portfolio gradually became more aggressive and now stands at 30 percent to 40 percent bonds and 60 percent to 70 percent equities. They're expecting a return of 5 percent on the fixed-income side and hoping for 8 percent to 12 percent on their equity positions.

In addition, they maxed out their RRSP contributions every year, and always did so one year in advance. They now have a combined $700,000 in tax-deferred RRSPs, and about $1.1 million in their taxable account. To make sure that spending half of every day investing didn't become a chore, the Wilkins have split their taxable account into two.

The "Retirement Account" (about $700K) is with their full-service broker, while their "Speculation Account" (the remaining $400K) is all their own. John enters "stop loss" orders on all their holdings in this account, and the investing decisions are all joint ones. The instigator of a particularly successful investment strategy will happily lay claim to "bragging rights" for the day, but that's about the only competition they get into. Theirs is a true investment partnership, and they want to keep it that way.

"It doesn't yet feel real"

Although they're still in the transition period, retirement is barely two months away. Marianne says they've established three key retirement goals: regular exercise at the fitness club; investing, of course; and gourmet cooking. More frequent socializing with long-lost friends and family is a fourth one, says John. But according to Marianne, the process of retiring "just doesn't feel real yet." She wants to keep busy and worries about the temptation to let things slip.

John laughs and says there's no worry on that score, she's never had a lazy day in her life. Marianne agrees, and says: "I'm going to do some volunteer work at the hospital, but I have to tell you, since we've slowed down workwise, John has found out that I *can* relax." John adds, "I'm glad we're retiring early because, for one thing, I didn't want to be sixty-something and trying to learn new hobbies." They laugh, because they know they're both worriers.

"What will happen to our investments if oil prices go through the roof?"

Fortunately, there are other sources of retirement income. John has negotiated a deal to get recurring income from the law office that is taking over his client base. But they worry about their investments, despite their success. Not everything has gone according to plan — a few years ago they invested in Nortel and WorldCom — and now they fear that market volatility will increase as more and more Boomers begin to invest in stocks. John also worries about what will happen to their investments if oil prices go through the roof.

Nevertheless, their investment strategy has paid off in spades, and they are big believers in diversification. John uses sophisticated stock-screening software to track and isolate new investment opportunities. "My research shows that a combination of technical and value investing can produce 2 percent to 3 percent higher returns. When you compound that difference over a long time horizon, the extra investment dollars can be substantial."

The Wilkins are an investment success, perhaps because they're masters at climbing the proverbial "wall of worry" that most experts say bull markets are made of. Or perhaps it's because they do really their homework. John and Marianne laugh and politely disagree. "We're a team, and we've always believed two worrywarts are better than one."

Nearly half of Canadians find life better after retirement

Almost half of Canadian retirees surveyed by Statistics Canada say life is better after retirement—and those who planned for it by developing hobbies and participating in various activities were most likely to find retirement enjoyable. The study questioned more than 4,000 recent retirees, and found 47 percent

206 LIVE WELL, RETIRE WELL

enjoyed life more after retirement than when they were working. Forty-one percent said they took the same pleasure in life before and after retirement, while only 12 percent reported they enjoyed life less after working.

Source: Lorrayne Anthony, Canadian Press.

WHEN I'M 69

Studies have shown that people are generally less stressed, exercise more and have higher degrees of life satisfaction when they retire. That's especially the case if you are healthy and have some financial flexibility. But there's one instance where we have very little flexibility at all.

Did you know your RRSP actually turns into a pumpkin when you turn 69? Okay, it's not Halloween yet, but be careful! By law, in the year you turn 69, your RRSP must be squashed like an old pumpkin that's past its due date. Officially, you must "collapse" your RRSP. The following deals with the conversion of RRSPs to RRIFs and annuities, so if you're well versed in these conversion rules, you can certainly skip this section.

When we turn 69, our financial life changes dramatically. The government figures that's the year you should start getting a retirement income stream, and what better way than to use the tax-deferred money you accumulated during your working years. To make sure you go from nest egg accumulation mode to nest egg payout mode, you must not only collapse your RRSP, you must arrange to take minimum annual payouts as retirement income. The good news is, the retirement income options offered by the government should provide you with RRSP-like tax-deferred growth.

Several hundred thousand Canadians who are turning 69 at or before December 31st each year must do one of three things: 1) convert their RRSPs to a RRIF; 2) convert them to an annuity; or 3) take a partial or full lump sum withdrawal. There are really only two financially sound choices: RRIFs and annuities. Taking a lump sum is to be avoided because you'll instantly incur and have to pay tax on the *entire* amount you take out.

CHOICE #1: CONVERT TO A RRIF

Converting your RRSP into a registered retirement income fund (RRIF) has become the most popular choice in recent years. A RRIF pays income for as long as you choose, and gives you the flexibility to determine the amount of income you withdraw each year from your retirement savings. A RRIF gives you pretty well all the benefits of an RRSP except one. You get the same tax-deferral as an RRSP, it can hold the same investments, and any money remaining after death can go to your estate. But — and it is a big BUT — instead of contributions each year, RRIFs require you to make minimum annual withdrawals.

The minimum annual amounts are set by the CRA. At age 71, for example, you must withdraw 7.38 percent of the total funds remaining in the plan, and it increases periodically so that by age 91, it is 14.73 percent, and by age 94, you have to withdraw 20 percent of your remaining RRIF funds. During your retirement, you can increase your income stream any time you choose, or decrease it later, as long as the payouts stay above the mandated minimum. And remember, you pay tax on all the money you withdraw from your plan each year, not just the income portion.

CHOICE #2: CONVERT TO AN ANNUITY

Annuities are structured and sold by insurance companies to pay out a steady stream of income to you. You can choose a "term certain annuity," which pays income up to age 90. Or you can opt for a "life annuity," which pays income for as long as you choose. In essence, this option means you hand over your retirement savings to a life insurance company and in return you get a guaranteed monthly income for life. As with RRIFs, the full amount of each annuity payment is taxed.

If you prefer maintenance-free, guaranteed income, annuities fit the bill. They provide a consistent stream of income without the need to continue making investment decisions. The downside is lack of flexibility, especially compared to RRIFs. You are locked in if you buy an annuity; they are pegged to current interest rates at the time you purchase them; you have no control over how your money is invested; you cannot change your mind about this investment at a later date; and when you die your estate gets nothing — the funds remain with the insurance company.

CHOICE #3: AN ANNUITY *AND* AN RRIF

Depending on your cash and income needs when you turn 69, you may decide it's best to take some of your RRSP money as cash, put some in an annuity and put some in a RRIF. Whatever choice you ultimately make, please don't discount its importance or complexity. Converting your RRSP is a major financial planning decision, and as such it requires in-depth consultation with a qualified advisor.

PROTECTING YOUR REGISTERED RETIREMENT SAVINGS

Meet Julie and Trevor Lee, ages 57 and 59, respectively. They have grown children, they have accumulated $600,000 in RRSPs, and each plans to contribute the maximum until age 69. Upon death, they could be assessed for over $300,000 in income taxes! When the Lees begin to convert their RRSP savings to RRIF income, they plan to take only the minimum income required. As most of their other assets are in property and equity, they do not have another source of cash to pay off the taxes payable on the income from their retirement savings. Once the Lees convert to RRIFs, the minimum income withdrawn is subject to tax. The Lees' goal is to maximize the value of the assets that they pass on to their children, rather than have taxes take away their hard-earned savings.

Their TD Waterhouse advisor recommended the RRSP Principal Protector. The RRSP Principal Protector is a life insurance solution, consisting of a universal life policy that provides a tax-free payout at death.

The Lees' maximum RRSP balance was projected, and the future tax payment was estimated at approximately $850,000 by the time the RRSPs must be converted to RRIFs. To offset that tax bill, an RRSP Principal Protector with a death benefit of $900,000 would be payable when the surviving spouse passes away.

The Lees could buy this protection with ten annual deposits of $12,500. The $12,500 is based on an investment return of 7 percent within the RRSP Principal Protector. The deposit amount and duration would vary with the actual investment performance.

Under these projections, the RRSP Principal Protector outperformed other investment alternatives at any and every age the Lees could live to, and would provide substantially more after-tax funds to their children. This solution is best suited to retirees approaching retirement age.

WHAT HAPPENS IF I HAVE PENSION PROCEEDS?

Under pension laws, after a period of time (usually between two and five years after joining the plan), all money in a pension plan becomes fully vested in the employee. This means that you have an unconditional entitlement to the money as and when any age or service requirements are met.

If you were a member of a registered pension plan (RPP), and your employment was terminated (and assuming your plan was fully vested), the proceeds of that RPP would be considered "locked-in." These locked-in funds can *only* be transferred into certain locked-in retirement plans. Retirement income options are also available, but they are complex and outside the scope of this guide. I strongly suggest you consult your financial advisor about the conversion and income options available.

INCOME INTEGRATION: A MONEY-SAVER FOR YOUR RETIREMENT

"What's the best way to withdraw income during my retirement?" It's a question I hear a lot from retirees. If you're like many, you're likely receiving income from a variety of sources including RRIFs, pensions, taxable investments and spousal plans. To minimize the tax you'll have to pay on all these streams of income, it's important to develop some kind of an income integration strategy. If you want to minimize tax, you have to ask yourself some basic questions.

Question 1: How much income will I be receiving from all sources?

Talk to your advisor if you aren't sure. But if you know the answer, add all your retirement income sources together as follows:

Income streams:

Add: your expected CPP payments	$ _____
Add: your expected OAS payments	$ _____
Add: your expected GIS payments, if any	$ _____
Add: your expected pension payments, if any	$ _____
Add: your expected RRIF payments, if any	$ _____
Add: your expected annuity payments, if any	$ _____
Add: your expected spousal payments, if any	$ _____
Add: your income from your investments, if any	$ _____
Add: income from rental properties, if any	$ _____
Add: income from part-time or full-time work, if any	$ _____
Add: your income from any other sources	$ _____
Total income from all sources above	$ _____

Question 2: How much income do I need to live on in retirement?

If you can't work out a monthly budget, a rule of thumb is that you'll need two-thirds of your pre-retirement income to live comfortably. But that rule doesn't apply to everyone. You may want to spend less, or the same as before you retired or you may even spend *more* in the first year or two of your retirement because you want to travel extensively or buy a second home.

Question 3: How much of the above income do I need to receive in my hands (right now) to meet my retirement needs?

If you answered, "I need all of it," then an income integration plan won't save you any taxes.

If you answered, "I only need some of it," then you should strongly consider developing an income integration plan.

What kind of plan? The strategy most frequently recommended involves deferring your taxes as long as possible. This allows you to maximize the growth of your investments and maintain your nest egg longer.

DEFER YOUR TAXES THROUGH AN OPTIMAL "DRAWDOWN" SEQUENCE

By selecting the proper *sequence* to draw upon your retirement income streams, you can maximize your current after-tax income and preserve your wealth as long as possible. Deferring taxes not only provides you with the largest nest egg possible, but also maximizes the size of your taxable estate.

The process involves selecting the sources of income that will produce the lowest possible taxable income. How? By withdrawing the income you need *at the lowest possible tax rate*. You should start with your pension income, then work your way up the food chain until you reach your registered assets.

Pension income

The first withdrawals for retirement income are any and all pension incomes such as employer pensions and government pensions including Canada Pension Plan (CPP) and Old Age Security (OAS).

Non-registered (taxable) assets

If your pension incomes do not provide adequate income for you at retirement, the next withdrawals should come from any non-registered assets you own. Why? Because not all the income you withdraw from this source may be taxable. As with any taxable account, part of it is made up of your own after-tax capital. The withdrawal order is based on the following:

- Spousal assets owned by whichever spouse is in the *lowest* tax bracket. The optimal drawdown is based on each spouse's current and future tax brackets. Normally, the assets withdrawn first are those of the spouse that has the lowest marginal tax rate, followed by the higher marginal tax rate spouse's assets.
- Order of the investments/assets: The sequence for non-registered assets is to first withdraw those with the highest cost base relative to market value. In other words, sell those assets that have appreciated the least in value. This reduces the capital gains tax incurred when and if you sell assets to produce income. Also, the lower yielding assets should always be withdrawn before the higher yielding assets. This process defers capital gains for as long as possible.

Registered assets

After taking into account the RRIF minimum withdrawal requirements, if the income available through the above means is still not enough, the next sources of income are your registered assets. For retired couples, the normal order for withdrawing registered asset income is to use the spouse's income with the lower marginal tax rate, followed by the spouse with the higher marginal tax rate.

If there's a tie based on tax rates, the assets are redeemed in order of their total return from lowest to highest. This entire process is used to forecast income and assets over the retiree's lifetime and needs to be updated annually based on your current spending requirements and tax situation.

PRE-RETIREMENT TAX PLANNING

If it's not too late, you should place your investments in the accounts that attract the least amount of taxes before you turn 69, or earlier. You should start with your asset allocation for your entire investment portfolio. Once you have your desired breakdown, try to hold the majority of your fixed income component in your registered accounts. Fixed-income type of investments such as bonds or GICs should be placed in RRSP or RRIF accounts, and the investments that generate the most tax-effective gains such as equities or equity mutual funds should be placed in non-registered accounts. Revisit Chapter 7 if you need a reminder of how dividends, capital gains and interest income are taxed.

A similar type of tax savings can also be accomplished in non-RRSP accounts by having the spouse with the lower marginal tax rate own the interest income investments, and the higher income spouse owning the equities/equity mutual funds that generate tax-preferred income such as capital gains.

A key to effective retirement income planning is monitoring and tweaking your plans as circumstances change. Each year your income integration plan should be reviewed and updated to reflect your current goals and objectives

"I HEARD THE NEWS TODAY, OH BOY!"

Today, everyone seems to have a different idea of retirement, and yet no one really knows how they'll handle being retired. Whether you're planning to retire at 50, 65 or 80, there's going to be an adjustment period. It may be small or it may be large, depending on your work personality, your employment situation and your attitude. And now, more and more employers are jumping on the bandwagon by offering diverse and creative options to its retirement-age workforce. IBM, for example, is encouraging its *current* employees to become teachers.

Just recently, IBM announced this fascinating new transition strategy, which is aimed mainly, but not entirely, at upcoming retirees. Selected employees would be encouraged to transition into a new career — as math and science teachers. The reasons for this are many. But a prime one is that many technology companies worry about America's future. U.S. students are falling behind the rest of the world — especially Asia — in the sciences. "Over a quarter-million math and science teachers are needed, and it's hard to tell where the pipeline is," said Stanley Litow, head of the IBM Foundation, the Armonk, New York–based company's community service wing. "That is like a ticking time bomb, not just for technology companies, but for business and the U.S. economy."

IBM will give plenty of financial support to employees who want to leave the company to become teachers. They will be allowed to take a leave of absence and get full benefits plus up to half their salary, depending on length of service. And they could get up to $15,000 (U.S.) in tuition reimbursements and stipends while they seek teaching credentials and begin student-teaching. Now that's an innovative way to transition into retirement!

A brush with history: Stephen Leacock fights "compulsory" retirement

On May 31, 1936, because of compulsory retirement at the age of 65, Stephen Leacock was forced to retire from teaching at McGill University. Not ready for retirement, he put up a fight, but the board of governors would not budge on their decision. Despite his forced retirement, other universities were more than willing to hire him, but he decided to concentrate on his literary career. The years following his retirement were his busiest yet. He proceeded to write and publish *My Discovery of the West: A Discussion of East and West in Canada*, for which he won the Governor General's Award. Later he wrote *Canada: The Foundations of Its Future* (1941), *Montreal: Seaport and City* (1942) and *Canada and the Sea* (1944).

Source: Library and Archives Canada.

TRADING PLACES: SUSAN AND HER WHIZ KIDS

"It's not about the money, it's about the broiler."

Susan made me laugh as she began to tell me an outrageous *Desperate Housewives* type of story. Just recently, she had to console a serially married male acquaintance of hers, just divorced for the third time. He was upset, but not about all the money he'd just forked over to his latest ex. As it turns out, the cause of his distress was the stainless steel broiler she took with her. Susan laughed and said, "Whoever said money can't buy happiness never owned a broiler."

Susan is full of life, smart as a whip and energetic as all get out. Single and just turned 65, she lives in a beautiful condominium in the heart of downtown Vancouver. Self-employed (part-time now), she's also does a lot of volunteer work and sits on three different boards. Through good planning and with the full support and agreement of her kids, she's created a unique way to enjoy a worry-free retirement. Here's her story.

I've no intention of retiring. I'm not interested in sitting home and doing nothing. Life's too good. And I need structure. I have two grown kids, both successful, one married and one single. Way back when they were teenagers ready to go to college, I made them a deal. I gave each of them $30,000 to cover their college expenses, along with the proviso that if I ever needed money, I could call it back in small amounts. Gifting, I think it's called. They agreed. I also told them if I never need the money, I won't ask for it back. My kids set up and funded a personal account so that if I ever did need it, at least some of the money would be there.

All in the family

My main goal in doing this was to make them financially responsible at an early age. I told them to set up RRSPs and now, in their 30s, they each have about $35,000 to $40,000 saved in their RRSP accounts. I've done okay myself, with assets and a portfolio totalling about $350,000. I've worked with my accountant and my broker to establish a portfolio mix I can live with. Right now it's 50 percent equities, 20 percent fixed income and 30 percent short-term notes and cash (that's in case I want to quickly purchase certain stocks at an attractive entry point). I have a $150,000 mortgage on the condo which works out to about $900 a month.

She knows she won't be able to afford the condo when she retires

I won't be able to afford that in a few years when I retire and have to rely on a RRIF or annuity when I turn 69. So the plan is this: one of my kids will take over the mortgage for me, and structure it so that taxes are minimized through some kind of an income-splitting strategy. How, I don't yet know, but my son-in-law is a tax accountant and he's confident a deal can be structured. My kids and I are also looking at buying a place together in the south of France. We love visiting there, so it makes sense to buy property. I guess you could say it's all in the family when it comes to my finances. One of the great things about being in transition is that I have the time — and the money — to travel. I'm really looking forward to visiting the Balkans this summer — it's one of two major trips I plan this year.

Life is good for Susan, but she and others like her have earned it. Susan helped her family earlier and now they're returning the favour. By making a real impact on the people she meets, men and women like Susan are changing the way our youth-oriented society looks at the older generation — a new generation, the non-retired retirees.

Top employers of mature workers

Winners of the 2005 annual Best Employers for 50-Plus Canadian Awards, sponsored by Canadian Association of Retired Persons (CARP):

- Carrier Trucks Centers Inc., Brantford, Ontario
- Catholic Children's Aid Society, Toronto, Ontario
- City of Calgary, Alberta
- Direct Energy, Toronto, Ontario
- Excell Services, Penticton, British Columbia
- Flexo Products, Niagara Falls, Ontario
- Home Instead, Toronto, Ontario
- Merck Frosst, Montréal, Québec
- Orkin/PCO Services Corporation, Mississauga, Ontario
- Seven Oaks General Hospital, Winnipeg, Manitoba
- Toronto Auto Auctions, Milton, Ontario

Source: CARP (Canadian Association of Retired Persons)

WHAT TO DO WITH YOUR HOUSE

Financial planners disagree on what to do with your house at retirement. Some feel the recent gain in home equity is greater than what people could save in a lifetime. So it should count as part of your nest egg. "It really is an asset, and it is part of savings," they say. Others think it's a really bad idea to factor your home in as part of your net worth — you're always going to need a place to live.

In *Fortune* magazine's *2005 Retirement Guide*, a number of experts were gathered together for a wide-ranging roundtable interview. Financial planner Harold Evensky had this to say about the role of the house in retirees financial plans: "Since most investors don't want to plan on having to sell their homes and live on the street in order to buy groceries, we generally do a financial plan without including a couple's primary residence."

Cash-strapped retirees can potentially use a reverse mortgage to tap some of the equity in their home. Some planners wonder why retirees should have to substantially lower their standard of living by holding onto a large, fully paid-up home, just to hand it off to heirs who have good sized houses already.

CARP OFFERS A DETAILED OPINION ON DOWNSIZING

Take a 50-something city-dweller as an example. With children gone, and still ten or more years away from retirement, Mr. X can expect to live another twenty or more years after leaving his job. And with a home that costs, say, $20,000 a year to maintain (mortgage, taxes, utilities, repairs, etc.), he will have to save close to $400,000 just to afford to stay put for that period of time. Even if Mr. X could sock away $10,000 a year in an investment with a return of 10 percent (ask any financial planner, they'll say that's optimistic), it'll take nearly twenty years to reach his $400,000 goal. By then, of course, his hoped-for retirement date will have come and gone, and who knows quite what twists and turns his health — let alone the economy — will have taken in that time.

But if Mr. X had sold and moved to a more affordable neighbourhood, he could have saved a large chunk of that $400,000. Here's how: If he'd sold his existing home at the asking price of $300,000 — and bought a smaller home (maybe a condo) for $180,000, he'd instantly have a sizeable amount of money to invest. The new home's running costs are close to half what they were (now around $13,000). All of a sudden, things are looking rosier for Mr. X's retirement.
Source: *CARP News*, May 1988

That sure puts things in a different light, doesn't it? But as I've said many times, one size does not fit all, especially when it comes to retirees. Do you remember Richard and Colleen, our two academics who fell in love in Chapter 1? You'll recall they purchased land on Martha's Vineyard, only to run out of money to build the house. But unlike those retirees who have chosen to downsize, they found a way to make a *second* home part of their retirement scenario.

They managed to combine some new savings with a second mortgage on their Boston home and began to make their dream a reality. They put the money into a talented young architect's hands and watched him build a strikingly beautiful cedar home amidst the Vineyard's oaks, pines and wildflowers. Today, as Colleen reduces her workload prior to retirement, she'll be able to join him at their special retreat more and more, for both work and play. Each has their own study where they will continue to write papers, organize conferences and perhaps even teach the occasional course. And they'll have plenty of time and energy to enjoy the many pleasures of their island paradise.

CPP reserve fund grows to $87 billion

The CPP reserve fund, which includes investment earnings and CPP contributions not needed to pay current pensions, grew by $5.7 billion to $87 billion during the quarter ending June 30, 2005.

During the past five years the CPP reserve fund has earned a real (inflation-adjusted) rate of return of 4.6 percent, which exceeds the 4.1 percent real rate of return the Chief Actuary of Canada states is required to help sustain the CPP over the long term.

The strategy announced earlier this fiscal year is to further diversify the CPP reserve fund into real return assets, such as real estate and infrastructure.

Since 1999, when the CPP Investment Board began its investment program, the CPP reserve fund has almost doubled to $87 billion, with about 60 percent, or $24.9 billion, of the increase coming from investment gains. The Chief Actuary of Canada estimates the fund will grow [nearly 70 percent] to approximately $147 billion by 2010.

Source: *CARP News*, August 11, 2005.

WHAT LIFESTYLE DO YOU WANT?

A Canadian-based research firm, The Brondesbury Group, has created some interesting and quirky lifestyle categories. Depending on the relative cost of living in your area — expensive like Toronto, or inexpensive like the Maritimes, for example — you would pick the higher or lower end of each of the following ranges.

"Happy homebodies" $22,500–$35,900

This group lives very simply, on a fairly small income. Main costs include personal care, meals and housekeeping. They spend more time reading or watching TV than most and they often go to church-related activities if they want to socialize — which are generally inexpensive.

"Social butterflies" $27,900–$43,500

These people spend half their time with friends, usually at each other's homes to keep entertaining costs down. If they get together for costly activities or expensive restaurant meals, they'll spend more. Even things like transportation can add up.

"Super shoppers" $33,200–$52,400

Shoppers spend about four hours a day in stores and malls, but they usually browse and don't buy, so costs can be low. But they'll still spend a lot more than if they kept their wallets at home. Canadians who retire this way usually need a much higher income.

"Go-getters" $24,000–$36,300

An active group, Go-Getters keep busy with hobbies and interests such as sports and recreational activities, cultural events, and arts and crafts. This can be inexpensive. Going for a good walk is free!

"The community-minded" $31,600–$49,200

Volunteers are out in the community for about six hours on most days. They may assist civic groups, hospitals or schools. This can be very rewarding and doesn't have to cost a lot. Transportation can add up, however, as can social outings with your fellow volunteers.

"Travellers" $$$— depends on travel costs

Travellers come in all shapes and sizes — and so do their incomes. Some may choose a cheap bus trip to a nearby attraction as the way to go. Others sell their homes, take up life on the road, or hit warmer climates like Florida. The sky's the limit — if you have the money to pay for it.

"Worker Bees" $52,900–$73,100

These busy seniors still work regularly. In fact, many put in a full eight-hour day. No wonder their incomes are the highest of any retired group of Canadians. They're still busy building wealth — and loving the challenge.

IT'S TIME TO MOVE ON

Okay. You've transitioned well. What happens now that the transition period is over and you're comfortably ensconced in retirement? Life is good, financially, emotionally and health wise. But there's something missing. You've made your mark in the world, but now perhaps you're thinking of leaving another mark.

Perhaps you're thinking about your heirs, or about making a major charitable contribution, or maybe about setting up a trust of a foundation. Or all the above. If so, it's time to create or update your estate planning strategy. But to keep the taxman at bay, you'll want to create the most tax-efficient strategy possible — not just for your sake, but for your beneficiaries, whoever they may be.

That's what the next chapter is all about.

CHAPTER
NINE

"Harmony and me
We're pretty good company
Looking for an island
In our boat upon the sea"
—ELTON JOHN, "HARMONY"

HARMONY
LEAVING A LEGACY: ESTATE PLANNING

"For harmony is a symphony, and symphony is an agreement"
—PLATO, *SYMPOSIUM*

To me, harmony is the serenely calm feeling that arises when the parts have been gratifyingly arranged into a whole. One of the best ways to achieve harmony in our lives is to leave a legacy. It can be artistic, like the Group of Seven; or political, like Pierre Elliott Trudeau; or intellectual, like Marshall McLuhan; or physical, like Wayne Gretzky; or spiritual, like Mother Teresa. It can even be social, like a local volunteer who is beloved by hundreds of friends.

For most of us, however, the legacy we can best leave behind is financial.

As you get older, you begin to long for some kind of immortality, and leaving a legacy gives you that. It may be possessions or memories. It may include family, work or friends. It may involve contributions as a parent, coach, foundation leader or mentor. It may be writing that book you've always put off. Whatever choice you make, it will define the path you take in the second half of your life.

About ten years ago, in the small town of Corbeil, Ontario, Marie-Louise Meilleur had a party. Hundreds of people showed up. Marie-Louise had reached the ripe old age of 116 when Guinness World Records named her the oldest living person in the world. The guests at her party included the local mayor, who was also the then premier of Ontario, Mike Harris. When she passed away a year later, she left behind a legacy uniquely her own: seventy-five grandchildren, eighty great-grandchildren and fifty-five great-great-grandchildren.

224 LIVE WELL, RETIRE WELL

The older we get, the more pleasure we take in experiencing the little things, like the fragrance of a newly blossomed flower, a beautifully written greeting card, the sounds of children playing in a schoolyard or the melody of a favourite old love song.

We all know about the five senses: sight, hearing, touch, smell and taste. Did you know there are actually more than five? The sense of heat and cold, the sense of pain and pleasure, the sense of balance and the sense of body awareness are distinct and documented phenomena, additional senses that are intertwined with some or all of the five primary ones.

I'd like to add another: the sense of fulfillment. Fulfillment is the feeling of satisfaction that comes from having achieved your desires. Fulfillment gives you a sense of completion. But how do you create a sense of fulfillment? By living your life to its full potential.

FULFILLMENT COMES FROM A LIFE WELL LIVED

People who live full lives usually live fully when they retire. They don't question the meaning of life because they're too busy *living* it. Viktor Frankl's famous book, *Man's Search for Meaning*, chronicles his time incarcerated in a World War II concentration camp. Imprisoned under the most horrific conditions, he needed to find a reason to live so his spirit wouldn't be crushed. He thought through the patterns of his life and came to this realization: Life never ceases to have meaning, even in suffering and death, because the meaning of life is found in every moment of living.

If one of my children asks, "What is the meaning of life?" I answer very simply, "The meaning of life is to live." Nothing more. And nothing less.

YOU CAN'T TAKE IT WITH YOU

Retirement is the time to think about others, because despite all the assets you may have accumulated, all the investment portfolios you may have grown, and all the funds you may have saved for a multitude of rainy days, at some point you're going to have to ask yourself one simple question:

What do I do now?

You can't take it with you, and even if you could, what would you do with it up there? Do you remember the Peggy Lee song, "Is That All

There Is?" There might have been a time when that question rattled around in your mind. But not any more. You've matured. You have a lifetime of accumulated assets. Even if you don't have much, you have your RRIF or your jewellery or the house you live in. Your estate can be measured in many different ways, but no matter who you are or how modest your assets may be, you *do* have an estate.

It's time to put that estate to work — for now and for the future. You've probably already made a difference to the lives of the people close to you, but now, through an effective estate planning strategy, you can make an even bigger difference. How? By ensuring that the interests of your heirs are protected; by minimizing capital gains tax; by ensuring your will is structured in the best way to look after your children and grandchildren; and by maximizing the value of your assets.

To do this, you need a plan. And your assets — house, condo, furniture, paintings, cash and jewellery, RRIFs, insurance policies, investments, collectibles of all kinds — are your estate. Put them together and you have an estate plan.

Fulfilling your potential
Self-actualizing people

- are realists
- are spontaneous and creative
- like solving problems, including the problems of others
- have an ingrained system of right and wrong
- aren't subject to peer pressure
- don't judge others

Source: Compiled from Abraham Maslow's hierarchy of needs.

ESTATE PLANNING OBJECTIVES

What are your estate planning objectives? You can make a final contribution to your children (or heirs), to a charity or alma mater or some other good cause. You can also set up a foundation or trust. There's also the perfectly understandable desire to give to the government only what is required of a lawful citizen, and not a nickel more. Estate planning allows you to realize these goals and much more. Having your affairs in good order when you pass on enables you to direct your money the way *you* want to, not the way the government wants to.

EVERYTHING BEGINS AND ENDS WITH A WILL

If you die without a will, legislation will determine how your assets will be distributed and you will lose the chance to minimize what must be paid to the taxman. A will does many things, including:

- Allowing for an orderly transition of assets to your beneficiaries
- Maximizing the value of your assets
- Minimizing tax and other costs before and upon your death

You'll likely have other objectives as well. Estate planning has sometimes been described as an art rather than a science — there are many rules but few apply to all individuals exactly the same way. When developing your estate plan, you must first think about yourself. That's because you need to keep the income and assets you need to enjoy the lifestyle that you want. A good estate plan ensures you don't end up giving away assets that you may later need.

Well thought out estate plans help you avoid leaving behind many legal, tax and other complications when your family is in a very emotional state. Poor estate planning has more serious consequences than wasted money. Years of family strife can begin when the will is read, sometimes never to heal. That's a legacy few would be happy to leave. A survey by Royal LePage Real Estate Services found that 81 percent of owners intend to give their vacation property to a family member. Of those, 21 percent said they expected a family feud to result.

In this chapter, we'll drill down to the fundamentals of estate planning: wills, powers of attorney, tax considerations, trusts, insurance and charitable giving. We'll also examine ways to protect your estate and reduce taxes so you can direct the financial part of your legacy to those you want to have it.

DEATH AND TAXES

Death waits for no one, but the CRA always manages to muscle its way to the head of the line. Unless you roll everything over to your spouse or common-law partner (and a few others we'll talk about later), property in your estate is deemed (for tax purposes) as having been "sold" immediately before your death. This means your capital gains must be determined, and any registered assets not assigned to a tax-free beneficiary must be taken into income.

When your registered retirement income fund (RRIF) is taken into income, for instance, its entire fair market value is added to your income in the year of your death. Your estate will pay tax on that RRIF money at your marginal tax rate, which will probably be the highest marginal rate because of the increase in your income due to the RRIF money itself. Any costs for settling the estate come on top of that, and probate fees, executor fees and legal costs can easily subtract another 5 percent.

Illustration: Estimate of taxes and charges to a sample estate

Asset	Value	Cost	Capital Gain
Principal residence	$300,000	NA	NA
Cottage/condo, recreational property	$250,000	$100,000	$150,000
Rental or other real estate	$200,000	$100,000	$100,000
Business/farm interest(s)	0	0	0
U.S. stocks (C$)	0	0	0
Stocks/bonds/mutual funds	$300,000	$200,000	$100,000
GICs, term deposits (non-RRSP)		$50,000	$50,000NA
RRSPs, RRIFs	$800,000	NA	NA
LESS: Mortgages, other debt		NA	NA
Total	$1,900,000	(3)	$350,000

1. ADMINISTRATION FEES: Probate, legal, executor
TOTAL ASSETS (1): $1,900,000 × 3% = $57,000
(Net of mortgages and other debts)

2. INCOME TAX ON REGISTERED SAVINGS
TOTAL RRSPs/RRIFs (2): $800,000 × 45% = $360,000
(Total value of registered funds are taxable at the marginal tax rate at death.)

3. INCOME TAX ON CAPITAL GAINS
TOTAL CAPITAL GAIN (3): $175,000 × 45% = $78,750
Capital gain (3) less exemptions × 50% (× marginal tax rate at death)

4. ADD: Mortgages and other debt not life-insured

5. LESS: Any permanent life insurance payable to estate

TOTAL Expenses against estate $495,750

You or your advisor can insert your own asset numbers in this example and come up with the tax liability plus cost totals for your own situation.

For many, the first impulse is to do everything possible to reduce probate fees. Because of this, I want to go through some effective strategies to reduce probate. But keep in mind, trying to avoid probate is not always a good idea.

PROBATE FEES

Probate is the government's way of certifying that your will is indeed your last will and testament. Probate also confirms that the executor you appoint in your will actually has the authority to carry out its instructions. If only one asset in your estate requires letters of probate to be issued, the entire estate covered by your will can be subject to probate fees. Provinces and territories impose a probate fee (though it's not always called that) that varies widely and is tiered so it grows proportionally larger as the size of the estate increases, except for two provinces that currently have maximum fees. Quebec's maximum charge is a modest $87, and Alberta's cap is $400. In Ontario, the province with the highest fees, a $1-million estate will pay $14,500 in what is now called an "estate administration tax."

PROBATE FEES IN CANADA (2004)

Alberta

- $25 for estates up to $10,000
- $100 for estates from $10,001 to $25,000
- $200 for estates from $25,001 to $125,000
- $300 for estates from $125,001 to $250,000
- $400 for estates greater than $250,000

British Columbia

- $208 flat rate on the first $25,000
- An additional $6 per $1,000 for estates from $25,001 to $50,000
- An additional $14 per $1,000 on the balance exceeding $50,000

Manitoba
- $50 on the first $10,000
- An additional $6 per $1,000 on the balance exceeding $10,000

New Brunswick
- Up to $100 on the first $20,000
- $5 per $1,000 on the balance exceeding $20,000

Newfoundland
- $90 on the first $1,000
- $5 per $1,000 on the balance exceeding $1,000

Nova Scotia
- $70 on the first $10,000
- $165 for estates from $10,001 to $25,000
- $275 for estates from $25,001 to $50,000
- $770 for estates from $50,001 to $100,000
- $13 per $1,000 on the balance exceeding $100,000

Ontario
- $5 per $1,000 up to $50,000
- $15 per $1,000 on the balance exceeding $50,000

Prince Edward Island
- $50 on the first $10,000
- $100 for estates from $10,001 to $25,000
- $200 for estates from $25,001 to $50,000
- $400 for estates from $50,001 to $100,000
- $4 per $1,000 on the balance exceeding $100,000

Quebec
- $87 for non-notarial wills
- $0 for notarial wills — they do not need to be probated

Saskatchewan
- $7 per $1,000 of estate's value

FOUR STRATEGIES TO AVOID PROBATE

First, a word of caution. Be careful that in avoiding probate fees you don't trigger more costly problems later on. Caution is especially necessary if a testamentary trust might be better for you or your beneficiaries. We'll talk about the advantages of trusts a little later, at which point you'll understand why a trust is often a better option than gifting.

1) Gifting

Gifting is the easiest way to get assets out of your estate for the most obvious reason: You no longer own them. The biggest danger with being generous is that you might miscalculate your own needs and run out of money in your retirement. It's hard to get money back from children who have sunk it into their mortgage. You also have to be vigilant to be sure that income attribution rules under the Income Tax Act won't apply. Gifting cash to anyone is completely unproblematic from a tax perspective because it comes from your after-tax money. Giving away other real or financial assets is more involved, as it triggers a deemed disposition.

Gifting securities to your adult child (or any other adult) is seen by the CRA as a sale even if no money changes hands. You're required to pay the capital gains tax on the fair market value of those securities on the day they changed hands. This fair market value becomes your child's cost base, and they'll be required to pay tax on all subsequent gains, interest and dividends from that day forward.

Giving financial assets to minor children or grandchildren does not release you from tax obligations. Attribution rules will kick in (see Tax Planning in Chapter 7). Not only must you pay tax on a deemed disposition, but you're also responsible for the tax on interest and dividend income generated by those investments until the minor turns 18, even though you no longer receive them, since it is attributed back to you. Capital gains, however, are taxed in the minor child's hands. Attribution rules are in place to prevent some types of income splitting in families, and you can inadvertently trigger them if you make gifts without considering the tax consequences.

One useful gifting technique involves buying a universal life insurance policy on the life of your minor child. By making generous deposits to the policy, you can take advantage of the policy's tax-sheltered investment growth. When your child is grown, you can transfer ownership of the policy to him or her with no disposition — or tax — attributed to you. Your adult child (or grandchild) can then either withdraw some or all of the money within the policy or borrow against the policy. Withdrawals will be taxable, but if your child has little or no income, the strategy ultimately should save taxes.

2) Joint ownership

Some forms of joint ownership allow assets to pass directly to the surviving owner without going through the deceased's estate. Real estate owned in certain joint tenancy and joint investment accounts are common examples, as are joint bank accounts.

Joint ownership has its dangers in the sense that you give up exclusive control of your assets. A joint bank or investment account is accessible by either owner and can be depleted by either owner without the knowledge of the other. You also will not be able to sell jointly owned real estate without the approval of the other owner(s). And there may be tax implications in switching from sole to joint ownership unless your joint owner is your spouse or common-law partner.

Adding someone to your savings and chequing accounts has no tax consequences. There's no deemed disposition because the assets are cash, and there's no change in income attribution. If the money was yours in the first place, so is the tax liability on the interest income.

The same isn't necessarily true with an investment account at a brokerage firm. In that case, adding another person who is not a spouse or partner as joint owner of the account could be deemed a sale of half the assets in the account for tax purposes and a capital gains tax could apply.

Seniors have to be especially careful, because capital gains can affect means-tested government benefits for seniors. Joint ownership of an investment account also requires you to decide how the ongoing tax liability on the account is to be shared among the joint owners, if it is shared at all. The CRA will generally tax the income of joint accounts in proportion to the owners' contributions to the account.

Want to leave your house to one of your children without having to pay probate fees on it? Re-registering the house in joint tenancy will accomplish this, but caution is required. If your child lives in a house of their own, they may have to pay capital gains tax on their half of your house when it is eventually sold. Why? Because they won't be able to claim the principal residence exemption if they already claim it on their own home. Their capital gain will be calculated based on the property's value on the date ownership was transferred to them. Land transfer tax could also be due upon re-registering the property unless the transfer was done for "natural love and affection" and no money changed hands.

You could be jeopardizing your security if you decide to let a child own half of your house, and that child is also married, and living with his or her spouse in your home. Your child's half of your home could also be considered the "matrimonial home" should he or she go through a spousal split. In many provinces, this means the spouse could end up claiming an interest in your house!

Giving joint tenancy to anyone other than your spouse or common-law partner will trigger a deemed disposition. When that property is your principal residence, there are no tax consequences to you because of the principal residence tax exemption. But if the property is not your principal residence, you are responsible for paying any capital gains tax owing on the "sale" of that half of the property, whether or not you received any money for the title transfer. Keep in mind, too, that your joint owner's creditors could lay claim to your now jointly held assets.

Avoiding probate by arranging joint ownership can be adding a level of complication to your life that may not be worth the savings. It may complicate the affairs of your joint owner as well, so consider it carefully beforehand. I would suggest you consult your financial advisor to assess whether it is a good option for you.

3) Name a beneficiary

You can start "thinning out" your estate by designating beneficiaries on your RRSPs, RRIFs and any other registered plans you may have. As a result, when you die these assets go directly to your designated beneficiary instead of passing through your estate. These assets stay outside your estate and probate fees on that money are avoided. If your beneficiary is your spouse, common-law partner or a financially dependent child or grandchild with a mental or physical infirmity, the money can be rolled over to their RRSP, RRIF or a lifetime annuity with no immediate tax consequences. By the way, the beneficiary isn't obligated to roll it into his or her own RRSP. He or she can choose to receive the cash and pay the tax.

Financially dependent children or grandchildren without disabilities can also receive your registered funds undiminished by deducted income tax. Financially dependent (but not handicapped) adults and minors who inherit registered money do, however, have to include that money in their own income in the year they get it. This may sound punitive, but it could actually save tax, since your dependants could be in the position of paying less tax than your estate. Beneficiaries who are minors have one tax break available to them. They can place your formerly registered money in an annuity that pays to the age of 18. In this way, they pay tax only on the taxable income received from the annuity each year and not in one fell swoop.

With a RRIF, you can name your spouse or common-law partner as what is called a successor annuitant. This allows him or her to simply take over your plan and continue receiving the income. If you don't name beneficiaries on the registered plan, the legal representative of the deceased plan holder can in some cases roll over the assets to a surviving spouse or common-law partner. If this doesn't happen, the assets are paid into the estate, taxed, subject to probate and then distributed, diminished by taxes and probate fees, to the estate's beneficiaries.

Remember, though, registered accounts are paid out to your beneficiaries at *full* value. The estate is responsible for paying tax on that money, which can amount to nearly 50 percent of the total value of the account. This can easily lead to a strikingly unfair situation when one child gets the RRIF and another gets the remaining estate assets, both of equal value before tax. After tax, the final tally will be very different.

There's another caution about assigning beneficiaries to your registered accounts. Those planning to fund a testamentary trust (explained in a moment) will probably want the registered money to go into the trust rather than directly to the beneficiary, but registered assets cannot be transferred directly into a trust. They must first go through your estate and then be moved into a testamentary trust net of probate costs, administration costs and income taxes.

4) Transfer assets to a trust

A trust is a legal entity that can be created to hold property on your behalf. Trusts play a big role in reducing probate fees because what is put into a trust is no longer part of your estate even though you may retain control over the assets and even receive income from them. Using trusts wisely can reduce probate fees but actually that isn't the *primary* reason for establishing them. Trusts can significantly reduce overall taxes and protect assets for your beneficiaries, so let's take a good, hard look at these useful structures. Two new types of trusts, "alter ego" and "joint spousal" trusts have recently emerged thanks to changes to Canada's Income Tax Act. One caveat: any probate reduction or trust strategy should only be considered within the context of a comprehensive estate plan.

234 LIVE WELL, RETIRE WELL

What exactly is a trust?

Trusts are remarkably useful for many people, not just the ultra-wealthy. Trusts are legal agreements that can protect you and your heirs from creditors, minimize probate fees and potentially create significant tax savings. You don't need a lot of money to justify establishing a trust. A rough minimum is $300,000, but this depends on a number of different factors that need to be worked out with your lawyer and/or accountant.

Trusts come in two basic flavours: testamentary and *inter vivos*. A testamentary trust is set up after your death through instructions in your will. A trust established while you are living is called an *inter vivos* or "living trust." The distinction between the two is important because they are taxed very differently.

Trusts have three parties: the donor, the trustee and the beneficiary. The donor is the person who contributes assets to the trust, while the trustee is the person who is "entrusted" with holding and managing the assets (according to the terms of the trust agreement) for the benefit of the third party, the beneficiary.

Almost any kind of asset can be put in a trust — financial instruments, real estate, valuable personal property, even a business — and trusts can be revocable or irrevocable. A revocable trust is simply one that can be dissolved or revoked at any time. An irrevocable trust is the opposite: it permanently transfers legal title to the trustee who holds and manages the assets for the beneficiaries.

Every twenty-one years, most trusts must calculate capital gains tax on the deemed disposition of their assets. Exceptions to this rule are qualified spousal trusts, alter ego and joint partner trusts. This limits the time capital gains can be sheltered and thus left unrealized. But this is just a tax reckoning — the investments within the trust don't actually have to be sold unless cash needs to be raised to pay the tax bill.

TESTAMENTARY TRUSTS

You can establish one or a number of trusts for your beneficiaries through your will. The most common of these are spousal trusts and trusts for your children/grandchildren.

Spousal trusts

Suppose you want to leave money for your children in your will, but you're worried that your spouse might run short of money if you do. Or perhaps you're afraid that your spouse won't manage your assets effectively after you're gone. There are any number of reasons for setting up a spousal trust. By putting assets into a trust exclusively for your spouse's benefit, you can be assured that money will be available for your spouse's needs. Once your spouse dies, then and only then will the remaining money be passed on to the children or other beneficiaries.

When you're establishing the trust, you direct the trustee as to how the money is to be invested and paid out. Some donors give the trustee a great deal of discretion; others grant very little. Some trusts are designed to pay out only the income from the trust investments, while others can pay out principal under certain conditions — usually at the discretion of the trustee. The income beneficiary and the capital beneficiary need not be the same. However, a spousal trust can become "tainted" if someone other than the spouse receives a benefit from the trust while that spouse is still living. Tainted trusts lose their tax advantages.

Apart from probate fees, no taxes are paid when assets are placed in a qualifying testamentary spousal trust. It is considered a tax-free spousal rollover. The income and capital gains earned within a testamentary trust that are not distributed to a beneficiary are taxed at graduated rates just as an individual would be taxed (though the personal tax credits don't apply). This is especially useful for spouses who have an income of their own and don't particularly need the distributions from a spousal trust, which would be taxed at a high personal marginal rate.

Money within a spousal trust can compound and be taxed at graduated rates, leaving more money for the spouse later on or ultimately for those who will inherit what is left of the trust. It's also possible for the spouse to receive income from the trust but elect to have that income taxed within the trust to take advantage of the graduated tax rates.

The assets in the surviving spouse's trust do not form part of that spouse's estate and will not be subject to probate fees. Had they not been put in a trust, those assets would have been subject to probate fees twice — once upon the death of the first spouse and then again on the death of the remaining spouse.

Spousal trusts can be established for married, common-law or same-sex partners.

Other testamentary trusts

Because the income that is not distributed within a testamentary trust is taxed at personal graduated tax rates, leaving money to your grown children or grandchildren through a trust can be very tax-effective. Money that isn't needed can stay sheltered within the trust, generating income and attracting less tax than that income would probably attract in your children's hands.

You can establish one trust for all your children, with specific instructions to the trustee for each child. Or you can set up separate trusts for each child, as long as administrative costs still make it worthwhile. Any income a trust distributes is taxed in the hands of the beneficiaries. For beneficiaries who reside in Canada, the nature of the trust income is retained: Capital gains, dividends and interest income all keep their tax identity. Trust income distributed to non-resident beneficiaries, however, does not retain its tax character, and withholding tax is levied on it as trust income.

WORRIED HOW YOUR KIDS WILL HANDLE YOUR MONEY?

Are you worried how your teenaged kids will spend the money you gave to them long ago when they were so sweet and well-behaved? Formal trust planning can spare you lots of anxiety. According to Teresa Gombita, Senior Tax Planner at Ernst & Young, the key is to document your intentions.

Many parents set up in-trust accounts to implement income splitting with their minor children only to realize when these children turn 18, the parents can't maintain control of the assets in these informal trusts. If a trust was formally established from the start, there would be a documented plan of intention as to what happens to the assets when the child reaches 18. If properly established, an in-trust account will allow funds to be set aside for a minor beneficiary with only income, not capital gains, from the funds being attributed to the person who established the account until the child turns 18. Second-generation income, or income on income, should also not attribute.

If you're wondering whether one or more of your children will "turn on, tune in, and drop out" because they've won the trust fund lottery, a formal trust, like the one described, can save you lots of sleepless nights.

DISABLED BENEFICIARIES

Mentally or physically disabled beneficiaries may already be receiving government assistance that income from a trust could affect. A "Henson trust," named after the plaintiff in an Ontario court decision, may help address this concern. With a Henson trust, a trustee makes the distributions to or for the benefit of the disabled beneficiary during his or her lifetime. The trustee has absolute discretion as to the amount and timing of the payments. Because a trustee has absolute discretion, the disabled person has no "beneficial interest" in the trust and distributions from the trust shouldn't affect the disabled beneficiary's entitlement to government benefits.

In Ontario, you can arrange a very specific type of trust that won't reduce benefit allowances for a disabled beneficiary. The Ontario Disability Support Program Act trusts have restrictive rules: The trust's capital must be an inheritance or the proceeds of an insurance policy and cannot exceed $100,000. Distributions from this trust will not affect the benefit allowance so long as they are used for approved disability-related expenses that aren't otherwise reimbursed.

LIVING (*INTER VIVOS*) TRUSTS

Trusts that are established while the contributor to the trust, the donor, is still alive are called *inter vivos* trusts, which in Latin means literally "from one living person to another living person." Where a probate will is a public document and everything in the will, including the terms of a testamentary trust becomes public after probate, *inter vivos* trust documents are private. *Inter vivos* trusts are also taxed differently from testamentary trusts. Any income that's retained in the trust is taxed at the highest marginal rate, not at the personal graduated tax rates applicable to testamentary trusts.

With some notable exceptions (e.g., cash), putting assets into any trust is considered a deemed disposition, which means that capital gains on assets put into a trust must be recognized for tax purposes. In the hands of the settlor, however, no tax is triggered when assets are transferred into spousal trusts (either testamentary or *inter vivos*) or to two new kinds of *inter vivos* trusts: alter ego and joint partner trusts.

238 LIVE WELL, RETIRE WELL

The big advantage with these new *inter vivos* trusts is that they help you exclude assets from your future estate with no immediate tax consequences. This reduces probate fees when your estate is settled; however, the assets cannot then be transferred into a testamentary trust. In exchange for saving some probate charges, your beneficiaries receive the trust assets directly and pay tax on the income paid from the trust at their marginal tax rate.

Unless your heirs have low incomes (or the amount inherited is very small), they'd probably prefer to be the beneficiary of a testamentary trust, because the one-time savings on probate fees is generally less than the annual tax savings a testamentary trust offers. This is a prime example of how the drive to avoid probate fees can create costly tax consequences for your heirs down the road. Always consider these factors when contemplating establishing a particular kind of trust.

Alter ego trusts

If you're 65 or older you can establish what's intriguingly called an "alter ego" trust. This kind of trust allows you to make yourself— and yourself alone — the beneficiary during your lifetime. At your death, the assets in the trust trigger capital gains tax, and the residual amounts are then distributed to your chosen beneficiaries. Remember, there is no capital gains liability to placing assets in this trust initially unless you elect to declare a taxable disposition at that time. In keeping with other *inter vivos* trusts, however, income retained by the trust is taxed at your highest marginal tax rate.

You lose the use of the spousal rollover for any assets in this trust, but it is an effective way to avoid probate fees. Anything in an *inter vivos* trust is not part of your estate and therefore not subject to probate. Not being part of your estate may also place these assets beyond the reach of those who might contest your will, though this has not yet been tested in court.

Alter ego trusts are also useful as a practical will, and they can be an effective substitute for establishing power of attorney. Upon your death, assets are distributed from this trust in keeping with your instructions to the trustee, just as would be done with a will. In setting up the trust, you can also instruct the trustee to look after your assets, pay your bills, etc., once you become incapacitated or mentally infirm, just as a continuing power of attorney for personal property would facilitate.

Joint partner trusts

Joint partner trusts are very similar to alter ego trusts except that now you and your spouse are the sole beneficiaries. The trust stays intact until the last spouse dies, at which time the assets are subject to capital gains tax and distributed to your heirs or other beneficiaries.

The advantages here are identical to an alter ego trust. Assets are kept out of the estate and thereby avoid probate and may afford protection should someone challenge your will. The drawback is that your assets cannot be placed in a testamentary trust after the last spouse dies, so your beneficiaries may end up paying more income tax than might have been the case with a testamentary trust.

Charitable remainder trusts (see also Chapter 7)

Putting money in trust for a charity while you are still alive has some advantages. You can get a charitable donation receipt upon contributing to the trust, and the trust assets will not ultimately be subject to probate fees. Once you've placed assets in the trust, you cannot touch the principal: It will be the charity's property. And, being an *inter vivos* trust, assets put into a charitable remainder trust are deemed disposed for tax purposes, so a capital gains liability may ensue.

This tax liability should be more than offset by the resulting tax credit, however, and the credit could possibly offset other tax liabilities you may have incurred. The amount of your charitable contribution receipt is based on an actuarial calculation of the present value of the assets. You can claim a charitable donation tax credit of up to 75 percent of your net income in the year of your donation and carry forward any unused portion of that credit for five years.

As long as you are alive, you can receive income from the trust, but you cannot encroach on the capital. When you die, the principal is given to the charity. This kind of trust can be set up jointly with your spouse or partner so the assets will go to the charity once both of you have passed away. Major charities have advisors who can help you sort out the tax and legal issues involved in establishing this kind of trust. A charitable trust can also be set up through your will as a testamentary trust.

Here's an example from the University of Toronto's excellent Web site:

Gordon, a successful U. of T. alumnus, is 86 and wants to set up a scholarship in his memory. He transfers property worth $500,000 to a charitable remainder trust. He immediately receives a tax receipt for $409,500. When he passes on, the trust terminates and the remaining capital is used by the beneficiary (the University) to endow a scholarship in his name. Certainly a win/win for both parties.
Source: www.giving.utoronto.ca/plangiving/trust.html.

Cottage trusts

Just about anything can be placed in a trust, and the family cottage is no exception. Putting a family cottage in a trust will not give you any tax advantages, but it could prevent some major family disputes. By either adding it to a trust with other assets or placing it alone in its own trust, you take the potentially fractious issues of ownership, maintenance and use out of family members' hands and put it in your trustee's.

When you put a cottage in a trust, it is considered "sold" for tax purposes, which may result in capital gains tax. And don't forget the 21-year rule: Trusts must pay capital gains tax on the growth of the trust assets every twenty-one years. Both these tax rules usually mean the family has to come up with cash to pay the taxes. For this reason, some families prefer to include the cottage in what's called an "estate freeze" (see below), which postpones all tax liabilities until after the death of the cottage owner.

Calculating the tax liability on a cottage that has been owned for a long time is not entirely straightforward. There was no capital gains tax in Canada prior to 1972, and prior to 1982, a family could have two principal residences and two principal residence exemptions (the good old days are long gone!). Also, don't forget to check if part of the capital gain has already been recognized. In 1994, many people crystallized capital gains in preparation for the elimination of the $100,000 capital gains exemption. Your tax calculations should take those changes in tax law into account.

Estate freezes

You can "freeze" your estate and thus capture the value of your assets for tax purposes. As a result, you can transfer all future growth and the associated tax liabilities to someone else. Why might you want to do this? It's a way of limiting the final tax liabilities of your estate while still having control of the assets and their income. This can be accomplished in a few ways, but many estate freezes are executed by setting up an *inter vivos* trust.

You take your tax lumps in the tax year you place your "estate" in a trust, but after that, all future tax liabilities fall on the trust's beneficiaries, usually your children. But don't forget, the income from the trust assets can still be distributed to you, and if you are also a trustee of the trust, you can retain control of your assets, too, subject to the terms of the trust.

Small-business owners in particular find estate freezes useful, but do not always employ a trust structure for the freeze. For example, freezes can be done by placing company shares in a holding company or by simply reorganizing the company's share structure. This method avoids a deemed disposition when the freeze is implemented. Family cottages can be put into a holding company in exchange for a mix of preferred and common shares, but those using the cottage could be required to pay rent or declare a taxable shareholder benefit. Large personal investment portfolios or other assets expected to grow in value are also possible candidates for freezes.

Tax-planning suggestions

- You may want to hold much of your assets jointly with your spouse and have them transferred at their adjusted cost base. But those arrangements may not lead to the maximum tax savings.
- If you have losses that can be carried forward, you'll probably want to trigger some capital gains to take advantage of those losses.
- Shares in a qualified small business corporation may be entitled to enhanced capital gains exemptions. If so, it might be worthwhile to trigger some capital gains on those shares before transferring them. Please consult your advisor for full details.

DYING WITHOUT A WILL

Dying without a will is legally called "dying intestate." The repercussions of not having a will might surprise you. Each province has statutory rules for the distribution of assets when someone dies intestate. Most provinces give a set value of assets to the spouse and then split the remaining assets among children and/or the spouse. Where this doesn't seem so alarming, the spouse's preferential share can be very modest in some provinces. In Alberta, it is only $40,000, compared to Ontario's $200,000. In the absence of a remaining spouse, children or parents, the estate is split equally among the deceased's siblings. The rules vary a little between provinces and depend on family circumstances.

These intestate rules are highly inflexible. Dying without a will could bring hardship to your loved ones, so if only as a courtesy to them, get a will. With some planning, it can actually be a good tax planning tool as well.

DON'T USE A WILL KIT

"Don't delay and don't use a kit," is Alan Walker's advice. Walker is Associate Vice President, Private Trust with TD Waterhouse Private Client Services. "Wills aren't expensive and the decisions you make are among the most important in your life. It's always worth getting good advice." He says wills must be properly witnessed and their instructions must be absolutely unambiguous. A lawyer can be very useful in helping you clarify your wishes and expressing them in a way that won't result in years of litigation or prevent your intentions for the distribution of your property from being achieved. A lawyer will also be able to advise you on how to structure your will so it's less likely to be successfully challenged in court after you die.

KNOW YOUR OBJECTIVES

Before seeing a lawyer, though, think about what you want to accomplish in your will, and then what the tax ramifications of those objectives might be. If you're leaving everything to your spouse, perhaps you might want to consider a spousal trust that will pay your spouse the income from assets that are held in the trust for the eventual benefit of your children. If you want to leave money directly to your children, it might be preferable to establish a trust for each child. That could save taxes and preserve the value of the inheritance.

You should have all your assets organized and a strong idea of how you want them distributed after your death. You might alter your plans in light of some advice from your lawyer, but it's good to know in detail what you are aiming to accomplish *before* seeing your lawyer.

Anyone with young children or disabled dependants has the added responsibility of naming a guardian in the will. It's a good idea to discuss financial arrangements with your elected guardian. Your guardian might feel more comfortable having your dependants' money placed in a trust or having a trust company manage the assets. If so, you can include those arrangements in the will if needed.

MULTIPLE WILLS

"Estate lawyers should consider the suitability of multiple wills for their clients," says Margaret Rintoul, a lawyer with the Toronto law firm of Aylesworth, Thompson, Phelan, O'Brien LLP. She says it's a good idea to look at making up a will for assets that require probate, and another will for those that do not. This way, only those assets requiring probate will be subject to probate fees, and not the entire estate. Just make sure the cost of making up separate wills is not greater than the probate fees you'd otherwise pay.

It's important to note that this dual-will strategy has been tested and upheld in court in Ontario. Even if it were overruled, however, an estate would pay no more probate tax than with only one will. Also, property held in different countries might best be dealt with in a separate will, though not necessarily for probate purposes. An estate lawyer can help you understand whether separate wills will work best for you and your situation.

THE EXECUTOR(S) OF YOUR WILL

You must also decide who will take charge of your affairs after you die and wind up your estate as directed in your will. Few people realize how demanding being an executor can be, which is why you should first get the agreement of the person you would like to be your executor.

Your executor should be reliable, fair and without bias to your beneficiaries, knowledgeable about financial matters, familiar with your family situation, and able and willing to take on what might become a lot of extra work. Your executor should live fairly close to you so visits to your financial institutions and other professionals won't be a major undertaking. Your executor must also outlive you, and since most people appoint their spouse as executor, it's a good idea to designate a contingent executor in case your primary executor dies before you do.

It's also possible to appoint multiple executors — your children, perhaps. That's not always a recipe for harmony, and the wisdom of this decision will depend on how well the children get along and their general agreement with your final wishes. If you do decide to appoint multiple executors, consider applying a "majority rules" clause or some other direction to help ensure a quick resolution to disagreements.

WHAT AN EXECUTOR DOES

1) Finds the will and arranges the funeral

An executor is responsible for arranging your funeral, so make sure your executor knows your wishes in that respect. A letter to your executor outlining the arrangements you would like is a good idea, and so is pre-arranging your funeral. Including instructions in your will is less than ideal because a will sometimes isn't located until well after the funeral has taken place. It's always a good idea to give a copy of your will to your executor.

2) Arranges probate

If any of your assets requires letters probate to be issued, your executor will have to have your will probated through the court.

3) Locates and secures the assets

The next thing your executor has to do is locate all of your assets and ensure that they are preserved. Leave a list of all your investment and bank accounts with account numbers, the phone number and address of the financial institution and a contact person. Leave written instructions to find your insurance policies, mortgage and loan papers, and all other similarly important documents.

An executor is personally liable to the beneficiaries, to administer and distribute the estate according to the will. The executor can be held legally responsible for any negligence made while settling the estate.

4) Pays all the bills and files the taxes

Your executor must pay all your debts from the money in your estate. Tax returns must be completed and taxes paid. Sometimes this involves filing more than one tax return, as it may be advantageous to file several types of returns for the year of death. Once the CRA is assured that all the taxes on the estate have been paid, it issues a clearance certificate.

This certificate is CRA's confirmation to the executor that all outstanding tax issues have been settled. The executor can then distribute the estate to the beneficiaries without any personal risk. An executor who pays out assets before the clearance certificate is issued risks being personally accountable should the CRA find tax still owing in the future.

5) Distributes the assets

With a clearance certificate in hand, an executor can distribute the assets to your beneficiaries with little worry about overlooked taxes. Your executor is obliged to distribute your assets in accordance with your will. It's not hard to imagine how torn an executor could feel having to oversee what he or she sees as an unfair distribution to people your executor might know and love. If you are contemplating what could be a controversial bequest, consider this when you choose your executor. Finally, your executor should prepare a summary of the estate and its disposition for the beneficiaries.

COMPENSATING YOUR EXECUTOR

Acting as an executor is a lot of work and you should make it clear that you don't expect your executor to do it all without professional help. Executors can be tempted to be penny-wise but pound foolish in trying to save professional fees while missing out on services that will save the estate money in the long run. The executor is entitled to claim some compensation from the estate, somewhere in the range of 3 percent to 5 percent of the estate's value.

It's quite possible your executor will feel uncomfortable about receiving compensation from your estate, especially if you suggest this while arranging for the executor's consent, and most likely before he or she knows how demanding the job will be. Out of consideration for your executor, stipulate in your will that the executor is entitled to fair and reasonable compensation.

WHAT A TRUST COMPANY CAN DO

Trust companies charge a fee for their service based on the size of assets under administration, but they can bring some impressive experience and tenacity to the table: They've been known to fight legal battles in court on behalf of minor or incapacitated beneficiaries and to safeguard the welfare of orphans by wresting control of businesses out of the hands of opportunists.

Trust companies look after the financial affairs of individuals, estates and businesses. You might appoint a trust company to take charge of your financial assets some time in the future in the event of your incapacity to avoid placing that burden on family or friends. Or you could appoint a trust company as the executor of your will if your estate is complex, if you are concerned about the unbiased execution of your wishes or just to spare someone close to you the responsibility of being your executor.

You may also want a trust company as your executor if you have a business that needs professional expertise to maintain until its sale. If you choose to establish a trust, either through your will or in your lifetime, appointing a trust company as trustee will guarantee the trustee will outlive your beneficiaries. Some trusts last for generations so continuity is important.

Trust services can include tax return filings, estate planning, bill payments, legal advocacy on behalf of clients or estate beneficiaries and, of course, the administration and management of financial assets.

Fees for trust services usually start at a basic minimum and then are tiered based on asset value and the level of service you require. When you consider you may be paying the fees of many professionals to deal with your estate, professional trustee services may not be expensive for the value they can deliver.

POWER OF ATTORNEY

A power of attorney is a legal document, signed by you in front of one or two witnesses (depending on the province) that authorizes one or more people to make financial decisions on your behalf if, because of accident or illness, or in the event that you become mentally incapable, you should become incapable of acting for yourself.

"Attorney" here does not necessarily mean a lawyer, just someone who will act on your behalf. The powers of your attorney can be as expansive or as restrictive as you specify, but they become void when you die. Your will and your executor take over at that point. There are two kinds of powers of attorney: one for your property and one for your personal care.

Power of attorney for property

This document authorizes the named person to act on your behalf with respect to your property. You might give a power of attorney to a trusted friend who will manage your affairs while you are on an extended trip or in the hospital, but the most common use is so your affairs will not come to a grinding halt should you become mentally incompetent. In order for your power of attorney to be valid when you become mentally incompetent, the document must stipulate that power of attorney is continuing or "enduring."

The power to act on your behalf can be as sweeping or as restrictive as you want. You can give a power of attorney for just one investment account or for every asset you own. You can name alternative attorneys or joint attorneys who can act either jointly or separately, as you decide. You can also instruct them to take some payment for their services or require them to do it free of charge (though the law entitles them to some compensation). Understand that there is always the possibility that your financial well-being could suffer through your attorney's lack of skill or outright dishonesty, so select your attorney with care.

The document becomes valid when it is signed and properly witnessed, unless it states it comes into force only on the happening of a certain event, like a determination of incapacity of the donor.

If you are on attorney for someone else, on their incapacity you should ensure that the incapacity is documented as required by the power of attorney and applicable laws. You must perform your duties with care or you could be sued by relatives or other beneficiaries of the future estate.

Power of attorney for personal care

This designates someone to act on your behalf in matters of personal health care. You may choose to include written instructions about your future care, perhaps in respect to resuscitation, heroic measures and pain management, or you can leave no specific instructions and rely on the judgment and compassion of your attorney.

The document becomes valid once it's signed and properly witnessed. Your attorney may use it when he or she judges you incapable of making your own personal care decisions. You may require your attorney to get a doctor's opinion confirming your incapacity before being able to exercise the power of attorney, and your attorney will probably wish to do this anyway for his or her own protection.

You may revoke this power of attorney so long as you are mentally competent by making out a new one, or saying in writing that you revoke it, and having it witnessed in keeping with the requirements of the original document. To be properly witnessed, there must be one or two adult witnesses (depending on the jurisdiction) who are not your attorney or his or her spouse, your partner, your child or someone with property under guardianship. Once you are mentally incompetent, you cannot revoke this power of attorney.

A power of attorney for personal care is a grim reminder of our physical vulnerability, but it is a critical part of estate planning. If you neglect to draw one up and become unable to make decisions about your own care, you may come under the care of the Public Guardian and Trustee. A close relative can petition the court to become your guardian — which could easily cost more than $1,000 — but you will have lost the right to decide who is entrusted.

Powers of attorney are very inexpensive to draw up with a lawyer. You can expect to pay about $200, and if you get your powers of attorney done in conjunction with a will, they may cost even less. A single, uncomplicated will with a continuing power of attorney for property and a power of attorney for personal care can be as little as $375 in small centres. That's a modest investment for the protection and peace of mind it will give you.

CHARITABLE GIVING

Why wait until you die to donate part of your estate to a charity? You could be denying yourself the gratification of furthering a cause you believe in while you can enjoy it. And you could be missing out on some hefty tax savings, too. While you're alive, you are allowed a charitable tax credit of up to 75 percent of your net income in any one year. And unused credits can be carried forward five years. In the year of your death, that limit increases to 100 percent of your net income, and excess credits can be carried back to the previous year to a maximum of 100 percent of your net income.

Large charities can usually accommodate just about anything you care to give them: cash, real estate, securities, valuable objects, insurance policies, royalties, even residual interests. Gift consultants employed by charities or tax accountants can help you sort out the tax implications of your gifts and advise you on different gifting strategies, many of which we'll cover here.

GIFTING STRATEGIES

The non-profit sector (including volunteer work) represents close to 9 percent of the Canadian economy. While charities desperately require additional contributions, Craig Alexander, Vice President and Deputy Chief Economist, TD Bank Financial Group, says the key question for Canadians is, "How do I get the most bang for my buck? We are entitled to ask how we can best invest in the charitable sector." To that end, Alexander believes a number of lessons from personal financial planning can be applied to charitable giving.

1) Develop a plan

As a starting point, every investor needs to build a financial plan, and charitable giving can be a core part of that plan. Outline your goals, then establish a road map to achieve those goals. But your financial philanthropic plan will not be static. It will change with life's events, so it should be reviewed, tweaked and updated periodically.

2) Understand the charity

How will your donations be used? How much support does the charity receive from governments and how reliant is it on personal donations? How much of the charity's funding goes to administrative outlays and how much is channelled to the end user of the charitable service? Bear in mind that administration costs are necessary for the provision of the services, but your charity should keep those costs under control. Conduct some due diligence, just as you would with any investment. Recent regulatory changes that require an increase in transparency by charities may make it easier for you to do that.

3) Diversify

Why limit yourself to a single cause? There are more than 80,000 registered charities in Canada, spanning a broad array of sectors, and many are experiencing financial strains. With charities in fields ranging from the arts to the sciences, as well as across all provinces and around the globe, there's a huge need for donations to multiple causes.

4) Give for the long haul

Donors should consider developing a long-term strategy for giving. The number one problem identified by charities is difficulty obtaining long-term stable funding. As a result, charities benefit tremendously when individuals make regular donations. This is not to suggest that periodic financial windfalls should not motivate additional giving, or that each and every individual donation needs to be part of a long-term plan. A balanced approach to giving is best, and to the extent that individuals want to provide sustained support, some thought should be given to the establishment of an endowment fund.

5) Maximize tax credits

Just as investors strive to maximize the return on their investment, charitable givers should maximize the availability of tax credits. On the initial $200 of donations each year, Canadians receive a federal tax credit of 16 percent of the donation, which can result in a combined federal and provincial tax credit of around 25 percent. Beyond $200, the federal tax credit rises to 29 percent, which can amount to a combined federal and provincial tax credit of approximately 45 percent. Donations do not have to be claimed in the year in which they are made and can be carried forward for up to five years.

As a result, individuals who make small contributions may want to wait to claim them on their tax return until they exceed the $200 threshold in order to maximize their tax credits. Similarly, donations by individuals in a household can be pooled together to exceed the $200 mark and claimed on the tax return of the person with the higher tax rate. There's also a benefit to giving during one's lifetime, rather than through an estate, to avoid probate and executor fees.

6) Be strategic

The bottom line is that Canadians will be more effective in their philanthropic efforts if they treat them as investments. Many wealthy individuals have applied their business and investment acumen to their charitable giving with considerable success. Bill Gates, Warren Buffet and many other billionaires have shared their wealth while pursuing a strategic approach to philanthropy in order to ensure that their money is well spent. However, you don't need to be a business tycoon to have the same success on a smaller scale.

GIFTS OF PROPERTY

Gifts of property will trigger a deemed disposition at fair market value that may result in a capital gains tax liability. (In the case of depreciable property, you may also have to deal with recaptured capital cost allowances.) The good news is that credit for capital property donations takes these tax liabilities into account. The 75 percent credit limit is increased by 25 percent of the taxable capital gains or recaptured depreciation resulting from gifted properties.

Donations of ecologically sensitive lands and certified cultural property may also get the same treatment under certain conditions. You must be mindful of triggering alternative minimum tax with such a large tax credit. Alternative minimum tax is a federal tax designed to ensure that taxpayers cannot reduce their taxable income below $40,000 by using tax shelters and other write-offs. Minimum tax does not apply in the year of death.

Think your house or cottage might make a nice venue for a charity? You can gift your property to a charity on the condition that you and your spouse continue to live there until death. You receive a tax receipt for your donation (at fair market value) when you sign over the ownership, but you get to continue to enjoy your property for as long as you like. You would, however, have to continue to maintain the property at your expense.

GIFTS OF SECURITIES

Special tax treatment for gifts of publicly traded securities (including mutual funds) has made it advantageous to donate the securities on which you have a capital gain, rather than donating the cash from the sale of those securities, because the capital gains inclusion rate for donated securities is only 25 percent instead of the regular 50 percent. Please note: In-kind donations to private foundations do not get this tax break.

GET CREDIT FOR DONATING SECURITIES

Although saving tax may not be your primary reason to give, it makes sense to give in a way that minimizes taxes. Here's what Tim Cestnick, one of Canada's foremost tax experts, has to say on the matter:

Make a donation of securities — stocks, bonds, or mutual funds — to a registered charity, and you'll be entitled to a special tax break. For example, if you donate shares that have appreciated in value, a capital gain will be triggered at the time of the dona-tion to the charity, since you'll be deemed to have sold the shares. Normally, one half of a capital gain is subject to tax. But in this case, our tax law cuts you a break, and just one quarter of your capital gain will be subject to tax. The result is that your tax bill on the disposition of the shares is cut in half. Further, the tax relief from the donation of the shares to charity will far out-weigh the tax hit on the shares.

Donate or sell? An example:
Gloria owns $10,000 of Publico shares, on which she has a $5,000 capital gain.

1) If Gloria *sells* the shares, she'll have to pay $1,150 in tax [($5,000×50 percent)×46 percent]. After she pays the tax, the charity receives $8,850. So adding in her charitable donation tax credit of $4,071 ($8,850×46 percent), Susan saves $2,921 in taxes ($4,071×$1,150).

2) If Gloria *donates* the shares, the charity gets the full $10,000 and Susan pays only $575 in tax [($5,000×25 percent)×46 percent]. After the tax credit on her donation, Susan's tax savings are $4,025 ($4,600×$575).

Donating the shares in kind has gained Gloria $1,104 ($4,025–$2,921).

Note: Example assumes Gloria has already made $200 in chari-table donations in the year.

GIFTING REGISTERED ASSETS

RRSPs, RRIFs and other registered assets that aren't rolled over tax-free to another person are taxed very heavily. All the money in these accounts is taken into income in the year of your death, which likely means you'll be pushed into the highest marginal tax rate if you weren't there already. As a result, this "income" will be taxed at the highest marginal tax rate in your province and your estate could easily lose just shy of half your registered assets to taxes.

You can avoid this tax bite by designating a charity as the beneficiary of your registered money. When the charity receives the money after your death, it will issue a charitable tax receipt that will offset the tax on those registered assets. The charity gets the full value of your RRSP or RRIF and your estate avoids income tax and probate fees on that money. This is an extremely tax-efficient way to give to a charity.

Perhaps giving away all your registered money is more than you would like to give to any one cause. In that case, you can name more than one beneficiary on your registered accounts and each will receive an equal share.

GIFTING INSURANCE

There are a few ways to give your insurance proceeds to a charity. Designating a charity as the beneficiary of your life insurance will give you a charitable donation for the death benefit, which can be claimed either in the year you die or taken back to your death. The charity gets the money promptly and, because the money never forms part of your estate, you pay no probate fees on the insurance proceeds.

It's also possible to make a charity the owner of your insurance policy, as well as the beneficiary. In that case, the value of your donation will be the cash surrender value of the policy along with any accumulated dividends and less any policy loans. If, however, that value exceeds the tax cost of the policy, you will be taxed on that excess as though you had received it as income. Once the policy is no longer yours, you can get ongoing charitable donation tax credits by continuing to pay the premiums. If the charity is the owner and irrevocable beneficiary of the life insurance policy, you will receive a charitable tax receipt for the premiums.

Robert Murray, Senior Manager, Structured Products, with TD Waterhouse Canada Inc., says gifting securities is more advantageous from a tax perspective than gifting insurance, so if you have the choice, he advises that you gift securities. Then, he says, you can replace the value of those donated securities with insurance that can pay your beneficiaries. That way, you've gotten the maximum tax benefit from a charitable donation and still have the same amount of money to give your beneficiaries, tax- and probate-free, for no more than the cost of the insurance.

SETTING UP YOUR OWN FOUNDATION

This may sound like the domain of Galen and Hilary Weston, but setting up your own charitable foundation is not only for the rich and famous. Minimums can be as low as $250,000. The advantage of a private foundation is that you, or a board of directors you select, can control exactly how your money is spent, and on what. The disadvantage is that you have to administer the foundation, organize and maintain a board of directors, and pay ongoing costs for tax filings and accounting services.

Your own foundation will receive donations from you, issue you donation receipts, and will then make distributions to the charities of your choice. A foundation allows you to build a legacy of giving. After you're gone, your heirs can continue to direct where the charitable dollars should go.

AN ALTERNATIVE TO YOUR OWN FOUNDATION

According to Jo-Anne Ryan, head of the Private Giving Foundation (PGF), over the next ten years the Boomer generation will inherit close to $1 trillion. Some of this money will be spent, but in the future, much of it will be passed on to charitable causes. But for many charities, *today* is the challenge, not tomorrow. Although Canadians have been generous the past few years, charities are having difficulty recruiting volunteers or meeting their donation targets.

Ryan offers a solution to this dilemma. Instead of waiting to donate through your will, why not donate while you are still alive and can enjoy the satisfaction of seeing your money go to a good cause? However, if you are thinking of setting up a private foundation to do this, she cautions that they are costly to set up and administer. And to make matters worse, the tax break you get for donating publicly traded securities is not available if you donate to a private foundation.

With this in mind, TD Waterhouse created PGF, an independent public charity that offers an innovative and simple way to support the causes that matter most to you. The PGF is registered as a public foundation, and allows you to enjoy many of the same benefits as a private foundation. Ryan adds that when you donate stocks, bonds and mutual funds to the PGF, the taxable capital gains on the donated securities are cut in half, to 25 percent from 50 percent.

Once you've established which not-for-profit organizations best represent your values and interests, there are some excellent options to consider. Your legal or financial advisor will help you:

1) Prepare a will
2) Establish a specific dollar amount or a percentage of assets
3) Establish the type and amount of any securities you wish to donate
4) Name a charity as beneficiary of your RRSP or RRIF
5) Name a charity as the tax-free beneficiary of an existing or paid-up life insurance policy
6) Purchase a new life insurance policy naming your favourite charity as the tax-free beneficiary

---

The benefits of the Private Giving Foundation

If you want to make a difference, and do it as efficiently as possible, the Private Giving Foundation (PGF) provides many advantages. The PGF:

- Simplifies your giving by making donations to one foundation.
- Establishes a legacy of giving by including your heirs in the process.
- Eliminates year-end pressure to select charities to support.
- Recognizes loved ones by naming the gifts from the PGF accordingly.
- Provides tax-free growth of your endowment, allowing for greater donations.
- Provides immediate tax savings from donations to the PGF.
- Reduces taxes on capital gains through the donation of publicly traded securities to the PGF.

You can even establish an account with the PGF that bears your family's name. A minimum, irrevocable donation of only $10,000 is all that's required.

Source: www.tdwaterhouse.ca/privategiving.

INSURANCE STRATEGIES

We've already seen that taxes can take a big bite out of your estate. Unless you can roll your assets over to a spouse or partner, you're likely to lose about half your registered assets to taxes along with any capital gains tax liability you might have. Add to that the cost of probate, legal fees and executor costs and your estate can be diminished pretty quickly. But something can be done about this.

Insurance can be used to replace the money lost to taxes and estate settlement costs, or it can form the very foundation of your estate. Death benefits on a life insurance policy are paid to Canadian beneficiaries tax-free. Sometimes the estate is named as the beneficiary. This is useful when the proceeds are intended to offset taxes on the estate or to fund a testamentary trust, particularly for the benefit of minor children. In most other cases, it is usually better to name a person(s) as beneficiary so the benefit does not have to be probated and creditors of the estate cannot lay a claim. It's also possible to name multiple beneficiaries in the event your prime beneficiary should die before you do.

Let's look at the following chart for an example. Plug in your own numbers to get a rough idea of your estate's tax liabilities and costs (if you are not able to take advantage of a tax-free rollover on any of your assets and you haven't made other provisions for putting your assets outside your estate). Now, with a ballpark idea of the insurance coverage you might want to obtain, you can decide what kind of insurance is most appropriate for you.

Estimate of Taxes and Charges to Estate

Asset	Value	Cost	Capital Gain
Principal residence			
Cottage/condo, recreational property			
Rental or other real estate			
Business/farm interest(s)			
U.S. stocks (C$)			
Stocks/bonds/mutual funds			
GICs, term deposits (non-RRSP)			
RRSPs, RRIFs	(2)		
LESS: Mortgages, other debt	(4)		
Total	**(1)**	**(3)**	

1. ADMINISTRATION FEES— Probate, legal, executor
TOTAL ASSETS (1): =
Net of mortgages and other debts   Rates 4%–8%

2. INCOME TAX ON REGISTERED SAVINGS
TOTAL RRSPs/RRIFs (2): =
Total value of registered funds are taxable   Marginal tax rate at death

3. INCOME TAX ON CAPITAL GAINS
TOTAL CAPITAL GAIN (3): =
Capital gain (3) less exemptions×50%   Marginal tax rate at death

4. ADD: Mortgages and other debt (4) not life-insured:

5. LESS: Any permanent life insurance payable to estate:

Total Expenses against Estate $

"TERM TO 100" AND UNIVERSAL LIFE

"Term to 100" and universal life are the two forms of insurance most often suggested in estate planning situations.

Term to 100 is designed to cover you for your entire lifetime. In most cases, the premiums are constant, and must be paid until you die or reach 100. If you stop paying the premiums, your coverage ends. (After age 100, the coverage continues without your needing to pay the premiums.) The premiums are higher than those charged for ten-year term insurance, and as with all term insurance, no cash surrender value is built up and there is no investment element.

Universal life combines term insurance with an investment element. It is permanent insurance because it covers you for life so long as your premiums are paid, either by you or the investment income generated within the policy.

Whichever type of insurance you select, if you have a partner, consider making it "joint and last to die." This means the policy pays when the last surviving spouse dies. For those who are able to use the tax-free rollover provisions, joint and last to die policies are usually suggested. Since a couple's biggest tax hit most often comes when the last spouse dies, this arrangement works well. Joint and last-to-die policies are also generally less expensive than single policies. This strategy might not be as expensive as you might think.

AN EXAMPLE

A couple, both 70 years old and non-smokers, would pay only $7,000 a year in premiums on a term to 100 joint and last-to-die policy that would pay out $300,000 based on current rates. A universal life policy would be more expensive because the investment element must be funded, but that can be paid for up front and the subsequent investment growth used to pay for the insurance premiums.

Universal life would be recommended for someone with more than adequate resources who is looking for ways to shelter income, move assets out of the estate or deal with the estate's tax liability. Moving GIC money, for example, into a universal life policy would shelter the interest income from tax while simultaneously removing that money from the future estate. Money that would have been subject to probate fees can now be paid out to the beneficiaries free of tax and probate. Of course, if the purpose of the insurance is to pay taxes on the estate, the policy would most likely be made out to the estate, in which case you've simply set assets aside through the policy to pay the taxes but allowed them to grow in a tax-sheltered environment and given them an added boost with the insurance element.

INSURANCE IN ESTATE FREEZES

If you've executed an estate freeze, you'll know *exactly* how much your estate's tax liability will be because it's been frozen in time. Insurance can be used to pay that liability. It can also be used to equalize your children's inheritance. Frequently, when business owners freeze their estate, new common shares in the family company are given to all of the children and any future growth will accrue to the children's common shares. (The parents retain preferred shares that are fixed, or "frozen," in value.) Seldom do all the children want an active role in the company, and this can force the ones who want the company to buy back the shares from their siblings at a cost they can rarely afford without going into debt.

Not many parents are in the position of being able to give the family business to one child and assets of equal value to the other children. Insurance can make this situation easier by making money available for the other children. Then the new business operator doesn't have the pressure of an unwanted debt and the other siblings have something closer to a fair solution.

GET INSURED WHILE YOU STILL CAN

All these insurance solutions hinge, of course, on your insurability. By the time you turn your mind to estate planning, you may no longer be insurable or a physical condition may make insurance too expensive. Even if you can't come close to estimating how much insurance your estate will ultimately need, you should seriously consider buying a small universal life policy for estate planning purposes while you are insurable. Many policies let you increase your coverage at any time without proof of insurability, so you can fine-tune your insurance coverage later on.

YOUR ESTATE PLANNING OPTIONS ARE VIRTUALLY UNLIMITED

After a lifetime of working, saving and investing, you should have the final say over where your money goes when you're no longer around to enjoy it. Spend some time making or updating your will, recording all the things your executor will need to know, drawing up powers of attorney and thinking about the beneficiary designations on your insurance, registered accounts and segregated funds, if you have them.

Understanding the tax and legal considerations of estate planning, the use of trusts and the advantages of some charitable gifting strategies could open up possibilities that might not otherwise have occurred to you. It may also give you the sober realization that these matters must not be put off indefinitely or those you love and the good causes you may wish to support could suffer.

A little time invested in estate planning now will save you and your family an awful lot of heartache later on. Planning is what retiring well is all about. And as I've said before, you don't need to make a choice between living well and retiring well.

You can do both.

CHAPTER
TEN

"I've been all around the world
Marching to the beat of a different drum.
But just lately I have realised,
The best is yet to come."
—VAN MORRISON, "SOMEONE LIKE YOU"

LIVE WELL, RETIRE WELL
MAKE IT HAPPEN

"Life is an open road—it's the best story never told
It's an endless sky—it's the deepest sea."
—BRYAN ADAMS, "OPEN ROAD"

LIFE'S AN OPEN ROAD FOR LLOYD AND JOANNE

Lloyd and Joanne Fillmore are city people through and through. That's why they decided to stay in the heart of downtown when Lloyd retired twenty-two years ago. They sold their house in Toronto's Beaches area, bought a maintenance-free condo and embraced the next stage of their life. Their only worry was whether they'd get on each other's nerves, now that they were together 24/7! They faced that problem in a unique way. The day after retirement, they jumped into the car and took an eight-week trip around North America.

The trip was financed by Lloyd's life insurance. He had an option on his policy which allowed him to take out a lump sum tax-free and still leave about a quarter of the cash value inside. "Why not take it?" says Lloyd. "It didn't change the coverage and it allowed Joanne and me to explore places we'd never seen — and explore a new side of ourselves as well."

When they got back, they felt excited to be free to do what they wanted, when they wanted. "I always felt we'd retire early," says Joanne. "Lloyd's pension was a good one, and since the company was restructuring he was given a financial incentive to leave early if he wanted. And boy did he jump on it!"

So after thirty-two years as a skilled draftsman at Ontario Hydro, Lloyd Fillmore put down his drafting pen for the last time, picked up his wife from the office where she worked and entered an exciting new stage in their lives.

"I HATE TO SAY IT, BUT WE'RE ENJOYING IT!"

The issue of getting on each other's nerves now that they were seeing each other 24/7 never materialized. In fact, "we found out we really liked each other," says Lloyd. "We'd always loved each other, but retirement brought us even closer. Strange to say, but we became even better friends." Joanne agrees. "We felt great about life. And we've always been busy people. We wanted to keep our minds active so we joined a world-wide competitive bridge club, we continued to play at our local club, and we are volunteer bridge teachers as well."

Lloyd chimes in, "I hate to say it, but after twenty-two years in retirement, we're really enjoying it. Our condo is as big as a bungalow so we can entertain easily. We've got a TV room and a computer room, and when we're not playing bridge or socializing, we're travelling or playing golf."

THE SECRET TO BEING HAPPY

Lloyd has a wicked sense of humour. He says the secret to a happy retirement is to "make a big deal out of everything in your life." There's never a dull moment in their lives, that's for sure. They've decided to stop spending money on indulgences, and concentrate on family, keeping fit and making sure their investments keep on working for them. "When we sold the house, we put the proceeds into stocks, and adopted a buy-and-hold approach. That strategy paid off for us, but even before that, I got kind of lucky with my RRSPs. I was getting nearly 9 percent on my five-year GICs and of course saved all kinds of taxes."

Joanne says their retirement number was set at 70 percent of Lloyd's working salary. "And when we added the pension benefits, the CPP and the RRIFs together, we matched up to that number very well. Our RRIF gives us the flexibility to change our monthly draw any time we want." It looks like the Fillmores have it all: financial health, physical health, a great family and an attitude to retirement that goes hand in hand with their personalities — totally positive. As Lloyd points out, "I always worked to live. I never lived to work. So I knew retirement would be a blessing, and retiring early was a double blessing!"

WELCOME TO THE THREE-DECADE RETIREMENT

In order to retire well you don't need a massive portfolio. But now, the three-decade retirement is becoming commonplace. What are you going to do during all those years? Research shows that how many friends you have, not how much money you have, is often a better predictor of how happy you're likely to be right after you retire.

That's one of the findings from a University of Michigan study by Alicia Tarnowski and Toni Antonucci. They collected data on 253 people over the age of 50, drawn from a nationally representative sample of U.S. households. As Boomers age, they should probably pay as much attention to their social lives as their financial portfolios, says Tarnowski. The study provides compelling evidence of this fact.

> The size of a recently retired person's social support network, not the size of that person's wallet or state of physical health, is the strongest influence on whether life satisfaction changes for better or worse. Our findings suggest that new retirees may need more emotional support than they did when they were working. Just having a number of people who provide emotional support, listen to your concerns, and let you know that you're still valued right after you retire, seems to make a big difference. It fits with other research showing that social support buffers stress, and even positive life changes like retirement can be sources of considerable stress.
> Source: www.pub.umich.edu/daily/1998

"To retire well, invest in making friends."
— University of Michigan study, 1998

EVAN AND SARAH ALWAYS LOOK ON THE BRIGHT SIDE

While Lloyd and Joanne are fortunate to be in good financial health, Evan and Sarah Ovinsky face a very different financial reality. Both are recently retired (Sarah is retiring this year), and they're about to see their cash flow diminish substantially — from a double income situation to zero working income in a few short years. Now, they must learn to live on one modest pension (Evan's) and one very small one (Sarah's).

What's inspiring about Evan and Sarah is that they aren't going to let their financial situation get them down. They know they must be careful with their finances but they'll continue to have an active social life, even when Sarah's final salary cheque arrives in the next few months. Here's their story:

"I was a victim of government downsizing back in the '90s," says Evan. "I'd had my salary frozen for eight years when the government asked me and a large percentage of other Ontario teachers if we would like to step down." Evan was an experienced vice principal at a Southern Ontario high school when an offer was made in April 1998.

"I was 53 years old, and I loved my job, but it took me a nanosecond to accept the offer. If I hadn't, I would have risked losing some of the pension benefits I'd built up over thirty years of service."

The first couple of months of early retirement were a little traumatic for Evan. Sarah worked as a corporate meeting planner for a big health care company, but Evan's structure had suddenly disappeared. He'd been working in the school system since he was 23 years old — his entire adult life.

"I REALIZED I HAD COMPLETE FREEDOM"

But then something happened to Evan. "On June 24th — I still remember the date — I woke up and realized I had complete freedom for the first time in my life." Here he was, still active and healthy, and now he could do whatever his heart desired. Yes, there was an adjustment — there was more time and less money. But Evan quickly realized it was a good tradeoff! "Now I'd have more time to for travel, and I'd also have more time to spend with my children and grandchildren."

In 1999, Evan and Sarah sold their big, 3,500-square-foot house in Mississauga, and bought a more modest (and cheaper) house in tree-lined Burlington, Ontario. They took stock of their financial position, and with Sarah still working, Evan decided to give his children some tax-free gifts so they could buy furniture and help pay off their mortgages.

"We hired an advisor to work with us. And since we're cautious investors, we re-constructed our portfolio to create a better balance between income and equities, and made sure we were properly diversified."

Meanwhile, Evan had discovered he had a talent for building and fixing things. He started a new business as a building contractor and roofer, and really enjoyed it. Some jobs were non-profit, for friends, but other jobs were paid. He couldn't complain. It kept him busy, and he was having fun. But then everything changed once again when they found out Sarah was to be laid off.

"She's in her late 50s now, so it's going to be hard for her to find another job. And of course, right now, she's going through a period of adjustment. But we'll survive. We'll do more than survive. We've got a great family, and while Sarah's pension is pretty minuscule, it's still something. Together with my pension, plus CPP, and of course the investments we have, we'll do fine."

Evan and Sarah are in great health, and Evan sounds really excited at the prospect of spending more time with Sarah — the love of his life. To retire well, you have to live well. And now that both will soon be retirees, Evan and Sarah plan to live a quality life indeed.

Riding the wave

We live in exciting and extraordinary times. The shape of society is changing right in front of us as the Boomer generation begins to retire. Even the usually staid *Economist* magazine is excited about what they consider a "once in a millennium" event: *Something unprecedented and irreversible is happening to humanity. This year or next, the proportion of people aged 60 or over will surpass the proportion of under-fives. For the rest of history, there are unlikely ever again to be more toddlers than grey heads. Already those aged 65 or over, who throughout recorded time have rarely accounted for more than 2–3 percent of most countries' people, make up 15 percent of the rich world's inhabitants.*

Source: "Forever Young," *The Economist*, March 25, 2004.

"THE RICH ARE VERY DIFFERENT FROM YOU AND ME"

I'm paraphrasing here from F. Scott Fitzgerald's *The Great Gatsby*. The actual quote is: "Let me tell you about the very rich. They are different from you and me." But let's not quibble. Fitzgerald's cynical view aside, the rich *are* different. Their attitude to money is different. In a MoneySense.ca article from May 17, 2005, entitled "Seven Habits of Wealthy Canadians," financial advisor James Yih highlights seven financial habits that separate the wealthy from the rest of us.

1) They save regularly

Having the discipline to save on a regular basis is not easy. Paying yourself first through an automatic payroll deduction plan, for example, is a great way to stay disciplined. Studies suggest that wealthy Canadians save about 20 percent of their income. How much do *you* save right now?

2) They live frugally

In the book *The Millionaire Next Door* by Thomas Stanley and William Danko, the millionaire next door is the person living in the same bungalow for the past twenty years. He or she doesn't dress in flashy clothes or drive expensive foreign imports. They don't spend and thus they don't show off.

3) They know where their money is going

Budgeting is key to saving money. Many of us don't bother tracking our spending, and yet we wonder where all our hard-earned money went at the end of the year.

4) They avoid debt

That includes credit card debt, loans and lines of credit on their house. Even with low interest rates, interest expenses on a variety of purchases can eat up thousands of dollars of your savings ever year.

5) They maximize income

Yes, I know, this is obvious. But *how* they do it is interesting. Studies in the U.S. indicate that most of the wealthy are self-employed. And a surprisingly high number of first-time wealth owners are immigrants who have not succumbed to the spend-first North American lifestyle. Their children may turn out to be another story, however. To increase your earning power, you might consider retraining, going back to school or maybe starting a business.

6) They own appreciating assets

They own, instead of rent. Not just their house, but their cars as well. Their investments are carefully thought out, and they usually stick to their investment plan.

7) They get professional advice

The wealthy can afford accountants, lawyers and financial advisors. But so can you. A dependable team of advisors can save you (and make you) more money than you thought possible. If you have chosen your advi-

sors well, the income and savings you receive from their services will almost always cover — and usually exceed — their fees. Although they use professional advisors, the wealthy ultimately make the final decisions themselves.
Jim Yih, MoneySense.ca, May 17, 2005.

I won't tell you no lie
But there's more to this journey
than is apparent to the eye
— Sting, "Rock Steady"

FOLLOW YOUR OWN PATH

How we transition into and ultimately enjoy our retirement is the big unanswered question. Only time and experience will answer that. But of one thing we can be sure: It will be nothing like anything our parents, grandparents and great grandparents experienced.

Because our retirement will be unprecedented, it's critical to plan for it like never before. If you follow and stick with the steps outlined in this book, there's no telling how rich and successful your retirement can be. The PATH, a simple and easy way to remember the four-step process, provides you with an organizational framework designed to offer focus and results. Picture. Arm. Transition. Harmony. I firmly believe it will help lead you to a richer life as well as a richer retirement.

By now you know I'm a big believer in repetition. It's the only way to get rid of bad habits and replace them with good new ones. If Beethoven can take four notes and turn them into his *Fifth Symphony*, then perhaps we can repeat four simple steps and turn them into a life-changing symphony of our own.

STRATEGIES FOR A RICH LIFE AND A RICHER RETIREMENT

Throughout this book, I've tried to break down and simplify the sometimes complex process of retirement planning. And it *is* a process. If you follow and stick with the four-step PATH I've outlined for you, you'll succeed beyond your wildest dreams. My motto is: "Think it, then do it." The thinking part is always the hardest because of that little voice within us. But if you block out the little voice, accept your limitations and acknowledge your strengths, your inner battle is won.

"Think it"

- Recognize and accept your limitations
- Acknowledge and make use of your strengths
- Accept — even relish — making mistakes
- Relax, then visualize your future
- Visualize, then incorporate, good habits into your life

"Do it"

- Set realistic goals
- Start with a simple, achievable plan
- Block out your negative inner voice
- Ditch bad habits by substituting good habits
- Find your life passion by turning "like" into "love"
- Avoid negative people
- Stick to the plan you created
- Reward yourself from time to time
- Tweak your plan
- Have fun

Common sense advice? I hope so! There isn't enough common sense in the world. We all get caught up in things sometimes, and that's when we lose sight of the forest for the trees. All I want is for you to live well and retire well, for there is nothing more valuable in this world than a life well lived. I used to know a cynical man who was always asking people, "What's the point? Why do you do bother? How can you actually like your work?" But then he shocked me one day when he asked me, "How do you know if you've had a well-lived life?" I said you feel it inside. Instead of a vague sense of disappointment with life, there's a sense of deep fulfillment.

But his question made me realize that I didn't always feel this way. A long time ago, when I was going through a very tough time, I got down on myself. My parents told me:

"When you fall, pick yourself up, dust yourself off and continue to move forward. You don't have to be the best but you have to do your best. It's only when you compromise and take short cuts that you cheat yourself out of fulfillment."

I thought about this for a while and knew they were right. So I got back up and moved on with my life. The moral of the story is, never give up. And it all starts with baby steps. If you like something, *stick with it*, and chances are you'll become good at it. When you become good at something, you're confidence rises. With confidence comes achievement and fulfillment. And the more you achieve, the better you'll feel about yourself. It's an upward (and very positive) spiral.

GIVING BACK IS WHAT IT'S ALL ABOUT

Do you remember Robert Edgewood, our multi-millionaire coupon-clipper from Chapter 4? He's planning for the future, and now that his estate has grown substantially, he's looking to set up trusts for his children. He's also exploring the possibility of setting up a charitable foundation. More Canadians than you might think are heading in this direction because they'd like to leave a legacy.

Dr. Albert Roche is one of those people. A semi-retired engineer, Roche has travelled all over the world teaching, delivering aid and managing development projects in countries such as Nigeria, Indonesia, Tanzania and Russia. Just a few years after receiving his doctorate in aerospace engineering from the University of Toronto, Dr. Roche travelled to Afghanistan and helped establish the Faculty of Engineering at the University of Kabul. It would become a life-changing experience for him.

Back in Canada, Dr. Roche put his mathematical skills to work in other ways. He became an astute stock investor and has amassed a fortune estimated at $13 million. But now that he's in semi-retirement, he is busier than ever.

> I'm totally involved in helping friends and community members become better investors. I do it voluntarily, but it's become almost a full-time job. However, my focus right now is on two things: I want to set up a foundation to help aid organizations I've worked for in the past; and I'm planning to go back to Afghanistan to help in the rebuilding of their engineering resources. Tragically, many of my professor friends were killed during the Soviet invasion in the 1980s. It's time for me to go back to the place that changed my life when I was a young man. I want to help any way I can.

Dr. Roche clearly has his heart in the right place. And now that he has the financial wherewithal, he can turn his humanitarian dreams into reality.

Whether you're years away from retirement, or already in retirement, it's never too late to reinvent yourself. It's never too late to fulfill your destiny, to give of yourself and develop a passion for living and giving. Maybe you don't have the energy you used to have. But if your energy is low, maybe it's not your age or responsibilities that are conspiring to make this happen. Maybe it's your lifestyle.

The word "lifestyle" has an interesting definition: "a manner of living that reflects one's values and attitudes." The process of living requires work. Getting up in the morning and cleaning the house is work. Buying groceries is work. Work doesn't stop in retirement, not if you're still alive and kicking. Just like lifestyle, the word "work" has an interesting meaning: "activity directed toward making or doing something." As long as you're active, you're "working" in some fashion. Why not be passionate about it? I like what Lloyd said earlier: "make a big deal out of everything in your life."

On that note, Steve Jobs, CEO of Apple Computers, gets the last word:

> The only way to be truly satisfied is to do what you believe to be great work. And the only way to do great work is to love what you do. If you haven't found it yet, keep looking.

BIBLIOGRAPHY

Anthony, Mitch. *The New Retire-mentality: Planning Your Life and Living Your Dreams...At Any Age You Want.* Chicago: Dearborn Financial Publishing, Inc., 2001.

Bassani, Giorgio. *The Garden of the Finzi-Continis.* Translated by William Weaver. New York: Everyman's Library/Random House, 2005.

Bateman, Gary L., and Garland, Lisa. *A Declaration of Taxpayer Rights: Your Family's Complete Tax and Estate Planning Guide.* Sixth Edition. Bateman Mackay Chartered Accountants. Burlington: Bateman Financial Consultants Limited, 2004.

Bell, Andrew. *Mutual Funds for Canadians for Dummies: A Reference for the Rest of Us.* Toronto: CDG Books Canada, Inc., 2000.

Brock, Fred. *Retire on Less than You Think: The New York Times Guide to Planning Your Financial Future.* New York: Times Books, Henry Holt and Company, 2004.

Canadian Securities Institute. *Professional Financial Planning Course.* Volumes 1 & 2. Toronto: CSI Publishing, 2001.

Canadian Cancer Society. *The Advisor: Charitable Giving Resource Binder for Allied Professionals.* Toronto: CCS Publishing, 2005.

Cestnick, Tim. *Winning the Tax Game 2005: A Year-Round Tax and Investment Guide for Canadians.* Toronto: John Wiley & Sons Canada Ltd., 2005.

Cruise, David, and Alison Griffiths. *The Portfolio Doctor: Your Prescription for Investment Health.* Toronto: Penguin Canada, 2004.

Dagys, Andrew, and Paul Mladjenovic. *Stock Investing for Canadians for Dummies: A Reference for the Rest of Us.* Toronto: John Wiley & Sons, Inc., 2003.

Farrell, Paul B. *The Lazy Person's Guide to Investing: A Book for Procrastinators, the Financially Challenged, and Everyone Who Worries about Dealing with Their Money.* New York: Warner Books, 2004.

Foster, Sandra E. *You Can't Take it With You: The Common-Sense Guide to Estate Planning for Canadians.* Toronto: John Wiley & Sons, 2002. Fourth Edition.

Gallwey, W. Timothy. *The Inner Game of Tennis.* Revised Edition. New York: Random House, Inc., 1997.

Gallwey, W. Timothy. *The Inner Game of Golf.* New York, Random House, Inc., 1998.

Gladwell, Malcolm. *The Tipping Point: How Little Things Can Make a Big Difference.* New York: Little, Brown and Company, 2002.

Hagstrom, Robert G. *The Warren Buffett Portfolio: Mastering the Power of the Focus Investment Strategy.* New York: John Wiley & Sons, Inc., 1999.

Hayes, Christopher L. *Money Makeovers: How Women Can Control Their Financial Destiny.* New York: Doubleday, 2001.

KPMG LLP. *Tax Planning for You and Your Family 2005.* Toronto: Thomson Carswell, 2004.

Lovett-Reid, Patricia, and Donna Green. *Surprise! You're Wealthy: Every Woman's Guide to Financial Independence.* Toronto: Key Porter Books, 2005.

Lynch, Peter, and John Rothchild. *One Up on Wall Street: How to Use What You Already Know to Make Money in the Market.* New York: Simon and Schuster, 2000.

Malkiel, Burton G. *A Random Walk Down Wall Street: The Time-Tested Strategy for Successful Investing.* New York: W.W. Norton & Company, 2003.

Matthews, Keith. *The Empowered Investor: A Guide to Building Better Portfolios.* Ottawa: Book Coach Press, 2005.

Milevsky, Moshe Ayre, and Aron A. Gottesman. *Insurance Logic: Risk Management Strategies for Canadians.* Toronto: Stoddart, 2002.

Moglia, Joe. *Coach Yourself to Success. Winning the Investment Game.* Hoboken: John Wiley & Sons Inc., 2005.

Nahirny, Dianne. *Stop Working, Start Living: How I Retired at the Age of 36, without Winning the Lottery.* Toronto: ECW Press, 2001.

O'Donnell, Jill, and Graham McWaters and John Page. *The Canadian Retirement Guide: A Comprehensive Handbook on Aging, Retirement, Caregiving & Health.* Toronto: Insomniac Press, 2004.

Orman, Suze. *The Nine Steps to Financial Freedom: Practical & Spiritual Steps So You Can Stop Worrying.* New York: Three Rivers Press, 2000.

Orman, Suze. *The Money Book for the Young, Fabulous & Broke.* New York: Riverhead Books, 2005.

Pape, Gordon. *Six Steps to $1 Million: How to Achieve Your Financial Dreams*. Toronto: Viking Canada, 2001.

Pape, Gordon. *Get Control of Your Money*. Toronto: Penguin Canada, 2003.

Praskey, Sally, and Helena Moncrief. *The Insurance Book: What Canadians Really Need to Know Before Buying Insurance*. Toronto: Prentice Hall Canada, 1999.

Siegel, Jeremy J. *Stocks for the Long Run: The Definitive Guide to Financial Market Returns and Long-Term Investment Strategies*. Third Edition. New York: McGraw-Hill, 2002.

Siegel, Jeremy J. *The Future for Investors: Why the Tried and True Triumph Over the Bold and New*. New York: Crown Publishing, 2005.

Soros, George. *Soros on Soros: Staying Ahead of the Curve*. New York: John Wiley & Sons, Inc., 1995.

Tyson, Eric, and Tony Martin. *Personal Finance for Canadians for Dummies: A Reference for the Rest of Us*. Third Edition. Toronto: CDG Books Canada, Inc., 2001.

Zelinski, Ernie J. *How to Retire Happy, Wild and Free: Retirement Wisdom that You Won't Get from Your Financial Advisor*. Edmonton: Visions International Publishing, 2004.

APPENDICES

"The most perfect character is supposed to lie between those extremes;
retaining an equal ability and taste for books, company, and business;
preserving in conversation that discernment and delicacy which
arise from polite letters; and in business, that probity and accuracy which
are the natural result of a just philosophy.... By means of such compositions,
virtue becomes amiable, science agreeable, company instructive,
and retirement entertaining."
—DAVID HUME, *AN ENQUIRY CONCERNING HUMAN UNDERSTANDING*

APPENDIX 1
How to calculate your net worth

1) Go to TD Canada Trust's planning section:
   http://www.tdcanadatrust.com/planning/rdmap.jsp#two

2) Then click on Net Worth Statement under the "Data Gathering" section.

Or complete the steps in the form below.

Net Worth Worksheet

Assets		Current Value
A. Liquid Assets		
Chequing account		
Savings account		
GICs and T-bills		
Cash value of life insurance		
Money market funds		
Other (e.g., money owed to you)		
Total Liquid Assets	(A)	_____
B. Long-Term Assets		
Mutual funds (excluding money market)		
Stocks		
Bonds		
RRSPs/RRIFs		
RESPs		
Company pension plan		
Other		
Total Long-Term Assets	(B)	_____
C. Property Assets		
Residence		
Vacation property		
Vehicles		
Jewellery/art/collectibles		
Other (e.g., furniture)		
Total Property Assets	(C)	_____
Total Personal Assets (A+B+C)		_____
Liabilities		
Credit card(s)		
Auto loan(s)		
Education loan(s)		
Investment loan(s)		
Other loan(s)		
Mortgage(s)		
Other		
Total Personal Liabilities		_____
Personal Net Worth		
Total Personal Assets		
Less: Total Personal Liabilities		
Equals: Your Personal Net Worth		_____

APPENDIX 2
Calculating your ideal RRSP contribution

1) Go to TD Canada Trust's planning section:
   www.tdcanadatrust.com/planning/rdmap.jsp#two

2) Then click on Retirement Contribution Calculator under the
   "Analysis and Solutions" section.

RSP Contribution Calculator

If you currently have a savings program in place, or are planning to invest an amount in your RSP, use this tool to determine how much will be available for your retirement.

Personal Information

1. What is your current age?

2. At what age do you plan to retire?

3. Number of years of retirement?

Retirement Expectations

4. What is the annual income you think you will require when you retire
   (in today's dollars on a pre-tax basis). $
   (As a general rule of thumb, you'll need 60%–80% of your pre-retirement
   income after you retire to live the same lifestyle you're living today)

5. Do you expect to receive some of this income from a company pension
   plan?   Yes No
   Typically, the breakdown between these sources are as follows: If you
   answered Yes to the above, the calculation will assume that you need
   40% from your RSP, 30% from your Company Pension, and 30% from
   Government/Other Sources. If you answered No it will assume that you will
   need 70% from your RSP and 30% from Government/Other Sources.
   If you feel that a different breakdown is more appropriate to your circumstances, you can change the assumed percentages by entering the new
   figures in the boxes.
   % RSP   % Company Pension   % Government

Current Contributions

6. What is the approximate value of your Current RSP holdings? $

7. What amount are you currently contributing to your RSP? $

8. Contribution frequency?

9. Annual inflation estimate?   %

10. Average assumed rate of return on retirement savings?   %

APPENDIX 3
Calculate your ideal RESP

1) Go to TD Canada Trust's planning section:
   www.tdcanadatrust.com/planning/rdmap.jsp#two

2) Go to "Setting Goals and Objectives" and click on Education
   Savings Tools.

APPENDIX 4
Fixed-income securities (CSA Guide)
Source: Canadian Securities Administrators

Type	Liquidity	Expected Return	Risk
1. Savings Bonds Savings bonds are issued in a number of forms by the federal and some provincial governments. They are evidence of a loan by the investor to the issuing government and are backed by the general credit and taxation powers of the government. Savings bonds are usually offered to sale to individual investors at regular times each year. Purchase limits often apply.	Savings bonds are generally not transferable. Some savings bonds may be redeemed by the holder at any time, while others may only be redeemed at specified intervals (e.g., every six months) or are not redeemable before maturity.	Most savings bonds guarantee a fixed rate of return for each year to maturity or specify a minimum rate of return that can be adjusted upward by the issuer if market conditions demand.	**Very Low:** Federal and provincial government backing of savings bonds means there is virtually no risk of default.
2. Bonds Bonds are evidence of a loan by the investor to the government or company that issues the bond. The issuer generally promises to pay a specified rate of interest to the bondholder and to repay a certain amount (the face value of the bond) at maturity. Bonds may be sold at prices higher or lower than their face value. Corporate bonds are typically secured by a pledge of specific assets. Some bonds offer holders the right to convert their bonds into common shares.	Bonds are normally sold through investment dealers or limited market dealers in an over-the-counter market. Some bonds offer redemption privileges.	Interest on bonds is usually paid at a fixed rate. (See comment on "yield," next page.) Bond values will fluctuate as returns offered on competing securities change. If interest rates go down, for instance, the market value of a bond would normally go up because its fixed interest payments would become more attractive to investors. The market value of a bond may also be affected by changes in the credit rating of the issuer. Conversion privileges enhance the potential for capital gains on a bond.	**Low to High:** The risk of a bond will depend mainly on the risk that the issuer will default on its payment obligations (default risk) and the risk that prevailing interest rates will increase, pushing the value of the bond downward (interest rate risk). Some bonds, commonly called "junk bonds," offer unusually high yields—typically because there is thought to be greater risk that the issuer will default on its payment obligations.

Type	Liquidity	Expected Return	Risk
3. Debentures Debentures are similar to bonds, but typically not secured by the pledge of specific corporate assets. They may, however, be secured by a "floating charge" on the issuer's assets generally.	Some debentures are listed on stock exchanges while some others trade in the over-the-counter market. In some cases, there may be no established market for a debenture or it may not be transferable.	Comments concerning bonds apply.	**Low to High:** Comments concerning bonds apply.
	Comment: The actual rate of return, or "yield," that you can earn on a bond or debenture will depend on the price you pay for it and the time remaining until it matures. For example, a debenture paying a 7% nominal rate of interest will pay you $70 per year for each $1,000 (face value) debenture. If you are able to buy that debenture for only $950, the actual rate of return you receive will be higher than 7%. Calculating the yield precisely can be complex, but your financial advisor should be able to do the calculation for you.		
4. Treasury Bills (T-bills) Treasury bills are short-term (less than one year to maturity) debt securities issued by the federal and some provincial governments. They do not pay interest but instead are sold at a price below their value at maturity. T-bills are issued by the government regularly and are typically sold in large denominations.	T-bills are not redeemable but they can usually be sold quickly through investment dealers.	Return will be determined by the difference between the purchase price and the value of the T-bill at maturity. Market values may be affected somewhat by changing market interest rates.	**Very Low:** There is virtually no risk of default and the short-term nature of T-bills limits risk of significant changes in market value caused by changing market interest rates.

Type	Liquidity	Expected Return	Risk
5. Guaranteed Investment Certificates (GICs) GICs are deposit certificates issued by financial institutions. Most GICs pay specified rates of interest to maturity, although some base the returns to investors on the performance of a benchmark such as a stock exchange index.	Most GICs must be held to maturity, but some offer limited redemption privileges.	Returns are often fixed, but in some cases are tied to the performance of a stock market index or some other benchmark.	**Low to Moderate:** GICs are guaranteed by the issuer and the principal is insured (subject to certain limits) by a deposit insurance agency such as the Canada Deposit Insurance Corporation. As a result there is very limited risk that the principal will not be repaid If the GIC's returns are tied to a benchmark, however, there may be risk that interest payments may be lower than anticipated or there may be no interest payments at all.
Comment: The return on a stock exchange index, such as the S&P/TSX composite Index is a statistical tool that measures the performance of a basket of stocks listed on the exchange. Some indices are designed to reflect the overall market, while others measure the performance of specific industry sectors.			

APPENDIX 5
Equity securities (CSA Guide)
Source: Canadian Securities Administrators

Type	Liquidity	Expected Return	Risk
1. Common Shares Common shares represent ownership of a company. As owners, common shares normally have the right to elect directors and to vote on certain major corporate decisions. They are also entitled to share in any residual assets of the company if it is wound up.	Common shares are normally traded on stock exchanges, ATS or in over-the-counter markets between dealers. For some common shares however there may be little or no market and/or the shares may be subject to restrictions on resale.	Return on common shares may take the form of dividends and capital gains (or losses). Many larger, established companies try to pay regular dividends to shareholders. Others may not pay dividends, either because they are not profitable or because they choose to retain earnings for reinvestment. Companies may also change their dividend policies from time to time. In many cases, returns will depend mainly on changes in the share price (leading to capital gains or losses when the shares are sold). The common share prices of all companies can go up and down, in some cases rapidly and substantially.	**Moderate to Very High:** Risk will depend on many factors such as the size, profitability and financial stability of the company, the capabilities of its management and its exposure to general economic downturns, foreign exchange risks and new competition. Common shareholders are the last in line (behind tax authorities, employees, creditors and preferred shareholders) to claim on the assets of the company in the event of insolvency.
Comment: Over 4,000 companies have their common shares listed for trading on a stock exchange in Canada.			
2. Restricted Voting Shares Restricted voting shares represent ownership, like common shares, but offer holders restricted or no voting privileges.	Comments concerning Common Shares apply.	Comments concerning Common Shares apply.	Comments concerning Common Shares apply.

Type	Liquidity	Expected Return	Risk
3. Preferred Shares Preferred shares typically give holder the right to receive a fixed dividend before any dividends can be paid to the company's common shareholders. Preferred shareholders are also entitled to a portion of the residual assets of the company if it is wound up. Holders often do not have voting rights, but in many cases are offered special features such as the right to redeem their shares at certain times or convert them into common shares at a predetermined price.	Comments concerning Common Shares apply.	Dividends on preferred shares are generally fixed, but the company may reduce or suspend dividend payments if, for instance, it fails to make adequate profits or needs to preserve its capital. The capital gains potential of preferred shares is usually less than for common shares of the same company, although conversion privileges, redemption privileges or other special features may enhance the potential for share price increases.	**Moderate to High:** Comments concerning Common Shares apply. Dividend payments may be reduced or suspended for various reasons (e.g., the company is not sufficiently profitable) and any reduction or expected reduction of dividends can have a significant impact on share prices. An increase in the rate of return offered on other investments can also affect preferred share prices as the fixed dividend of the preferred share price becomes relatively less attractive. Preferred shareholders are in line behind tax authorities, employees and creditors in claiming on the assets of the company in the event of insolvency.
4. Flow-through Shares Flow-through shares are special type of common shares that may be issued by oil and gas companies or mineral exploration companies. These shares allow certain tax deductions for qualifying exploration, development and property expenditures to "flow through" from the company to shareholders.	Comments concerning Common Shares apply.	Returns will depend on the potential tax benefits to the investor, and the capital gains or losses that may result for the success or failure of the exploration program. Potential tax benefits will be greater for those in the highest tax brackets.	**High:** Resource exploration and development programs are generally high risk. In addition, there are risks that the company's expenditures may not meet the strict requirements of the tax legislation and tax deductions may be disallowed. Flow-through shares are most suitable for experienced investors who can take maximum advantage of the tax benefits and who can withstand the loss of some or all of their investment.

APPENDIX 6
Options, Warrants & Rights (CSA Guide)

Source: Canadian Securities Administrators

Type	Liquidity	Expected Return	Risk
1. Options Options are securities that give the holder the right to buy (a "call" option) or sell (a "put" option) an asset at a specific price for a specific period of time. Many options on common shares, other financial products and commodities are traded on exchanges. The holder of an exchange-traded option may sell it, exercise it to buy the underlying asset or let it expire.	Exchange-traded options can usually be sold or exercised on short notice. Some options are not traded on an exchange and may not be transferable.	Options do not pay dividends or interest. Returns will depend mainly on changes in the market value of the underlying asset. The market value of an option will tend to decline as it approaches its expiry date.	**Very Low to Very High:** Risk depends on the underlying instrument and the use of the option. If used as a hedging tool, risk is reduced. If used to speculate, risk increases.
2. Warrants Warrants give the holder the right to acquire other specified securities at a specified price for a specified time. Rights are issued in proportion to the number of shares already owned by each shareholder.	Comments concerning Options apply.	Comments concerning Options apply.	**Very Low to Very High:** Comments concerning Options apply.
3. Rights In the rights offering a company gives its shareholders the right to buy additional shares from the company at a specified price within a specified period of time. Rights are issued in proportion to the number of shares already owned by each shareholder.	Some rights are listed for trading on a stock exchange and may or may not trade actively. In some cases, rights may be subject to resale restrictions or holders may be subject to restrictions on their ability to exercise the rights to acquire additional shares.	Comments concerning Options apply.	**Moderate to Very High:** Comments concerning Warrants apply.

APPENDIX 7
Further research

Here are some recommended online investment sites

PERSONAL FINANCE
* Moneysense.ca
* http://finance.canada.com/
* http://www.investored.ca (Investor Education Fund)
* TheBoomer.com
* GlobeInvestor.com
* www.td.com/economics
* http://money.canoe.ca/PersonalFinance/
* http://www.macleans.ca/finance
* Investopedia.com
* http://money.cnn.com/
* http://ca.finance.yahoo.com/
* http://biz.yahoo.com/funds/investing.html
* MarketWatch.com
* http://www.morningstar.com/
* http://online.wsj.com/public/us
* http://www.nytimes.com/pages/business/index.html
* http://www.berkshirehathaway.com/2003ar/2003ar.pdf

RETIREMENT SITES
* http://canadaonline.about.com/od/retirementfinance/
* http://www.sdc.gc.ca/en/isp/pub/factsheets/retire.shtml
* http://www.forbes.com/retirement/
* http://www.morningstar.com/cover/retirement.html?pfsection=Retire

MISCELLANEOUS SITES
* www.sedar.com

RISK SITES

- http://rider.wharton.upenn.edu/~prc/PRC/WP/WP2003-8.pdf
- http://www.casact.org/coneduc/ratesem/2002/handouts/ sanderson2.doc
- http://www.riskglossary.com/

GENERAL SEARCH SITES

- www. google.ca
- www. yahoo.ca

STATISTICS

In Canada:

Statistics Canada: http://www40.statcan.ca/
Industry Canada stats: http://strategis.ic.gc.ca/
CPP rates: http://www.sdc.gc.ca/en/isp/pub/factsheets/rates.shtml
TD Economics.com: http://www.td.com/economics/

International

Davidson Data Center and Network
http://ddcn.prowebis.com/
Provides an integrated, fully searchable online database on transition and emerging markets. The site has three main components: a data locator, an archive and a clearinghouse. DDCN facilitates the discovery of existing data sets, preserves and makes widely available micro data and macro statistics from these economies free of charge.

Organisation for Economic Co-operation and Development (OECD)
www.oecd.org
The Statistics Directorate of the OECD collects worldwide economic statistics and standardizes them to make them internationally comparable. These are published in both printed and electronic form.

United Nations
www.un.org
This page provides links to national government official statistical Web sites.

INDEX

A
accident insurance, 141
accredited investor, 116
adjusted cost base, 171, 187
ageism, 23
Air Canada, 97–98
Alexander, Craig, 55, 249
allowable business investment
  losses, 188
alter-ego trust, 233, 234, 238
American Stock and Options
  Exchange (AMEX), 109
Ammeter, Debbie, 30, 157
amortization periods, 167
annuity
  beneficiary, 232–233
  and collapsing RRSP,
    206–208
  and retirement strategy, 45
  and RRIF, 207–208
  and RRSP, 207
  tax savings, 141
  three-year rule, 160
Antonucci, Toni, 265
Arato, Pat, 197
asset allocation
  and base case, 78
  vs. diversification, 70–72
  and market capitalization,
    112
  purposes, 70
  and returns, 67–68
  and risk adjustment, 78,
    87, 88
asset-backed security, 98–99
asset classes

and correlation, 72–73
described, 93–94
and returns, 59, 68, 69
asset mix, 69
asset portfolio, 70
at-retirement strategy, 45
attribution, 159–160
attribution rules, 164, 165
Automatic Millionaire, The, 16
average return, 58

B
Bach, David, 16
Balls, Andrew, 65
bandwagon thinking, 62
Bank of Canada, 28
Barnes, Martin, 64
Bassani, Giorgio, 122
Bauman, James, 38, 44
beating the market, 85
behavioural finance, 61
beneficiaries, 232–233, 237
Berkshire Hathaway funds,
  63, 65, 150
Bill, 29, 78, 80–81
Billings, Gary, 199
Bogle, John, 70, 71, 77, 151
bond funds, 99
Bond Index Accounts, 127
bonds, 72, 87
Boom, Bust and Echo, 31
Boomers, 23, 30, 31, 32, 267
borrowing, 21, 52, 173–174
bottom-up managers, 107
budget and pre-retirement
  planning, 44

Buffett, Warren, 59, 63–64, 65,
  82, 111, 138, 150–151, 152, 250
buy-and-hold strategy, 52,
  150–153
"buy high" trend, 61

C
Cadsby, Ted, 87
Cakebread, Caroline, 184
calls, 117
Canada
  financial obligations,
    16–17
  percent of world market,
    74–75
  retirement investing,
    21–22
  and United States, 21
Canada Deposit Insurance
  Corporation, 106
Canada Savings Bonds, 50, 88,
  94–95
Canadian Education Savings
  Grant, 175–176, 175–177
Canadian Index Accounts, 127
capital and retirement number, 28
capital gains
  and losses, 187
  exemption, 186
  tax, 76, 77, 148, 149, 166
carrying charges, 188
cash, 80, 93
Cestnick, Tim, 127, 187, 251
charitable donations, 188,
  248–255

charitable foundation, 253–254
charitable remainder trusts, 179, 239–240
charitable tax credit, 248
child care expenses, 180, 188
closed-end funds, 103–104
club memberships, 183
CNIL (cumulative net investment loss), 187
Colleen, 17–18, 216–217
comfort levels, 44
Common Sense on Mutual Funds, 70, 151
company car, 182
compounding, 57, 89
Consumer Price Index, 64
continuing education, 201
conversion rules, 206–208
corporate bonds, 95–96
correlation, 72–73
cost, defined, 58
cottage trusts, 240
Couch Potato portfolio, 86
CPP, 22, 30, 132, 164, 217
credit card loans, 49
critical illness insurance, 134–137
cumulative net investment loss (CNIL), 187

D
Danko, William, 268
death benefit, 128
debt, 21, 49
debt "junkie," 21
deemed disposition, 237
deferred sales charge (DSC), 105
defined contribution (DC) plans, 23
Del Greco, Kathryn, 185
derivatives, 117
disability insurance, 130–133, 135–137
disabled beneficiaries, 237
diversification, 65, 70–72, 85–86, 87

dividend income, 148–149
dividend reinvestment plans, 170–172
dividends, 169–173
dividend tax credit, 169–170
dollar cost averaging, 173
donations tax credit, 178
drawdown sequence, 210–211
DRIPs, 107, 170–172
Dudack, Gail, 171
dying intestate, 241–242

E
early retirement, 31–32
earned income, 155–156
earnings potential, 124
economic power shift, 57
Edgewood, Helen, 52, 54
Edgewood, Robert, 51–54, 203, 271
education expenses, 189
"efficient frontier," 69
efficient market hypothesis (EMH), 108, 111
emotional investing, 60–61, 66, 82–85
employee benefits, 181–183
employee pensions, 22–23
employer loans, 182
employment expenses, 188
employment status, 147
Empowered Investor, The, 60
equities as asset class, 94
Equity Index Accounts, 127
equity investments, 54–55
equity mutual funds, 102–108
equity securities guide, 285–286
estate freezes, 240–241, 258
estate planning, 224–259
ETFs, 108, 109
Evensky, Harold, 216
exchange-traded funds. *See* ETFs
executors, 243–246
expense deductions, 187–189

F
Feldman, Amy, 64
Fesenmaier, Jeff, 62
Fillmore, Joanne, 263–265
Fillmore, Lloyd, 263–265
Financial Expertise Scale (financial IQ), 25–26
Fitzgerald, F. Scott, 267
fixed income, 93
fixed-income products, 96–98
fixed-income securities guide, 282–284
Florinda, 137
Foot, David, 31
foreign tax credits, 188
Frankl, Viktor, 224
Freud, Sigmund, 85
front-end load (FEL), 105
fulfillment, 224
fully invested, defined, 62
fundamental analysis (stock prices), 113–114
Future for Investors, The, 57

G
Gallwey, Timothy W., 41–42, 43
Garden of the Finzi-Continis, 122–123
Gates, Bill, 250
George, 82–85, 146
GICs
  defined, 94–95
  as fixed-income asset, 93–94
  insured, 106
  and life insurance, 127, 258
  and low interest, 51
  as money park, 88
  and pre-retirement plan, 211
  and RRSPs, 157
  and taxes, 148
GIFs, 107–108
gifting, 230, 251–252, 252–253
gifts (in cash, in kind), 178
Glassman, James, 108

global diversification, 73–75
Global Financial Well-Being
  Study, 30
global markets, 73–75
Gombita, Teresa, 236
Gorman, Bob, 78
Gottesman, Aron, 124, 127
Government of Canada
  bonds, 95–96
Great Gatsby, The, 267
Greenspan, Alan, 61, 65
Gretzky, Wayne, 223
Gross, Bill, 64
Group of Seven, 223
growth managers, 107
guaranteed investment certifi-
  cates. *See* GICs.
guaranteed investment funds.
  See GIFs
guided imagery, 38

H
Hacker, Jacob S., 21
Hagstrom, Robert, 71
Harris, Mike, 223
health care costs, 65
health plans (provincial), 135
hedge funds, 116–117
Hendricks, Mike, 32
herd instinct, 61, 63
high-yield bonds, 97–98
Hodges, Michael, 21
Holmes, Sherlock, 85
home business tax deduc-
  tions, 184–185
Home Buyers' Plan (HBP),
  167–168
home ownership, 166–169
Hood, Duncan, 85
house prices, 64
"human capital," 124

I
IBM, 212–213
income integration, 209–210
income splitting, 157–159,
  164–166
Income Tax Act, 233

income trusts, 99–101
incorporating, 185
index fund, 70–71, 77, 108
individual pension plans. *See*
  IPPs
inflation
  and bonds, 55–56
  and global policy, 28
  impact, 89
  and investments, 57
  and low-interest trap, 51
Inner Game of Golf, The, 41
Inner Game of Tennis, The, 41
in-retirement strategy, 45
insurance, 121–142
  accident, 141
  as asset protection, 122
  as charitable donation,
    253
  and estate freezes, 258
  and estate planning,
    255–259
  and long-term care,
    139–140
  payouts, 138
  premiums, 183
  as tax deferral, 123
  and tax savings, 141
  as tax shelter, 128
  varieties, 123
  and women, 139
Insurance Logic, 124, 127
interest
  income, 148
  rates, 27, 64–65
inter vivos trust, 234,
  237–241
investing, 50–51, 57–58
investment
  holding company, 187
  loans, 173–174
  mix, 68
  risk, 30
"invisible hand," 110–111
IPPs (individual pension
  plans), 185
irrevocable trust, 234
iUnits, 99, 109

J
Jobs, Steve, 272
joint ownership, 231–232
joint partner trust, 234, 239
joint spousal trust, 233
junk bonds, 97–98

K
Kanter, Larry, 63
Keynes, John Maynard, 110
Kieran, Patrick, 31
Kiss, Jason, 152
Klonowski, Francis, 123

L
Leacock, Stephen, 213
LEAPs, 83
Lee, Julie, 208
Lee, Peggy, 224
Lee, Trevor, 208
Lennon, John, 43
Letterman, David, 189
level load (fund sales charge),
  105
life annuity, 207
life expectancy, 31
"Life Expectancy, Health
  Expectancy...", 25
life insurance, 123–128
  converting from term to
    permanent, 129
  and death benefits, 256
  group plans, 124
  as loan collateral, 129
  lump-sum withdrawal,
    263
  and professional associa-
    tions, 124
  purpose, 124
  relative costs, 129
  and tax, 178–179
  and terminal illness, 128
lifestyle, defined, 272
lifestyle categories, 217–219
Lisa, 29, 78, 79–80
Litow, Stanley, 212
living benefit (insurance), 135
living trust, 234, 237–241

"long" defined, 116
long-term care insurance,
139–140
Long-Term Equity
Anticipation Securities
(LEAPs), 83
low-interest trap, 51
low load (fund sales charge),
105
Lynch, Peter, 59, 85, 86

M
Macklem, Katherine, 65
managed RRSPs, 156–157
management expense ratio.
See MER
Man's Search for Meaning, 224
Marciano, Simone, 196–198,
199
marginal tax rate, 147–148, 154
market capitalization, 111–112
market trends, 66–67
Market Volatility, 58
Matthews, Keith, 60
"maximum equity growth," 79
McCartney, Paul, 43
McLuhan, Marshall, 223
meals and entertainment
expenses, 183
mean (average) return, 58–59
medical expenses, 180
Meilleur, Marie-Louise, 223
MER, 99, 104–106, 109,
114–115
Milevsky, Moshe, 124, 127
Millionaire Next Door, The,
268
mining, oil and gas expenses,
189
money, attitudes to, 23–24
money market, 80
money market securities, 95
mortgage-backed securities,
98
mortgage funds, 99
mortgage payment vs. RRSP,
168–169
moving costs, 182–183

Munger, Charles, 63
Murray, Robert, 253
Mussolini, 122
Mutual Fundamentals, 87
mutual funds
benefits, 102–103
costs, 104–106
defined, 102
and insurance, 106
management fees, 104
management styles,
103–104, 106–107
and RRSP, 157
sales charges, 105–106
taxes, 104–105
and volatility, 66–67
mutual fund wraps, 114–115

N
naming a beneficiary,
232–233, 237
net-worth calculator, 278–279
Nifty Fifty, 61–62, 111
Nifty-Fifty Re-Revisited, The,
62
no load (fund sales charge),
106
non-registered assets, 210–211

O
OAS, 22, 164
open-end funds, 103–104
options, 117
options, warrants & rights
guide, 287
Orange, Jacqueline C., 49–50
Orlick, Terry, 38
over-diversifying, 70–71
Ovinsky, Evan, 265–267
Ovinsky, Joanne, 265–267

P
Partington, John, 38
PATH, 12, 17, 32–33, 269
pay yourself first, 49–50
PEG, 82, 83
Pembina Pipeline Income
Fund, 52

pension
costs, 65
funds, 78
income, 210
plans, 208–209
P/E ratios, 83
permanent insurance, 128
personal service business, 187
pooled wraps, 115
portfolio
income-oriented, 79
maximum equity growth,
79
model (for wraps), 114–115
no formula for, 81
and tax planning, 145,
152–153
power of attorney, 246–248
pre-retirement planning,
43–45
price to earnings growth
(PEG), 82
principal residence exemption, 166–167
Private Giving Foundation,
254–255
probate
avoiding, 229–241
and executor, 244
fees, 228–229
and gifting, 230
and joint ownership,
231–232
naming a beneficiary,
232–233
and trusts, 233–240
procrastination, 88
property as charitable donation, 251
province of residence, 188
puts, 117

Q
QPP, 132

R
"rational" investor, 110–111
real estate bubble, 21, 63–64

real estate investment trust.
See REIT
rebalancing, 76–77
registered assets, 211, 252–253
registered education savings
plan. See RESP
registered pension plan
(RPP), 209
registered retirement income
fund. See RRIF
registered retirement savings
plan. See RRSP
REIT, 100, 101–102
RESP, 164, 169, 147, 174–177
retired, defined, 15
retirement
adjustment period,
212–213
attitudes to, 16
as career shift, 201
delaying, 202
downsizing for, 216
estate planning, 224–259
house as asset, 215–216
income, 159, 209–211
investing, attitudes to,
21–22
lifestyle categories,
217–219
needs, estimating, 27–28
and negativity, 31
phasing in, 201
planning, as process,
269–271
procrastinating about, 24
and social life, 201–202
three-decade, 264–265
transition to, 199–203
"retirement blues," 199
"retirement number," 22,
26–28, 29, 44
retiring allowances, 183
return and risk, balancing,
69–70
reverse mortgage, 216
revocable trust, 234
Richard, 17–18, 216–217
Rintoul, Margaret, 243

risk, 69–70, 77–78
risk-adjusted returns, 77–78
risk/return trade-off, 66–67
risk tolerance, 25, 30, 66, 88
Roche, Albert, 271
Rosentreter, Kurt, 146
RRIF, 75, 157, 206–208
RRSP, 23
borrowing from, 161
and capital losses, 164
for children, 160
collapsing, 206–208
contributing, 162
conversion, 206–208
early withdrawals,
161–162
and global diversification,
75
and income splitting, 163
and insurance, 126
key benefits, 160
maximum contributions,
156, 160, 162
vs. mortgage payment,
168–169
naming beneficiary, 163
over-contribution,
160–161
and pensions, 161
personal allowable limit,
158
and portfolio, 163
portfolio returns, 79
self-directed, 157
spousal plans, 157–160
and tax refund, 162
and tax-sheltered contri-
butions, 153–155
as tax strategy, 153–164
ten biggest mistakes,
162–164
and term deposits, 157
RRSP calculator, 280
RRSP Principal Protector,
208
Rukeyser, Louis, 86
"rule of 72," 51
Ryan, Jo-anne, 254

S
sales taxes, 189–191
Sanderson, Scott, 69
saving vs. investing, 50–51
savings, 29, 49–50, 157
Sean, 137
sector rotation managers, 107
securities as charitable donation, 251–252
segregated funds, 107–108
segregated wraps, 116
self-actualizing people, 225
self-directed RRSPs, 157
self-employment, 183–189
"sell low" trap, 61–63
"Seven Habits of Wealthy
Canadians," 267–269
Seven Strategies to Guarantee
Your Investments, 87
Seychuk, Allan, 65
share purchase plan (SPP),
170
Shiller, Robert, 58
"short" defined, 116
Siegel, Jeremy, 56–57, 76
SIPs, 107
small business tax rate, 187
small-capitalization stocks, 111
Smith, Adam, 110
smoking, 31
Soros, George, 59–60, 86
Soros on Soros, 60
spousal RRSP, 159
spousal trust, 234, 235–236
spouse, defined, 158
SPP (share purchase plan),
170
Standard & Poors Depository
Receipts, 109
Standard & Poors Index
Accounts, 127
Stanley, David, 171, 172, 268
starting a business, 201
Stiglitz, Joseph, 110
stock market fads, 63
stocks, 109–117
vs. bonds, 87
and correlation, 72

for the long run, 56–58

fundamental *vs.* technical analysis, 113–116

and growth opportunities, 111–114

and investor behaviour, 110–111

and market capitalization, 111–114

portfolio, 70

preferred *vs.* common, 109

prices, analyzing, 113–116

and rate of inflation, 111

and "rational" investor, 110–111

trading, 151–152

value of shares, 109–110

Stocks for the Long Run, 56

Sudhir, 138

Susan, 213–215

Systematic Investment Plans (SIPs), 107

T

tangible assets, 94

Tarnowski, Alicia, 265

tax

after death, 226–228

deductions, maximizing, 177–180

liability, 83–84, 89

minimizing, 52–54

planning, 145–191, 211–212

strategies (sure-fire), 147

tax-efficient investing, 146

technical analysis (stock prices), 114

term certain annuity, 207

term deposits and RRSP, 157

term life insurance, 125

term to 100 insurance, 257–258

testamentary trust, 234–237

theory of fallibility, 60

Thorfinnson, Michael, 152

Thornton, Grant, 165

three-decade retirement, 264–265

three-year rule, 159–160

top-down managers, 106

top employers of mature workers, 215

top ten investment mistakes, 87–89

Toronto Stock Exchange (TSX), 109

traditional retirement, 38–39

trailer fees (fund sales charge), 106

transition plan, 200–203, 204–206

Tremblay, Monique, 30

Trudeau, Pierre Elliott, 223

True New Economy, 57

Trump, 86

trust company as executor, 245–246

trusts, 233–240

tuition expenses, 189

U

undervalued businesses, 63

unemployment, 23

universal life insurance, 126–128, 257–258

V

value managers, 107

visualization

concentrated, 37

explained, 38

and no retirement, 40

and phased-in retirement, 39

power of, 41–43

and sports, 38

and traditional retirement, 38–39

volatility

and diversification, 70

and time, 75–76

trends, 58

volunteering, 196–198, 201, 205

W

Warren Buffett Portfolio, The, 71

wealth, 16

Weston, Galen, 253

Weston, Hilary, 253

whole life insurance, 125–126

Wilkins, John, 203–205

Wilkins, Marianne, 203–205

Williams, Terri, 168

will kits, 242

wills, 226, 241–246

Worker's Compensation, 132

wrap fees, 115

wrap programs, 114–116

Y

Yih, James, 87, 267

Z

Zack, 147–148

Zweig, Jason, 64

585- 5833

FREDA